KENYA

A MOUNTAIN TO CLIMB

Kenya A Mountain to Climb

Spiderwize
Remus House
Coltsfoot Drive
Woodston
Peterborough
PE2 9BF

www.spiderwize.com

A CIP catalogue record for this book is available from the British Library.

The views expressed in this work are solely those of the author and do not necessarily reflect the views of the publisher, and the publisher hereby disclaims any responsibility for them

ISBN: 978-1-912694-95-2
eBook ISBN: 978-1-912694-96-9

KENYA
A Mountain To Climb

ROD WOOD

Spiderwize
Peterborough
2019

Other Books by Rod Wood

Kilimanjaro. My Goal. My Story.
(republished as Kilimanjaro. My Story)

Fishing the Net (WITH JANE REEVES).

To my new Granddaughter Amelia,
and to the future of the African elephant

Contents

Prologue

It's 6.30am on July 5th, 2012. The sun is rising over the Rift Valley in East Africa, and in front of me, getting ever closer is the summit of Kilimanjaro. It is within my grasp, my childhood ambition, to stand at the 'roof' of Africa, Uhuru Peak at 5,895 metres above sea level.

And then I have reached it.

I had done it, I stood proudly at the summit having my photo taken by our trusty porters who guided us to the summit. Proud? Yes but knackered to the extent that I couldn't really take in what I had achieved until the following day, staring up at the peak towering above me. Snow covered but surrounded by azure sky, it was an incredible sight from the garden of the Glacier Club in Moshi. Neil and I sat drinking a bottle of Kilimanjaro beer, and asking each other, "Would you do it again?" It had been hard and the answer from both was "no".

But that was five years ago. Although I had related a lot of the climb in my first book, *Kilimanjaro My Story*, and it had given me enormous satisfaction in being able to write a book - again something I thought I was incapable of - there was a yearning to do something similar again.

To be honest, that had existed ever since we had touched down at Heathrow in 2012, and somewhere in my mind I had promised myself to go back to see the Game Reserves I had missed out on then. Also, to see elephants in the wild, whose very existence seems to be becoming harder and harder despite their magnificence, because as humans, we like the ivory and they happen to carry it as part of their anatomy.

Somewhere in the depths of my mind, it was telling me that the promise was to do the trip in 2017, and I have now reached that year. Something inside me was now setting new challenges, and there was a drive to succeed in whatever those challenges were.

I cannot emphasise enough, as I have related in the Kilimanjaro book, what an enormous impact that climb has had on my life. A childhood ambition yes, but when it came to it, especially with Margaret and Graham (two very good friends) pushing me into doing it, there was a great reluctance from me to have a go. I had lost confidence in myself and had gone through a bout of depression. I couldn't find a lot of good in my life, and could only see failure around every corner, especially in myself.

But I did do it, I found it hard but thoroughly enjoyed it, the success, the camaraderie. Those memories are still so fresh in my mind. The achievement of writing a book still moves me when I read bits of it.

"Was it really me that wrote that?" I asked myself. Also, the emotions people have told me they felt as they read my account of my climb. They felt they became me, willing me to achieve my ambition, they had felt what I felt, doing the climb themselves alongside me. Tears, joy, anguish and sadness are all emotions people had said they have experienced while reading my account of the climb and how it had affected me.

This, the new me that they now see, is not the same shell of a man who set off for Africa in June 2012. The man that came down that mountain and made a thank you speech to our leader, Chunga - the first inkling of a change that has gone on and on in me. Now positive, not accepting failure, so driven by a will to succeed. Separating what is important and not important in life, and now not dwelling on that which doesn't matter. I have confidence and belief in myself and am now actively pursuing the advancement of well-being in the work place, to try and prevent other people having to go through what I had endured. Yes, a person reborn who now knew what he wanted, what was realistic, and mapped out how he would achieve his goals.

As one acquaintance said in his review of *Kilimanjaro. My Goal. My Story*: "Coming back down the mountain and his final few hours back at the hotel you realise that this is a totally changed man to the one who tentatively started out on this adventure several months before."

I had fallen in love with Africa and the people I had met there, not just on the Kilimanjaro climb, but also when I had visited Egypt with my then lady friend but now fiancée Jane the previous year in 2011. Yes, there were rogues amongst them, but overall these people were friendly, helpful to the extent that they couldn't do enough for you, and happy to share their countries with you (not forgetting of course the enormous benefits that tourism brought to their economy). There are people who endure hardship, famine, corrupt economies, drought and so much more, but are still so welcoming. We in the so-called civilised world could learn a lot from them.

I am a vet by profession, working in a large animal practice in Shropshire. After my trip to Tanzania, one of my work colleagues visited Mozambique to help in a project to help the native population develop their own dairy industry, firstly by giving them a cow, showing them how properly to look after it, gain more milk that they could then sell and slowly improve their lives while producing a product which was required by more of the population. I had, after my trip, professed an interest in this project myself, a chance to see more of the continent, to help them in their development and to try and repay something back from my chosen profession into helping the so called third world countries. Alas for me, due to the changing political situation in the country, the project was abandoned as it was deemed unsafe to send further vets in to help the project. I was disappointed, though pleased to see that some of those helped had visited these shores courtesy of a Veterinary group that we are part of, to see some farming over here, and even go on a trip to Old Trafford (my Tanzanian friends also seemed to be United fans, such is their worldwide popularity). How much that link remains I don't know. For me it never happened.

So there was a yearning to go back, especially to see the Game Parks I hadn't had the time to see on my previous trip.

Over four years, clients and friends had asked me what my next project was and where was I going to climb, to which I would often reply that despite on the anniversaries of being at the roof of Africa, I always seemed to be as high as I possibly could, the Dolomites, mountainous Crete, a small hill in Rhodes - the biggest one I could see around. I didn't particularly enjoy walking uphill, but kept on doing it. Then, over time, my reply would be: "In 2017, I'm going back to Africa."

"Kilimanjaro again?" they asked.

"I don't know yet, but I will certainly be seeing some wildlife," I said.

It was fascinating in my travels meeting other people who all seemed to know someone else who had tried Kilimanjaro. Some had failed, some succeeded, but all had said how they were told how hard it was. I only met one other person who had done the climb themselves, a charming lady who was taken there as a 50th birthday present with her husband. Though she did find the going tough, like me she had succeeded, though not on the longer route that I had done. Even over here, success, even the attempt seemed to enter you into some sort of select club where you could swap stories. It seemed to gain you some sort of respect, even though so many people have now done the climb. But I could also relate how it had changed me. I would have regretted it for the rest of my life if I had chickened out and not attempted it.

I now have a firm belief that if you have a dream or goal, then you should go for it. Even if you don't succeed, at least you have tried and given it your best shot and can take enormous satisfaction from that. Otherwise, it will always be a what if? That thought had carried me forward, a new man. I had discussed with my son, who had worked in the City, this very ideal. I think he had itchy feet and had a desire to test himself too. Life had become stuck in a bit of a rut and he wanted to get out of it. He took himself and his surfboard up the Pacific coast from Chile to Ecuador (though the board was abandoned on route) meeting new people, ascending parts of the Andes, visiting Machu Picchu, but unfortunately it was too wet to go down to this great historical site. Then he had returned to England, and needing money, gone back to his original job in London. Then itchy feet took him first to Costa Rica surfing, then into working in a ski chalet in France for two winters. But his sense of adventure ("Did he get it from me?"), took him towards joining the Territorial Army and the Paras, until a knee injury put a damper on that.

But like me, he now wanted to fulfil those ambitions he had. He had his dreams, and may he succeed in them, me also, and it was time that I was thinking of another challenge.

The promise I made to myself to go back to Africa was still in my mind. I had looked at walking over the Ethiopian highlands or climbing a mountain called Toubkal in the Atlas Mountains in Morocco. But the pull, the draw, was the Game Reserves, and the more 2016 progressed the more I felt the following year, 2017, was going to be the year I would go again - five years after Kilimanjaro. My promise to myself would be honoured, and it didn't take a lot of thought not to attempt Kilimanjaro this time, but the second highest African peak, Mount Kenya. Not as high but from what I could gather, a harder climb. Decision made, I would give it my best shot.

That was the promise to myself, but as I had changed, then so had my life and my relationships. Re-united with Jane after five years apart, and honouring her undying love for me, we were now together and did enjoy our shared holidays. But I was going to climb a mountain, and although she now enjoyed walking - especially if Pokémon were involved - the thought of climbing Mount Kenya wasn't really her. Unfortunately, as we were getting into walking long distances together, Lake Vyrnwy, then the Dorset

Coastal Path, she slipped while we were walking down to Durdle Door. She broke her ankle very badly, to the extent that after five operations it was as good as it was going to get, but far from perfect. She had to try and develop a new confidence in walking again, and although her doctor had suggested she would be up to climbing the mountain herself, realistically we both knew it was a non-starter.

After much discussion we thought we would come up with a dream holiday, the experience of a lifetime, Mount Kenya (I would climb, she would wait in a hotel at the bottom), then cross into Tanzania and see the Serengeti. We would see elephants in the wild and fulfil another dream of mine, before going to Zanzibar and spending a week on the East African coast, enjoying the sun, the sea and each other. It sounded very exciting, something to really look forward to.

It would be summer 2016 when I retraced my steps back into Shrewsbury and Peake's Travel, as I had done when I went to Kilimanjaro, to see what they could arrange for us along the lines I have just mentioned. I met a lady, one of their service long haul providers, Sue Kinton, who told me it was probably too early to start thinking about the idea yet in terms of booking, as the tour companies would not have formalised their deals yet. "Come back in the autumn when they will be more aware of flights and what hotels they would use," she said "and then we should be able to see what is available and find your dream trip for you". And for another two and a half months, our plans were put in abeyance.

But that burning desire to go back to Africa was growing stronger and stronger. The dreams of seeing its animals in the wild, in their own habitat was drawing me to the extent it had to happen, come what may. I had promised myself 2017, and it was going to happen. By October I was chomping at the bit to get back to see Sue and see what she could arrange. I got in to see her just before we were going to take a short break down to Dorset for Jane to conquer her demons and walk down to Durdle Door, the scene of her accident almost 12 months ago to the day. Sue took down my requirements, early summer, a small party for the climb (it was nice to get to know the gang, five of us, when taking the Lemosho route up Kilimanjaro, and getting to know our trusty porters as well, though not as well as I would have liked). She would see what she could find out and put some sort of package together for us. She would ring me when she had heard back from the tour organisers.

I waited patiently, until one day I received a text from her saying: "What did you think of the plans I have e-mailed you?" I hadn't received them and rang to tell her that. She would try again, and they did duly arrive. I was eager to open the mail, read what she had sorted out, and was gobsmacked with what a company called 'Africa and Beyond' had put together as a possible package. It encompassed my climb while Jane remained in the hotel at the bottom, then took us into Tanzania and the Serengeti, and finally to Zanzibar, and an all-inclusive luxury hotel near the beach, before flying back home to England.

Perfect, I couldn't wait to find out, I was more than excited.

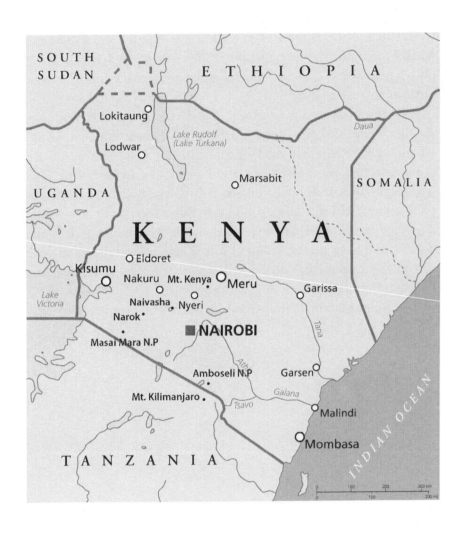

1

Planning and Arrangements

Yes, what the operators had sorted out looked perfect. We would fly out from Heathrow to Nairobi and then be transferred to a hotel on the western side of Mount Kenya, the Naro Moru River Lodge. This would be Jane's base for the next six days, while I, after an initial night there, would undertake my mountain trek, and if successful would be back for one night there to re-unite with my lady before heading back to Nairobi. From there, we would catch a flight to Kilimanjaro Airport (it would be nice for me to revisit this place and say hi to my mountain again - an emotional reunion). We would spend the night in Arusha before heading off to the lands of the Rift Valley I had dreamed about. First the Serengeti and then the Ngoro Ngoro Crater. We would pass through villages, farmland and plantations of bananas, maize and coffee, before arriving at the Manyara Wildlife Safari Camp. Manyara, which Hemingway had described as: "The loveliest place I had visited in Africa."

Here, our first experience of game drives, African wildlife in the flesh and then the campfire when we returned. Then the Serengeti, and if we were lucky, the start of the annual wildebeest migration across the plains of Africa. Lion, elephant, giraffe, gazelle, eland, to name but a few, even a hot-air balloon trip if we wanted. Two days then Ngorongoro, again for two days in a luxury farm lodge, with more game drives while staying in the world's largest intact volcanic caldera. Hippos in small lakes, more and more for us to see. Then onto Lake Burunge for one last night on safari, to see more wildlife and have the chance to interact with local communities, learning about their culture - real Africa.

Then it would be goodbye to our safari as we would fly from Kilimanjaro to Zanzibar to spend a few days, being spoilt at a beach club and spa situated on a long, unspoilt stretch of sand. A tropical landscape, our intended destination was named the 'Best resort in Tanzania' in 2005 at the World Travel Awards. Then after a time of luxury, our return, back to Kilimanjaro, Nairobi and London. We would have had our dream holiday, it looked perfect, everything I had wanted from this trip, the climb, a diversity of safaris, then to be pampered and spoilt on the East African coast.

I had already asked work, with this holiday in mind, if I could have an extra week of unpaid holiday, as age was creeping on and I couldn't cope with the rest of the year on less than two weeks holiday. They were quite happy with that, and gave me an extra two days of holiday per year. We had been summoned to a staff meeting one day, which as ever was late starting, so I went to relieve myself, only to return to the staff room to find everyone in there staring at me. I joked that it wasn't my birthday again and sat down for the head honcho to announce that it was a special day, someone today had now been working for the firm for 10 years, and the management wanted to acknowledge that achievement and loyalty. Gosh, how embarrassing, it was me, and it hadn't even crossed my mind today. I was later told in private of my reward, extra holiday, no watches etc.

I read the email when it came from Sue. I was sold, this really was the holiday of a lifetime, something I really, really wanted to do. Everything about it was perfect. Well almost everything, there was one thing missing from the email, the price. I texted Sue, it would follow, sorry, she thought it was with the itinerary.

The trip was seriously expensive. Perhaps not for some, and it would be a holiday of a lifetime, but I hadn't envisaged it costing this much. Yes, I knew the pound had fallen seriously against the dollar, the currency that these African countries tended to work in, and that Tanzania had seriously put up tourist taxes, (25% I had heard), but I wasn't thinking we would have to pay in the region of £12,000 between us, especially considering the cost of my Kilimanjaro trip, including my flights those five years previously. It was miniscule compared with this price. Were our dreams about to be shattered? We also had the little thing of a wedding to plan after I had proposed to Jane in Paris the previous summer, and although she had said it wouldn't be 2017 because we had too much on, I said we would marry that year. A pity we couldn't consider this as a honeymoon, but no, it was too expensive for us to even contemplate.

We had to go to Shrewsbury, so arranged to go and meet Sue and discuss our intended trip. I told her that what she had organised was exactly what I wanted, except the price. She understood and even told us that the price had gone up nearly £3,000 in the time she had been researching the trip, and there were no guarantees it wouldn't go up again, though it would be difficult to increase the prices the airlines charged us if we had paid for all the flights already.

We talked it through, where we could make shortcuts, and came up with what we thought may be more acceptable. Jane would fly to Nairobi at the end of my climb, meet me at the airport and then we would fly on to Tanzania together to complete the rest of the trip as planned, but in a different hotel which would again save a little bit of money. Sue would find out a new price for us, getting back to us as soon as she could.

I waited impatiently over the coming days for the new estimate. It did finally arrive, and although still pricey, yes, we would accept that price, now nearer £10,000, but very conscious of all the add-ons there would be such as visas, injections for Yellow Fever, anti-malarial drugs, the list would go on. I rang Sue up with one or two queries, but when answered, accepted the new quote and paid my deposit.

Just after putting these plans in place, while organising this Kenya trip, XLVets (a body our practice was part of and who had organised the Mozambique project mentioned earlier) joined up with another charity, Send a Cow. They would go to East Africa (Kenya, Uganda and Rwanda) over the coming two years to help these people develop their bovine industry. Why now, when I had already committed to going back to Africa for my climb? Why now resurrect this aid project which I had already professed an interest in? But after not a lot of thought, I emailed the organiser and said that I would still be interested in going, but preferably in 2018, and may consider it as my last action as a vet before retiring. I mentioned my Mount Kenya project, and I could use it as a means of raising some money for the charity.

A positive response, almost straight away, though I was offered the chance to go to Rwanda in October 2017, rather than Kenya in May 2018, as Kenya may still be fresh in my mind. No, after a little thought, I would stick with Kenya and 2018, the retirement thing I hoped for but would have to see how life progressed. And yes, thank you for the thought of trying to raise money on the climb, every little helped. I was signed up, and would be going to Kenya two years running, I was excited by the thought of that, very excited.

But as we turned into 2017, Jane seemed distracted, more than just because her parents were not in the best of health. She returned from visiting them one Saturday to announce that she realised what was at the back of her mind at last, and it was the thought of the cost of the trip, and the fact that she couldn't afford it. The trip would set her finances back for some time to come if we did go. No, she couldn't go, what did I think?

To be honest, it was more than stretching my finances as well, but could I or would I pass up this opportunity to see the real Africa? I had it in my mind that if I didn't do it now, then I would never do it – and that I would regret for the rest of my life.

I was really torn between going or not. I knew what I had promised myself, and so went to enquire about the cost if Zanzibar was dropped, after all there was no point going there by myself. The point about that part of the holiday was to relax together, spend a week on our own in luxury. Sue did come back to me yet again, but still the price was very high as it was just me, I was being penalised for Jane cancelling, and at every destination I was now having to pay a singles supplement. This was blowing my mind, I really wanted to go and was committed to doing Mount Kenya because the fundraising was already online. I had written an article on Kilimanjaro and overcoming depression in the *Veterinary Times* in early 2017 and had set up a Just Giving page which I had publicised in the article. Jane thought that I could just go and do the mountain and come back again, just be away for a week, then come back and we could then go somewhere else together.

What to do?

After days of anguish and having decided I would do the trip less Zanzibar as planned (I had to see my wildlife), I suddenly one morning while lying awake in bed thought "no". But what if they could sort out a couple of days on safari after the climb, staying in Kenya. Perhaps a ten day stay? I suggested this to Sue, again she would see what she could arrange. Eventually she came back to me with a two-week trip, incorporating three game parks when the climb was done. The price was far better and they had dropped a lot of the flight cancellation penalties from Jane's trip, also some of the single supplements. At last, I thought I was sorted, I would accept these plans, a good compromise (and Jane had managed to arrange a holiday with one of her friends, Helen, matron of honour to be).

Confirmation for Kenya 2018 as well, so all was looking good for me. I could at last get down to sorting the finer points out: vaccinations, visas, equipment and clothing.

I was pleased at last that it was becoming a reality. Yes, I was sad there would be no Jane, but I was going to realise a dream, and a promise to myself, and I think at the end of the day even if that sounded a little selfish, the disappointment of not going would have stayed with me for a considerable length of time, if not forever.

Sorted - or so I thought.

While out on my rounds one day, I received a call from Sue informing me that with this itinerary the climb was fine, but for the safari to take place, they needed a minimum of two people, and at the moment there was just me. I could arrive two days early, no problem and they would bear any extra cost, hotel upgrades as it turned out, or stick with the dates arranged and see if anyone else signed up. At the onset with the climb I had said that I didn't want to be in a large group, the five of us on Kilimanjaro was brilliant in the camaraderie we built up between each other, helping each other when one was down, or struggling, especially Neil and altitude sickness. We built a bond that if one failed then we all had, and those last few hours at Addis Ababa were special, yes, then only four but that time together was special before we boarded the plane to Heathrow and then went our separate ways. They told me there would be a minimum of me, and a maximum of seven. But on the safari - I didn't want too many - they said seven in a truck, but there could have been a hundred trucks, a convoy hammering across the plains. The thought of only two of us sounded great, more intimate with our guides. I could get their personal stories, and WE could see more of what we wanted to see, without falling out with everyone.

I wanted this trip sorted out, with no risk of late cancellation. After all, it was only (though I didn't know at the time) a few days before the Kili trek that they had got a large enough party with Chris and Claire signing up that it was confirmed it would go ahead. I would have been devastated if it had been called off at the last moment, and almost certainly wouldn't be the person I am now if I hadn't done that climb then. No - go for the trip that would go ahead without any what-ifs, so long as work said it was okay to go earlier, then I would move forward two days. They had no problems with that, so ringing Sue back, we would finalise everything around our new dates, and take the hotel upgrades in my stride.

Were we there at last?

There were just a couple of points I needed to sort out.

Firstly, the first day was a bit ambiguous, almost giving an impression that I would get off the plane, travel to the hotel, and start walking up the mountain straight away. That sounded a bit harsh, but on enquiring, we found that I would be starting the climb the next day. Secondly, from my intended itinerary, I would be leaving Amboseli early on my last day to arrive back in Nairobi around midday, but my flight wasn't until nearly midnight. Twelve hours to kill, luggage in tow, and I had heard, rightly or wrongly that this city wasn't the safest for single travellers. Would they put me up for the day in a hotel, and then would they take me to the airport, or would I have to find my own way there? Were there any other suggestions of what I could do?

The suggestion of going to a Game Park was made (Nairobi Game Park) situated in the city, but was very expensive at £185 for an afternoon (and even if there were a high concentration of black rhinos there, I hoped that I would have already seen them elsewhere). Alternatively, I could visit the house of author Karen Blixen of *Out of Africa* fame - mental note to get hold of the book as my holiday read.

After much thought over three weeks, I contacted Sue to say I would go for the latter, the Karen Blixen tour. They would take me and my luggage, and then drop me off at the airport when finished. With only five and a half weeks to go before travelling, I was finally sorted after the best part of six months trying to arrange it all. Thank you, Sue, for your patience.

Oh boy, I think I need a holiday to get over trying to arrange this one! But we had got there in the end, and now all I could do was really look forward to it, and I was! The visa application, done online this time, was quite straight forward, with even my computer skills coping with the process, other than downloading a couple of documents onto it, but Jane helped me with those. Vaccinations, other than an initial check-up with my doctor, Tom Underwood again, were put in the hands of the practice nurse. An appointment arranged, we went through together what I may need. Yellow Fever was the biggest concern, and certainly if I had still been flying from Kenya into Tanzania, then it would have been essential. When I had the vaccination for Kilimanjaro, I was told it would last for five years, it would just have expired. But somewhere along the line, they had extended this to 10 years, and I am not sure if now it lasts for a lifetime. We excluded that one. Hepatitis B, Polio, Diphtheria and Tetanus, yes, I would need all those so both arms were going to suffer. Rabies was the other question: Did I think I would be bitten by any animals while out there? Well, it certainly wasn't my intention, so we gave that one a miss as well.

Lastly, Malaria. Again, what was the risk period? While on the mountain I would be above mosquito habitat, but what about the first 24 hours before we started climbing, at what height was Naro Moru Lodge? If above 2,000m, no risk, if not then there was. I didn't know the height, so we assumed we would need it, and I was to start the course of Malarone before the climb, continuing until after I returned to England for another week.

I had put together most of the kit I needed, bought what I thought would be useful in the future, meaning all I would need to hire would be a sleeping bag that would keep me warm in the extreme temperatures at the summit. It seemed pointless buying stuff that I would need for only the last few hours of the climb, in the night in sub-zero temperatures.

Checking with Sue, I think we were almost there. It was time to get fit and ready to climb.

2

Preparations

I GUESS MY preparations for Kilimanjaro were geared specifically for a climb, starting with general walking in my vicinity in Shropshire, the Wrekin, other local hills, and one or two walks I got from a Shropshire Walks book I had been given. There was some structure to it, trying to walk at least twice a week, building up to a week on Exmoor, staying with my parents, doing more hill walks, then the Coleridge Way over two days. One last hard climb up the Watkins Path on Snowden and my preparations were complete.

I had found Kilimanjaro, other than the summit climb and the Barranco Wall, reasonably comfortable walking, helped by our pole, pole pace (slow, slow) because of the lack of oxygen in the air. But now, with an easing of my work duties at weekends and with less nights on call, I was slowly having to give in to getting older and I had more time to prepare. But there were two other changes now. Firstly, Mum and Dad had also moved to Telford to be closer to me and my brother. Doing any training on Exmoor like last time was not an option. Secondly, I now walked often anyway, partly because I found I now enjoyed it more, and partly because I found it helped ease a back problem that raised its ugly head every now and again. I also hoped it would help reduce my weight and that dreaded middle-age spread.

It would not now be uncommon for me to walk most nights, even in the dark evenings of winter when I had returned from work. A walk, even just around the block, was now very common, and in the safety of street lighting I could do 30 - 40 minutes most evenings before settling down with Jane. I would walk to the town centre, not far away, rather than using the car. Generally I used my feet whenever I could.

On top of that, Jane had got me a Fitbit for Christmas, partly with the climb in mind, and hoping it would give me the push to train for the mountain. Set at 10,000 steps a day, it gave me a target to achieve from my daily walking. But having not suffered with altitude sickness five years previously on Kilimanjaro, despite the fit guys with me that had, I was conscious that I didn't want to get myself overly fit, though carrying less pounds would be an advantage and good for my general health anyway. If I could lose just over five kilos in the five to six months I had until I went to Kenya, I would be quite happy with that.

So, yes, I did start walking a lot, and as the days and evenings got longer I started going further and further. I had discovered the Telford Town Park at last, having lived in Telford for all these years, and found with the variety of tracks and paths, I could walk without going the same way twice. The bonus was that I found us residents of Telford were really blessed with a wonderful park, with trees, ponds, hills and historic structures such as the Stirchley Chimney showing off our industrial heritage. It offered so much of interest. Even sometimes when walking into town, being a faster walker than Jane, who could walk up a path in her own time looking for Pokémon as she went, I could take the long route around a lake and re-join her by the town centre. And all this was just on my doorstep.

I was walking a lot, so in the early months of the year I wasn't too worried about how much I needed to step up my exercise. But one other problem was about to arise. I was on-call for a weekend in early January and was coming back from a calving late on a Saturday night when I noticed that my right eye seemed sore, as if I had something in it, blurred and quite watery. I was aware that a piece of cow muck may have splashed into it (and it can be quite acidic) a couple of days earlier, so I bathed it several times a day with saline, hoping for an improvement. But then it was noticeable that even in daylight my vision in that eye was blurred. I mentioned it at work and was forced to put it in the accident book. After a couple of days with no improvement, they persuaded me to go to my GP to get it checked out. Ringing for an appointment, the triage doctor referred me straight to an optician, and asked me to ring back if I couldn't get an appointment so she could try and get me to the local emergency eye clinic at Shrewsbury hospital. No joy anywhere, and even the hospital wouldn't be able to fit me in for 24 hours. At last one Boots optician shop informed me that they were changing premises, had no optician in, but that as I had spoken to him he had a duty of care to find me somewhere, and thankfully he did.

Jane carted me into Wellington; I needed a driver as I was told I probably wouldn't be able to drive myself as I would have drops put in my eyes that would dilate my pupils. We found the opticians and while I went in, she took herself off to get her nails done. A preliminary examination with a lovely lady optician showed no damage to my cornea, but although it was only six months since I had had an eye test, she said she would repeat it. "Read the lines as small as you can," she asked, covering my left eye. I could see the big top letter and that was it. Swopping eyes, I could manage down to the last but one line, that was a bit of a shock.

She put the drops in my eyes, gosh that really stung, and then I waited back in reception while they started to take effect. Ten minutes later I was back in again. After a long look, and she was rather taken aback by the sudden onset of it, there I had a well-developed cataract in the centre of my right lens. I was lost in thought, I wasn't expecting this, and I mulled over all the connotations it could have on my life. Could I drive? Could I work? My African adventure, marriage, there was so much it could influence. I was stunned. Yes, they are fixable, but how long until I would be sorted out, cataract removed and replaced with a new lens?

I was told that it had progressed far enough already that I was at the op stage now, it wouldn't have to deteriorate further until they decided that they would have to operate. Yes, I could carry on driving, yes, she saw no reason why I shouldn't continue my adventure. Hopefully I would go on the waiting list and should have it dealt with in 18 weeks maximum.

Jane arrived back and carried on as if nothing had happened, me, I was rather numb with it all. We finished at the opticians with her saying that if I had any other queries then please get back in touch with her. Jane dragged me into Iceland, although what flavour of ice cream we would buy was the last thing on my mind with so much churning over in it. Would there be radical changes in my life? Well, I couldn't do much now other than inform work, and wait, wait for my appointment to come.

The next day I was off anyway, a trip into Shrewsbury was planned to meet a PR lady about my books. The first snow of winter and I was still upset with my news, so Jane drove. I had a chat with the management team at work on how I was feeling, then went back to day to day life. Then on Sunday we took a trip to Coventry to see the Wasps play rugby, and I have to admit I did struggle to watch the game, which was dull, and the floodlights shone straight into my eyes. The game was a bit of a blur, my good eye was trying to compensate for the bad one. At least there was another Wasps win, and I could savour the atmosphere of the crowd. This could affect me in work and in play.

The next day at work first thing I had an appointment with management. Could I work? Could I drive? There was no beating about the bush, how blunt was that. I would manage, may need to adjust my computer to cut out reflections, and may need to take the odd break if on it too long and it was causing some eye strain. Then, and I was still trying to do my walks, I was sent off to Lincoln to assist with the Avian Influenza outbreak there. Déjà vu with the foot and mouth in 2001? The phone call came, where would I like my appointment, Telford or Stoke?

"Which would be quicker?" I asked.

"Stoke," they replied.

"Then that is my choice," I said.

An appointment in early April was arranged for what sounded like another assessment, still 10 weeks off, and then I still didn't know how long it would be until the op. There was nothing I could do but wait, hoping I wouldn't need to change any other plans, mainly my trip to Mount Kenya. It was déjà vu as another outbreak came and I was the designated Welfare Officer in the culling of 18,500 turkeys, the latest case. Glasses steaming up inside protective suits and full-face respirators when one eye was suffering anyway wasn't easy, but after a few minutes the view did clear.

I would have to say in all my years of vetting that I have never seen such a devastating disease, as the turkeys deteriorated with the illness so quickly, to the extent that a bird that seemed 'healthy' in a couple of hours could be very ill, and not long afterwards would be breathing its last. There were many birds in front of me changing their health status so quickly, horrific. A very hard few days, though I did get to see a bit of the city in a quieter moment, with some spectacular views of the cathedral standing out above the fog, lit up in the dark. And Steep Street, very aptly named.

To cut a long story short, the appointment was cancelled, rescheduled and after a lengthy Saturday morning at Stoke, courtesy of one of my best friends, Dave, kindly driving me there, and those drops again, they decided to try and do the op before I went to Kenya, nine days before in fact. The effects of the drops, the weather outside, and the lack of phone reception in the hospital meant I had to ring Dave from outside to pick me up. With my pupils dilated, and the sun so bright, I couldn't even see the phone let alone dial a number to get him. I did at last find a dark corner in the bike sheds to ring him, only to find that he was just outside the main door enjoying the sun, no more than 20 yards from where I had been, but I couldn't see a thing. The bright sun, it was hurting, and it was just as well I hadn't driven myself there, I think I would have been sitting in the car park a considerable time waiting for my vision to improve.

It was nice to have a chance to chat with Dave, and a Stokie thing, on the way to the hospital he had introduced me to Oatcakes, I had never had them before, but filled with bacon they were delicious. We found a little shop in a back street which we eventually managed to find from his wife Lisa's instructions, and as we walked in I was staggered to see seven members of staff, preparing, cooking and selling these breakfast treats. Dave informed me it was like bread to Stoke people, and certainly in our brief stay in the shop the number they shifted was incredible. There were all sorts of fillings, you could have a full English in one of these things. It seemed a very lucrative business.

And on the way home, a well-deserved pint, of course still avoiding sunlight because my eyes were still hurting. It did wear off some hours later when I was at home. But once again, thanks Dave for helping me out in my moment of need.

At least now I had a date set for my operation, nine days before I was due to fly, and the nurses didn't seem unduly worried about that. If they got a cancellation, they would try and get me in earlier, but for the time being, at least the operation was arranged, and I hoped this would help me in day to day life. As we moved into summer and a long dry and sunny period, I can't deny that the eye was not causing me more discomfort.

As I have said, I had got into walking again, and did so to some extent or another as often as I could, though it was rather tedious having the limited number of routes I could do on the dark nights of winter restricted to where there was good street lighting. I was not unduly worried therefore about getting into the stride of it again. Walk I must and walk I would do!

3

Training Commences

MY FIRST SERIOUS walk, one I had done before a couple of times, and did before my Kili climb, was a walk through the Ironbridge Gorge, encompassing some 11 or 12 hostelries on the way. My son wanted to walk and stop somewhere on the way for a meal over the Christmas period, so along with Jane (her first strenuous walk since breaking her ankle), and Richard's girlfriend, Tamsin, we set off on this walk on Boxing Day. Chilly, but at least dry, we managed a comfortable eight miles on this route, though we weren't quite as successful on the meal front, only managing to find food that would be served sometime in the near future at the last but one pub (the last was closed as well). It was nice to spend time with Richard and Tamsin, good to get Jane walking again, and good to have started my training though my departure date was still nearly six months away. No after effects for either of us.

I would try to build from here, just increasing fitness and come late spring would then try and bring some hill walking into my programme, practising for the inclines of the mountain.

I had also been to the Health Centre again to get checked out by my GP, Tom Underwood, and with a clean bill of health (just about!), could start seriously planning my trip.

ONLY FIVE MONTHS TO GO:

Arriving home in the dark after work, in the cold and sometimes wet, it could on some evenings be hard to motivate oneself to get out there and do the hard yards. I suppose that is where the Fitbit came in useful as you became ever-controlled by the number of steps you had done, and you had to achieve your daily target, 10,000 for me. This often meant having to walk four to five kilometres on the streets, and in the dark. That is where it did get boring, doing the same, or virtually the same route each night. Weekends would give me the chance to walk the Town Park, exploring more and more different routes, going further and further, and discovering more areas of natural beauty - especially around the several pools in the park. Some Saturdays I would get up to 10 kilometres, and rarely followed the same route twice. I was beginning to see why this park scored so highly in the national competition for town parks the previous year. And generally, even for winter, the paths were good, and you were not plodding through mud all the time.

The weight was starting to come off slowly, but at least I was going in the right direction. If the actual travel arrangements were frustrating me, at least as I knew I was going, I could start thinking of what equipment I would need, what I had, what I would buy, and what I would beg, borrow or steal (hire out there). I could take my time to try and spread the expense over the coming months until departure.

Clothing was the big issue, as I found five years previously, you can carry a lot up that you don't use until the final ascent when the temperatures are so low when you are walking through the night. Especially with the warm outer layers, one would be wearing a size or two above normal, as you were wearing so many layers beneath them. I wore seven layers for the summit walk on Kilimanjaro. You almost certainly would find these garments too big in the future for general walking, unless considering another climb like this, and I wasn't, so it would be silly to spend upwards of £200 on a waterproof, and again on a duck down inner garment, when both would be too large for me in the future. Something that I would consider carefully over the coming weeks were visits to the outdoor pursuit shops to see what was available, plus other little extras like sleeping bag liners, light pillows and water sterilisation tablets. I had decided to hire a sleeping bag out there as the ones in the shops with suitable tog ratings were mega-expensive.

I had my boots, my walking sticks and other things I hadn't used in the past five years, but which would now come in useful, and I now had a new mattress. More would follow. January, and I was five and a half months off. Yes, I was starting to get into the walking, and there were not many days I didn't get to my intended 10,000 steps a day. I was even getting up to the dizzy heights of 100,000 plus per week, more weeks than not, plodding the streets of Telford at night, and then one or two long walks through the town park at the weekend when I could walk in daylight. I even passed my first 20,000 step day, though I would have to be honest and admit some of those steps were dancing to my favourite local band, The Endings, and their Irish music. But steps are steps and the dancing gave the heart rate a good workout. Aerobics!

The only big failure week was the week when I was on call at the weekend and could not travel far from the phone or car unless called out. This was also the weekend that I discovered that I had an eye problem!

I had for some time been trying to read a book Graham had given me as a present, *The Last Train to Zona Verde* by Paul Theroux. He has written a lot of books on his travels around the world, also a lot of fiction. This one, I would have to admit, I had been trying to read for some time and was struggling to get into it, but I decided I would have a real go at it and finish it. He describes a journey he undertook from the Cape up the west coast of Africa through South Africa, Namibia, Botswana and then Angola on his journey towards the Congo and the intention to go further north. He describes a variety of landscapes, spotting cattle in the bush until he crosses into what he describes as 'The Red Line' into a different Africa the "improvised, slapped together Africa of tumbled fences and cooking-fires, of mud and thatch, of heat and poverty, of roadblocks, mobs and anarchy." Landscapes where animal life cannot survive, of real poverty amongst the indigenous population but with the mineral resource the country possesses, a very rich country but only to those in power, and those involved in corruption. To most of the population, and from what he describes, if the money was distributed fairly to offer help to everyone, it wouldn't exist, just poverty, real poverty. Hope – little, but still an enduring happiness in these native people.

This wasn't the Africa the tourist books describe, of wildlife, safaris, the Garden Route, even Kilimanjaro (where again the locals were such wonderfully happy and helpful people).

At the end of his trail, he found it too depressing to go on. Congo and its corruption could be even worse than what he had seen already. It was a sad end to the Africa he had loved as he didn't feel he could return at a later date.

It made me question whether this is the Africa I want to go back to? And if I went back, would it spoil my opinions of my brief encounter with the continent? Was the aid we sent - and our governments should really ensure it gets to where it is needed - really of any value to these poor people even if it reaches them? Shouldn't we spend our money on how to find and collect water, and then how to use it better, to improve their agriculture so they could produce more of their own food? Help the people at grassroot levels, not line the pockets of the powerful, the rich and the corrupt. Otherwise, Africa would always be a continent of upheaval, of war and of famine.

Did I really want to go back? The enduring answer, after some thought was yes, because even if one could forget the people, there was the wildlife that had inspired me through all my life so far, and I wanted to see it for real while, and I can only apologise if I repeat myself, while it was still there in its native surrounds, the Serengeti, the Masai Mara, and all the other famous Game Parks. I wanted to see elephants, before our obsession with ivory destroyed their populations, in their natural habitat. Rhinos and their horns, the same, and despite tremendous efforts by conservationists, how much longer would we see them? The great natural predators, lions, cheetahs, leopards, all slowly but surely dropping in number as man doesn't seem to want to live in harmony with them, just destroy them.

Here in the Great Rift Valley was to me one of the great wonders of the world, thousands and thousands of animals living in their natural habitat, the carnivores, the grass eaters, the hunters and the hunted.

I wanted to see it all for real while I still could. And I guess on the positive side, wasn't my trip with Send a Cow in 2018 all about what I hoped our aid would be? I would be going over to help them develop their own agriculture. I hoped this project would bear great fruit to the people of Kenya, Uganda and Rwanda where we were being sent. A fortnight of my time, I hope will give a lifetime of benefits to many, if the powers that be allow their development. I was still going, but the message in Paul Theroux's book would stay with me throughout the preparation, and I would expect for a long time after that. I know nothing of colonial Kenya and will endeavour to try and find out more when over there. We may have already exploited the country ourselves. I have heard of the Mau Mau risings, but only by name.

I trust I will come back with a more thorough history of a nation, that now let's face it, beats the hell out of us if we put a running track, cross country course or marathon in front of them. January was passing, I was walking and reaching my targets most days. Things were going well!

FOUR MONTHS TO GO:

Luckily, as of yet there was still no sign of a winter to speak of. Yes, there were frosts, but no snow, and I was still being lucky that on my return from work I wasn't being drenched when I went on my walks. The walking was going surprisingly well in fact, with me usually clocking up the required number of steps each week, especially with those long Saturday walks when I could step and follow the rugby and football scores while out. Refusing to pay Sky the ridiculous amounts they charge for their sport, and in my opinion ruining football by the amount of money they put in, giving players stupid salaries and allowing managers to buy rather than coach players, sport on a Saturday afternoon was a thing of the past. Wasps would generally play their home rugby games on a Sunday, and fixtures were few and far apart over the coming weeks. So finding time to walk was easy, neatly fitting around attempts to decorate the hall, the landing and the lounge. My only dilemma was trying to work out how fit I wanted to be, and I still wanted to lose weight.

It was surprisingly hard to find much about Mount Kenya, I did find a little on Google about the walks up, but little else. I would have to be honest, I was far more interested in reading and re-reading the itinerary of the Game Parks in Tanzania and making the hard decision of whether to cancel that part and just climb.

It was also at this time that we fixed a wedding date. Jane thought another year would slip by before we tied the knot, but I had said next year (2017) when I proposed, and I meant to be true to my word. We were both working on Valentine's Day, so we had arranged to go out to our favourite restaurant, Renaissance, in Shrewsbury on the following Saturday. Julie, our hostess, had made a couple of comments about the wedding.

"We will marry in the summer and have our evening do here in this restaurant", I said to Jane. I did want my closest friends there, those that had helped me through depression those five years and more ago, and had stood by me for years, but other than them, we could have a small do and it would be this year. I guess that made my mind up on Tanzania, it was too expensive with the wedding as well, and I would see what could be arranged about doing a Game Park in Kenya and cutting out some of the flights. Thank you again Sue for sorting it all out for me.

THREE MONTHS TO GO:

It was now March and the trip still seemed a long way off. Preparations would be interrupted by a couple of weekends away, a promised weekend in Salisbury with Jane and a golfing weekend in Essex with the boys, though with work I wouldn't get down there till late on the Friday night. In fact, both weekends I did still manage to walk.

In Salisbury, Jane and I walked a long town walk, following the river north before heading up the historic hill fort of Old Sarum on a beautiful spring morning, sunny and bar the wind at the top of the fort, very pleasantly warm. We had a nice pint in a pub in the market square, before going to see the cathedral and museum, and being able to admire Constable's portrait of the building. I was amazed at the detail with each brush stroke. It was far better than the cold and windswept day at Laycock and then Stonehenge we had had the previous day, before the rain caught up with us mid-afternoon and we had another enjoyable meal at a restaurant called the Old Charter House. Everyone was so friendly in this town. Not even a sniff of Novichok on our visit!

Then a golf and rugby weekend with the boys. Even with them, you do walk a long way around a golf course, laden with a golf bag, and the way I played, a lot further than I needed to, but all good exercise before the walk into Dunmow in the evening for beer and sustenance.

But news arrived in the post that I didn't want. Stoke hospital had changed their booking system and subsequently had cancelled all their eye appointments. I didn't know when my appointment would be, let alone the operation. I really had hoped that it would all have been done before I travelled, now I just didn't know.

I could only wait patiently and see, if you'll excuse the pun. Fingers crossed it would still be done before Kenya, I certainly wanted it before the wedding, and not to be photographed standing beside Jane with a patch over one eye.

TWO MONTHS TO GO:

April arrived, just over nine weeks to go now and it still seemed some way off. But here I decided it was about time I started to find out something about this mountain and this country. Scouring Amazon, I did find a couple of books on Kenya and Mount Kenya. I waited for them to arrive.

I needed to get my vaccinations done as well, and malaria tablets, I mustn't forget those, although I did have some left from my last trip, where, due to the altitude we were at, we were above mosquito height so didn't need them. This time, I wasn't sure what altitude we would be at, especially in the Game Parks, so decided that I would go prepared.

I went to an appointment at the Health Centre with a nurse, computer on and we worked through which jabs I needed and those I didn't. Hepatitis, polio, tetanus and diphtheria, one a triple vaccine, two injections, one in each arm. She would sort out a prescription for the malarial tablets for me, this I would have to pay for.

I had decided to combine this with a long walk, the walk we had done at Christmas with my son in the Severn Gorge. This time I was going to start at home, walk to the Health Centre, then onto Blist Hill and start the walk from there, down the bank to the river. Then I would follow the Severn back up to Ironbridge, stopping for a well-deserved pint of Wainwrights bitter at the Black Swan, sitting out enjoying the sunshine, before continuing up the bank, through the woods and then joining the Silkin Way back through the Town Park and home. Four hours but I did it, easily, other than two arms which were now starting to ache a bit. Spring was here, it was dry and there were flowers in the woods: celandine, wild garlic, wood anemones, cherry in flower and even my first bluebell of the year. The scents were gorgeous, yes, for once an early spring.

Jane was off at the end of the week, and it was my long weekend off so on the Friday we took ourselves off to Lake Vyrnwy and were going to walk around there, as we had done now nearly 18 months ago just before she had broken her ankle. Again, spoiled by the weather, a little chilly on the shaded western side, but once we rounded the far end and were heading back towards the car, in the sun it was lovely. I suppose inevitably at some stage Jane was going to start feeling it, and sure enough she did so having reached the entrance to the Lake Vyrnwy Hotel. I left her there to walk back to the car, crossing the dam, taking a young couple's photo for them as I passed, and then back to the car park. Lots of people surrounded my car, strange, but it was because I was parked next to an old Bentley, an estate car I suppose you would describe it as, with wooden trim, huge headlights. A beautiful ancient beast. I think the audience assembled as I approached, thought I was the owner, and that they would be able to have a look inside as well. Disappointment when I unlocked my Qashqai and drove off to retrieve this redhead by the side of the road and whisk her up to the hotel at the top of the drive.

Not a cloud in the sky, lambs in the fields below, and in perfect sunshine a wonderful view of the lake from the balcony of the bar. Spoilt a second time this week with the weather, and two very long walks, though this one largely on the flat. It wasn't falling off, but I was certainly losing some pounds, I felt good. I carried on steadily through the month but as April progressed, what had seemed so far away for so long, now seemed such a short time to go, and diminishing rapidly all the time. Seven weeks was soon six, then five as the month ended.

My brochure had finally arrived. The brochures, travel information that had come through with the booking described a walk each day from point A to point B, an increase in altitude of x amount in metres, but not a lot more. It sounded relatively easy.

Then the books came and as I flicked through them, read a few pages, then a couple of chapters, I was starting to think that this wasn't going to be so easy! It sounded harder than Kilimanjaro, and after all, I was five years older. Snow, glaciers, shingle slopes, it sounded tough going.

What I still didn't know were the distances we would be walking each day, how long that would take each day (I had a rough outline on Kilimanjaro), and I say we, it could just be me and my porters. That I wouldn't know until I arrived there. What I did know now was that the rainy season should just about be over unless I was very unlucky, and, as far as my safaris were concerned, I was probably just going to be too early for the great wildlife migrations, described as the greatest wildlife show on earth. That was a shame and something I would have to admit that I hadn't even considered when booking, but something I really would love to have seen. Perhaps they will set off early this year, just for me.

But the climb was starting to concern me, would I cope with it? The terrain looked so rugged in one of the books I had got, a book called *On God's Mountain*. I was starting to worry, especially as I hadn't done a lot of hill work yet, my planned trip to Dorset to do the South West Coastal Path as part of my training, the ups and downs of the cliff paths, had fallen through. It would have to be what Shropshire could offer in the time that I had available, fitting it in between work and other commitments, back to climbing The Wrekin, Pontesbury Hill, The Lawley and Caer Carodoc. I would have to hope that would be enough.

My first attempt at the Wrekin was hard work but I managed it without stopping, which I was more than pleased with, and to stop and view Shropshire from the highest point, magnificent views, landmarks in every direction you looked. Just over an hour up and down, so not that strenuous, but at least a start. The next time, on the way home from work one Friday night, and having got to the top, I decided to take the longer route and continue down the other side on what can be a treacherous downhill slope, slippery even when dry as underfoot was so hard, with just the top layer of soil giving as you trod your way down. Again, I was pleased I had carefully negotiated my way down an arduous walk, and then back along the Forestry Commission track back to the car. Undulating up and down but rewarding with the sight of the bluebells in the woods at their magnificent best. A blue carpet on the slopes above and below me.

A good pace as well, so I was well happy with myself.

I had an appointment for donating blood mid-month, it was the last time I would be able to give for a few months as my African travel would preclude me for six months from my return. It's always nice to get that thank you text, and then to say where my blood has been used. That would be it now for this year.

Having decided to try and raise some money for charity on the climb, for a local hospice and for the Send a Cow project, fundraising was also going well. I hadn't managed to get the local exposure on Radio Shropshire I had hoped for, but my farmers were being exceedingly generous, and if I had set myself a target of a couple of grand to split between the causes, then I was well on my way towards that. I hoped that showed the amount of respect I had from the local community, so it was very pleasing (or they felt sorry for the old codger trying to relive his youth, but I think it was the former).

Having done the circular route up and around the Wrekin, I also wanted to do it in the other direction, so I would have to tackle the steep slope, but vowed I would only do it with my sticks. Time to get them out! They would give confidence where there was unsure footing. Again, after work one night I set off to do this walk, though as we were having a dry and sunny April, it seemed everyone else wanted to walk the Wrekin too. I eventually managed to find a space to park the car, but it was quite a walk to the start of the normal walk. Up the steep stony path to where it divides to my normal route up the hill, and the way most were going, or following the undulating path around it, through the bluebell woods, and eventually to the start of this steep climb. Out with the sticks, set at the height I could remember I had used them at before, and upwards I set off, looking for grip from bare tree roots crossing the path, stones, anything bar the bare earth of the path. I was doing well, I had heard of no end of people who had injured themselves here and was surprised at the footing attire worn by those I passed, offering no grip whatsoever. But a hard slog, and I emerged at the top of the path, unscathed, puffing a little, checking heart rate (okay and soon returning to normal), I felt really pleased to have done it, and without stopping. Well done Rod!

I had been with Dave a few years ago and had picked up a couple of Telford walks. The first I had done four years previously, an unattractive walk in Telford, and the second, the Hutchinson Way, a walk from Wellington to Newport, heading first towards the Wrekin before taking a route through the centre and north of Telford, eventually arriving in Newport after 18 miles. I had wanted to try this route, and it would give me an opportunity to test my stamina, like when I had done the Coleridge Way before tackling Kilimanjaro. What I needed though was a lift to the start and to be picked up at the end. Luckily one Sunday, Jane had to look after her mother while her brother gave her father a break and took him out for the day. I would have a go, and so set about printing off the directions from the internet, as having moved to a new house, I had mislaid the original I had.

She would drop me off in Wellington before going to Newport to look after Mum and await my arrival either at the end of the walk or at her parents' home. It was some 18 and a bit miles; I hoped to be dropped off at half ten so that I would arrive around four to half past.

With my small rucksack with a bit of food and a couple of bottles of water, I was ready to go, dropped off by the leisure centre, and not late, on what was a beautiful spring morning. We hadn't had any rain for a few weeks and at present it seemed to alternate between cool cloudy days and sunny ones, but always with a cool breeze. Today I was lucky, sunny, a slight breeze but it must be in the mid to high teens centigrade.

I set off, as the walk would have it in the opposite direction to Newport, heading down footpaths between housing estates before joining the old Watling Street and then striking left towards the Wrekin car park. Once out of the houses with the beech woods of the Ercall on my left, on my right views along and over the M54 and westwards towards the Welsh Hills, and the yellows of the rape fields now in flower. A steady uphill walk on road before heading left by the Wrekin, walking another half a mile and then heading up into Ercall Woods.

The directions said the route would be well signposted, but all I found were markers for another circular route through the woods, though I did recognise some of the names as places I needed to pass. Follow the steady incline and then bear left it said, I was going at a good pace, enjoying the rays of sun penetrating through the tree canopy, and the bluebells on the woodland floor.

I went left and found myself fast approaching the road I had walked along to get here. Turning back and retracing my steps, I headed off on another path, bumping into a lady who didn't know the area, busy photographing butterflies at close range. Retracing my steps again, this was getting a bit like the path through the woods on the Coleridge Way five years ago before Kilimanjaro. I wasn't supposed to go near the top of the Ercall, but I did, and ended up basically following my nose, towards where I thought the Wrekin golf course was (I used to be a member).

Up and down dry paths through the woods, I eventually came out by the motorway and Golf Links Road. At least I knew where I was and was able to find a path around the golf course and towards Steerway Farm which I knew was on my route. Woods, ponds, wild garlic, it was very pleasant, but I arrived at the farm only to find the path was closed. There was only one way I could go, and I soon bumped into an old couple out for a stroll talking to a young couple I was sure I had passed soon after my entry into the woods an hour and some more ago.

I told them where I was going, and they were a bit surprised that if I was going to Newport from Wellington, I was where I was. But having told them of this 'Hutchinson's Way', they understood, wished me luck on my mountain climb and guided me along the path towards another which would cross old meadowland and back into the woods. It would then join a bridle path which would take me towards the town centre. I thanked them and set off again in pursuit of their directions, straight forward and not unattractive until heading back into the woods.

I found the path turning and it followed the course of a stream, by which I mean the path was the stream. Was I starting to tire of this walk? Yes, but I knew it wouldn't pass too far from home a little later if I was really fed up.

Back on terra firma, I came out of the woods and followed the path as directed, only to meet a bloke called Dave who told me this path was closed as well. I told him what I was doing this walk for, and he kindly escorted me up another path and into old open cast mining ground. We chatted about my climb, and the previous one up Kili, before our paths diverged, with him telling me to follow the left fork to reach where I needed to be. A nice bloke, thanks, and I was back on track, though I felt somewhat behind the clock for my pick up at Newport.

I crossed a road, then a proper made up path, my pace was quickening again, perhaps I could make up some time. Drink, I must drink in this heat, a snack and I was back on course until I reached Lawley village. I had never seen this development properly, and it reminded me a bit of Portbury in Dorset which I had been to in its infancy. I was very impressed with the mix of architecture and designs... except they had built it on the path I was trying to follow.

I did find my way out, emerging near to a footbridge I was supposed to cross, and did, only to find the next part of the walk had been built on as well. All I could do was to follow the main road towards the town centre and a road I knew, where I knew I could pick the proper path up again. At least I now knew that I wouldn't have to look at a map again for at least a couple of miles. Easy walking now, and if I had been going for well over two hours, I felt good.

Yes, passing the road my brother lived in, I knew where I was going, on past the town centre (and home), past Telford Central and towards Priorslee - I would soon be near the halfway point. Here again the directions went a bit wayward, but I enjoyed a lovely walk by The Flash, beside the lake in Priorslee, admiring the abundance of waterfowl before finding my way around St Georges. I circled the Astro Turf hockey pitch, which I had always wondered about due to my interest as a former hockey player, before finding the path I should be on again and heading downhill towards Granville Park. I had a slight wobble at the end of the path before realising I was supposed to almost double back on myself, but I was motoring now.

Here, the path opened out onto grassland, leaving the woods behind at last and four hours after finding my first 'Hutchinson Way' sign. Now well marked paths ran parallel with horse tracks towards Granville Park proper, again, somewhere I had never seen before.

What I had first thought to be a redundant site of past open cast mining turned out to be a picturesque walk over meadows, through woods and passing remnants of old canals supporting some local birdlife.

Here it would be wrong not to mention the evidence of our industrial heritage I had seen on various walks in my preparation. From the Bedlam furnaces in the Ironbridge Gorge, the foundries of the industrial revolution, the Victorian village at Blist Hill (a very popular tourist attraction in town now), to the brick works in the Granville Park, all now preserved for our future generations. Even in the Town Park there was the old railway station of Dawley and Stirchley chimney, a focal point when walking as it always seems visible, and frustratingly, not far away. The old slag workings, all so much history and if Telford is a new town, it does boast much works of both Brunel and Thomas Telford.

Though I can never envisage calling this place my home, I have been more than impressed and interested in the amount of our country's history which is so close at hand. I transgress but must mention it to anyone who visits.

I continue along my path, past a huge solar panel installation and then into Muxton, before leaving Telford and heading across fields towards Newport. Fields are obviously a cause of dispute when developers want to build on them, but the locals have the opposite opinion. Who will win? Silly question I suppose, here in Telford it is always the developers.

Across a stile, through rape towering either side of me, the monument on the hill at Lilleshall is fast approaching and the end of the journey doesn't seem that far away, an hour and a half maximum. Despite the wrong turns and the paths disappearing, my ETA I guessed would be about four thirty, maybe earlier. I felt good and my pace was quickening. Arriving in Lilleshall and heading out across fields towards Newport, I texted Jane to update her on my progress; I wouldn't be long.

She rang back, her Dad was home and had cooked the lunch they were about to eat. She wanted to go home, she was leaving and would meet me at the Red House pub. No discussion. I had failed, I wasn't going to get to my intended destination, my target of 18 miles. As I turned around and retraced my steps back into Lilleshall and then through the village towards the pub, I felt very disappointed. The first time I hadn't succeeded in my target. I suppose if my walking was going as well as I had hoped I wouldn't have felt so down about it, but I wasn't doing the mileage I wanted to be doing. Never mind.

As I walked through the pub door all I could do was smile and enjoy the cider she had bought me, thanking her for picking me up. I had walked a long way and still felt fresh. There were no after effects over the next couple of days either. That was a positive.

A MONTH TO GO:

What seemed ages away was now approaching at pace. I had to walk uphill, lots. I would be wearing the Wrekin out as I was fast running out of time to do anything different. Fundraising was going well, I think I had everything I needed, and I was also trying to arrange a wedding, my wedding, to Jane of course, a fortnight after my return. Too many distractions meant I would probably go slightly undercooked, especially as my eye op was also in that time frame.

Worryingly, I went off for two days golf at Celtic Manor with the boys, and some of the hill climbs on the course I found very hard work. I guess I wouldn't be pulling a golf trolley up Mount Kenya though. A very enjoyable couple of days were had where we were made to feel like professionals, with lovely company, food (the beer could have been better), and our upgrade to one of the hunting lodges was just pure luxury. How many times did I have to use the hot tub? Whenever I could, even when we had returned from the pub late at night, and first thing in the morning. Lovely views over the golf course while gently simmering!

We did get wet, and with just over two weeks to go, it continued to be wet, but I had to grin and bear it and get out and walk, and climb the Wrekin, again, and again.

Now ten days away, and with my op tomorrow, I would have to see how much more I could do, hopefully I'd have the chance to walk a little. A long walk through the town park again, down the Silkin Way; I suddenly realised after all these walks along the same path that this must be following the old railway line, cuttings through rock now covered with lichen, ferns and bracken. Now many young Sycamore saplings joined those well-established trees of the same, and the Ashes moved gently in the breeze.

I enjoyed the noise of all the songbirds flitting around, the friendly blackbirds looking for a morsel and robins now losing their plumage. All part of the joys of spring, and strangely as the weather gets better and nature marches into summer, I seem to have the park more and more to myself. I am not going to complain. More new paths to explore, I think even on my return I will continue to investigate this nature reserve so close at hand.

I am trying to read more about the country I am about to visit, though I can't find vast amounts of material, especially about the mountain I am to climb. But from what I could discover, this country was appealing to me more and more, with the wish to explore and discover when I got there.

But now, another distraction, my eye op is upon me. And, my faithful old Vectra has finally given up the ghost, 245,000 miles, she was getting a bit warm, very warm. Head gasket gone, and she isn't worth enough to consider having it repaired. Externally, she still looks so good. A good servant to me, but time to move on and sort my sight out.

TEN DAYS AND COUNTING:

The eye operation was upon me, not that I was worried about it at all; the sight in my right eye wasn't getting any better, especially with the long summer days where everything was far brighter. An early 6.15am start into Stoke for the operation, with Jane dropping me off and then I'd phone her on completion and she'd come to collect me. Driving for me would be off limits for a few days, as would work.

It looked like I was second in line on the morning list, so my wait wasn't long. After several bouts of drops in my eyes to anaesthetise them, I was ready to go in. Gown on, into theatre and prepped, then with a nurse holding my hand in case I needed to cough, or if in pain (I would squeeze her hand), they would begin. How bright was that light in my eye? I wanted to close it but couldn't and shouldn't; they wouldn't be able to operate if I did.

"We've removed the lens" she said, then "the new one is in", and the bars on the lights were suddenly obvious, and thankfully they were done. I can't say I didn't feel a little of it. A patch over the eye and back into the waiting area for final instructions before Jane arrived. Then home.

I would be able to see better again!

I suppose it did affect my other eye a bit, so I felt very useless trying to put a bottle of beer back on the shelf in Aldi and missing by a couple of inches! Luckily, I hadn't let go! I got home and all I could do was sit, and close both eyes, awake but resting. We took ourselves off to Cineworld in the afternoon to watch the latest *Pirates of the Caribbean* offering, and the walk there was good.

I could take the eye patch off the following morning and peeled off the tape in anticipation of what I would see. Amazing, a vast improvement, the eye was slightly bloodshot and uncomfortable but otherwise looking good. I would take myself off for a walk and see how I got on. I was encouraged that it was now far easier without glasses than with them on.

I can't thank the staff of North Staffs Hospital enough for all they did for me, in these days where everyone wants to knock the NHS, they were excellent.

Now down to a week till departure, and one last long walk of two and a half hours, though that did include a stop at ASDA to get some US dollars for the trip, and there was a spring in my step as I did some 12.5 kilometres without much effort.

Shrewsbury the next day, I had received a message from Peake's travel to say come and collect my tickets. Sue greeted me, and we went through the arrangements, the e-tickets etc, checking I had got my visa, then just chatting about safaris. She also wanted to go to the Serengeti to see wildlife and asked me to promise that I would pop in on my return with some of my wildlife photos.

Again, a huge thank you to her for sorting the holiday out, with all the changes that took place along the way.

On the way home, I had wanted to climb the Wrekin once more, up over and down the other side, then do it in reverse with my walking sticks. Not as much hill work as I had hoped to do but this would be my last chance. The other side was steep and you needed good grip, but as I went to put my walking boots on I found I had brought two left feet with me. Donkey!

Against my better judgement, and so that I could climb, I went in my ordinary shoes, sticking to the stone track where I would get some decent grip, and again found it relatively easy. I soon reached the top where I got chatting to a man who was using the Wrekin for training as it was closer than Snowden for him. He said the path onwards was okay, so I risked the descent down the other side in shoes, and yes it was a little slippery at times with no grip, and I did end up on my backside once, but no harm done.

I wouldn't climb back that way without proper equipment, so took the undulating path back around the bottom. A nature walk! I looked at the holes bored in trees by woodpeckers, they had been busy, and admired a pair of song thrushes in full voice. As we were passing into summer, the bluebells were gone, leaving us with the smell of wild garlic wafting through the air, surrounded by the fresh greens of early summer leaf of our deciduous trees making up this natural woodland.

Despite the footwear, I had enjoyed the walk and found it comfortable. I guess that was my last walk before I would go any-where of significance. It was also the last opportunity with work and spending time with Jane before we parted for our respec-tive breaks.

Time to think of packing, and then of getting to Heathrow.

Time was flying, in a few days I would be on the mountain, everything would be for real.

I hoped I was ready. I know I would have liked to do more, more miles, more climbs, but unfortunately, too many things got in the way. Time to go!

4

Near Departure

IT WAS 5AM - 3am British time - and we had just touched down on Kenyan Airways Flight KQ101. It was dark and I hadn't seen much out of the plane window, other than just a few lights and cars travelling along a road, as I had the central seat. There wasn't much to suggest this was a bustling city of over four million people.

It had been a long 24 hours. Jane and I had said our good-byes before she had set off to work for her last 48 shift before she would depart to Spain with her friend Helen for a week. I remembered my flight day before departing for Kilimanjaro five years ago, where I had twiddled my fingers for a morning, packed and unpacked more than once just to kill time. This time I had decided to go into work for a couple of hours. I would do one of my normal routine visits, then go home, shower, load the car and check one or two things to do with the fast-approaching wedding, then I would be off. Dull and threatening to rain, I headed off towards Heathrow, ignoring the radio and all its election fever.

I had cast my postal vote some time ago, was worried the call for an election was ill-conceived by Mrs May, and that the Corbyn bandwagon was really rolling, promising everything, bugger the cost (a personal view). I feared for a hung parliament and would have put money on it, but there was nothing I could do now, so I forgot about it.

For once, it was an easy journey through Birmingham on the M6, onto the M42 and M40; the journey was proving uneventful. There was the usual sigh of resignation from my Sat Nav lady as

I ignored her advice once again and headed for the M4 at High Wycombe rather than join the M25, not a tough decision! An easy trip off the motorway and down the A4, I could remember the hassle I had finding this place five years ago, mainly because I was on the wrong road.

I arrived and parked, with a berth to unload, and left the car. Bags into the transit van and I was ready to go to the airport. But hang on a moment, I have forgotten something, my ticket! A quick sprint back to the car to retrieve that and I really was ready to go.

Work wanted a photo of me to put on their social media pages as I was fundraising, so having arrived at terminal four, I showed the driver how to use my phone camera, and a picture he took. I should have checked his effort as once through security I found he had taken a picture of his own thumb. Luckily, I had taken a photo of the kit outside the car before I loaded it at home, that would have to do.

Check-in and security were a breeze, even the liquid and my eye drops for post-op care. I had made good time, so found a quiet spot, not easy. I sent my final messages to those important people in my life, and switched my phone off. A beer and some calamari would see me through to flight food, I was set and ready to go.

Time to think of this place I was going.

So, what of the country I was about to visit? Kenya. I had been to two African countries so far, Egypt with Jane six years ago for a cruise on the Nile, and Tanzania when I had climbed Kilimanjaro, but I had not seen a lot of the country other than the nearby town of Moshi, the scenery between the airport and our hotel, and the road to the mountain. I exclude Ethiopia because although there for a few hours, I saw no more than the confines of the airport. In both countries, I had enjoyed meeting the people of the country, and had found them both helpful and friendly.

Now a different country with different people. Though the Maasai passed frequently between Tanzania and Kenya with their nomadic existence, the warriors I would meet on my trip could freely boast of being able to walk the short distance of 70 miles from their homestead on the Mara to the Serengeti in less than a day. Kenyans do have a great reputation as long-distance runners, but did I believe that? I'm not sure I did (my guide would tell me the great Kenyan runners were not Maasai, but from tribes further north).

Kenya was part of the African Rift Valley area that had interested me since I was a child, especially its wildlife, and I had been a keen reader of the three Elsa books, *Born Free*, *Living Free* and *Forever Free*, as well as other stories of wildlife conservation - especially on elephants. Now was my time to visit. I wanted to see what I could of the country, meet its people, and chat to as many as I could. Kenya had a colonial past, being part of the British Commonwealth, before gaining independence in 1963. Its mountains, like Kilimanjaro, had been the subject of many explorers in the early 20th century, especially by German explorers.

Over the previous couple of decades, politically, the country had been somewhat unstable with disputed election results and the violence after the 2007 election. After the 2011 election there did seem some sort of truce and the fortunes of the country seemed on the up. The Kenyatta administration had undertaken a policy of trying to get roads and electricity to all folks, a task in motion. Was there still corruption in government? Is there an African country that it doesn't happen in?

But soon after my intended visit, there would be another election, and how the country would fare after that only time would tell. But as a visitor, there had been several periods in Kenya's near history where travel was not recommended by our government. There were pirates in the north of the country, hijacking ships and putting them up for ransom, originating from Eritrea but attacking any shipping in the Gulf.

More seriously was the threat of kidnapping of foreigners on the beaches of Northern Kenya by the Islamic military group

Al Shabaab. At times the advice said visiting this area was a definite no-no.

More recently, in the early months of 2017, there were reports of a spate of attacks on ranches by armed nomadic herdsmen. One such attack was the killing of a former British Army officer and owner of a safari business who was shot on his own land in the central county of Laikipia (I wouldn't be far away from here) when he rode out to assess damage caused by the herdsmen. These attacks were partly precipitated by a drought forcing pastoralists to invade private farmland to find grazing for their animals, but these were largely restricted to a few localities.

The Kenyan Tourist board had said that the well-known wildlife conservancies and tourist facilities in the rest of Laikipia were not affected and remained peaceful and calm. Advice came that other areas were perfectly safe, the Laikipia area would take some time to recover, but would not be an area recommended at present. The Kenyan tourist industry would continue to develop, despite past difficult security situations.

The Republic of Kenya was named after Mount Kenya (or Kirinyaga), lying between Ethiopia and Sudan to the north, Somalia to the east, Uganda to the west, and Tanzania to the south. Nairobi, the capital city, was named after the Maasai 'Nyrobi' meaning 'the place of cool waters'. Nairobi is the highest city in East Africa, 1,700 metres above sea level, and is a fast growing and modern city with a population of over four million people.

Other main cities are Mombasa on the coast, Kisumu, Eldoret and Nakuru. A coastline of 536 km, an area of 583,000 sq. km, of which 13,400 sq. km are inland waters, including part of Lake Victoria.

The coast is hot with an average temperature of 27-31 degrees centigrade. Nairobi has an average temperature of 21-26 degrees centigrade. The equator runs through the country, but in winter, July and August, Nairobi can seem quite cool. Elsewhere, the temperature depends on altitude.

Kenya has a population of 41 million (July 2011 est.) of whom

40% are under 14 years old. With a growth rate of 2.56%, this is one of the highest in the world. 50% of the population live under the poverty line and there is an unemployment rate of 45%.

It has an ethnic make-up of over 42 tribal groups, which are distinguished by two major language groups, the Bantu (Kikuyu, Meru, among others) and Nilotic (Maasai, Turkana, Samburu etc.).

English is the official language, Kiswahili the national language.

It's mainly a Christian country, but Hinduism, Sikhism and Islam traditional beliefs also exist.

The landscape of Kenya is divided into two halves, the eastern half which slopes gently down to the coral-backed seashores, and the western section, which rises abruptly through a series of hills and plateaus to the Eastern Rift Valley. The west of the Rift is a westward sloping plateau, and the lowest part is covered by Lake Victoria. The highest point, my target of Mount Kenya, is the second highest mountain in Africa.

The main rivers are the Athi/Galana and the Tana, but the mountain provides much of the country's water, including natural water from the run-off from the large area it covers. Other lakes as well as Victoria are Turkana, Baringo, Naivasha, Nakuru and Elementeita to mention but a few.

There are coastal forests, extensive savannah and dense rainforests on the eastern and south-eastern mountain slopes, and finally alpine zones on land higher than 3,550m. All give a vast diversity of different scenery in this one country. These environments offer over 80 animal species, ranging from the 'big five', all of which I hoped to see, to tiny antelope. There's over a thousand species of birds to see, and I am told it wouldn't be uncommon to see more than a hundred-different species in a single day.

I was about to discover it all for myself.

5

The Flight Out

BOARDING - THE usual hassle of people trying to get on before their number was called, but eventually we were all in situ. There's a strange business class on Kenyan Airways, just separated from us plebs by a sheet, but they did get VIP treatment. I sat just behind on the outside row, between a young Asian lady and a middle-aged gentleman on my right.

Unlike the shy, introverted Rod of five years ago, lacking self-confidence, this was the new me, over depression and about to start on an adventure. This is what I had promised myself those five years ago on my return from my climb. I guess I was tired, so by the time we had taxied to near the end of the runway, I was asleep! But a delay in take-off due to a congested runway meant I was soon awake again and wouldn't sleep again on the rest of the trip, much as I tried.

The lady on my left slept, read and managed to get her petite body in all sorts of positions to rest. The man on my right, it was the TV screen for him. Our meal arrived and with some confusion over the lady's drink, I was given two bottles of red (small) which she, after having just water, decided she liked the look of too. After an altercation with a stroppy stewardess, then with the help of a charming steward, we did eventually manage to sort her out; she had her wine and enjoyed it.

I started to chat to my male companion, Chris, an Englishman now settled in the States in Chicago, but with family in London and Brighton of whom he had just visited before now flying to Kenya to visit his son for four weeks with his wife (sitting the other side of the aisle). We chatted about his job, and mine, how he would probably stay in the States now, but near retirement move to somewhere warmer away from the very cold Chicago winter. His son had a short-term contract in Kenya, so would show them around Nairobi during their visit. They would visit the Masai Mara and the coast at Mombasa. I said I was envious. With them being on the Mara some three weeks after me, they would get the chance to experience the migration, a wonder of the world. I thought that I would be too early.

We talked about my books, and my intended climb of Mount Kenya - the risks, the excitement, altitude sickness and a book to follow. I enjoyed his company while we chatted, and we had soon passed over Europe and over the Med, then Africa.

I really wanted to sleep but however much I tried, it wouldn't happen for me. How tall people cope I don't know, but I struggle to find room for my massive five feet seven inches to be comfortable when flying. All I could do was close my eyes and hope as this seemingly endless journey continued over the Sahara and south.

At last there was the call to fasten seat belts and prepare for landing. We had arrived in Nairobi. A quick disembark, and having said goodbye to Chris and his wife, who didn't think their son would be over pleased at getting up at this time of night to pick them up, we wished each other luck on our respective travels. It was surprising how many times we then bumped into each other as we made our way through immigration, baggage reclaims and out into the city.

The airport was quiet and seemed small in the dark from what I could see. The exits seemed a bit like walking out of Telford bus terminal. But outside......chaos.

My instructions were vague, I would be met at the airport and driven to my hotel. Inside, outside, it didn't say and there was no one inside. Outside, there were any number of people looking for people to pick up, and of course the opportunist salesmen. I should carry a badge saying 'Don't hassle me', I only buy what I want so if I need anything, I will come to you, go away!

One entrepreneur asked me what I was here for and offered me a trip up Mount Kenya for $125 - too good to be true. I told him I was already fixed up while scouring the pavements for someone who looked as if they may be waiting for me. Thank god, with my persistent salesman still in attendance, there sitting on the other side of the road was a man with a sign 'Mr Wood'. I made my way through an endless stream of cars to find him, he was my man.

"Bilal," he said.

"Rod Wood," I replied.

Introductions over, he took my bags and lead me away to his vehicle, the hotel vehicle. He asked if I wanted to sit in the front. Why not? I could chat to him and get a taste of Kenya. My adventure was on the road, but first we had to escape from this car park, along with many others. After Bilal had obtained a ticket, we had to first make our way through a barrier and then into a stream of traffic all waiting to pay some way up the road. Those with passes went straight through, but we had to queue, waiting to see a lady who didn't seem to be fussed how quickly she worked, and not helped by those who didn't have the right money.

But this lady had a gun, so whatever she said was fine by us. Slowly the darkness of night was lifting to reveal Nairobi to me, Kenya's capital, and with first light the signs of the city came to life.

I enquired with Bilal how long it would take to get to the hotel. "Five hours," he said. That wasn't the reply I was expecting, thinking a couple of hours maximum would see us reach our destination. We soon hit Nairobi traffic, and what chaos that was. We were in three lanes, or was it five at times, as people interchanged lanes, overtaking lorries either side as they tried to make haste. We had to head towards the centre before traveling north towards Mount Kenya. Every roundabout was absolute chaos but the attendant traffic police kept the roads moving, with no apparent signs of any collisions - I don't know how.

Bilal weaved us in and out of traffic, making steady progress past a national sports centre, a city garden, and even what looked like through the trees, a golf course. I could only compliment him on his driving, saying that I was glad it was him and not me at the wheel. And all this time, the city was getting ready for work, getting busier and busier as streams of people walking along the roadside headed to factories and schools in preparation for the day ahead. We passed some industry, but my first impressions of this major African city were low, dirty, dusty, untidy, and with little sign, other than a few tower blocks in the distance, of a thriving capital. Then we swept around and passed over the road we had just been on. At last we were heading in the direction we wanted to, the traffic in front of us slowly thinning out.

But the other direction was just total congestion. Bilal told me that Fridays and Sundays were the worst two days for this congestion, with people heading out of the city for the weekend, then returning on Sunday. Today was now Friday! But the sun was now shining, and we chatted as he drove us out of town. He told me they were coming up to an election on August 8th; parliament had just been dissolved and now there would be much campaigning for government, for county elections of which there were 47, and for women representatives.

He was interested to find out that we had our election all but 24 hours previously. I wondered what the result was. When would I be able to find out? He told me of the corruption in Kenyan politics, the rich got richer, the poor stayed poor. Millions of Kenyan schillings were poured into the election campaigns. The hope at the end was that there would be some national stability, unlike back in 2007 when after the result was declared there was much confusion and then unrest as the result was deemed to have been fixed. If not perfect, at least at present there did seem to be a degree of calm, which was what the country needed, and he hoped that would continue after the votes were cast. Signs of the election were everywhere though, on huge billboards, cars, buses and people's work jackets, the whole thing was in your face.

Nairobi seemed endless as we continued along the Thika

Road. More and more people by the roadside walked across barren wasteland, all seeming busy. Kenya has very strict speed limits, with many police on the roadside checking speed, and there are many sleeping policemen, which as our journey continued, I found were very useful overtaking spots, especially of lorries. They were also very good positions for people to try and sell, as they stood in between lanes selling bottles of water, fruit, newspapers, anything to make a schilling or two. I was surprised there were no accidents, but everyone must try and make a living I suppose!

We passed the Safari Park Hotel and Casino where I would be staying on my return to Nairobi before my safari began. A grand looking place, but misplaced amongst the squalor that surrounded it. There was to be a big fundraising event there the following day for President Kenyatta.

The further we drove out, the more we saw signs of the nomadic herdsmen with their cattle, sheep and goats, finding whatever grazing they could for their wards, whether it be on the side of the road or pastures away, but whichever, the grazing looked sparse, dry and yellow. It amazed me how many of these small herds we passed, even on the outskirts of a major city. They were tended by their herdsmen, driving them on towards their next mouthful or towards a watering place, which again looked like unappetising, brown muddy water.

At last we were free from the city. Bilal had stopped by one of the road salesmen to buy me a paper, the Daily National, and I read that as we continued to talk. The headlines were mostly on the election and various rally's being held, the promise of electricity and roads for all from the present government, and them extolling the virtues of all they had done. There was a section on the failing maize crop and how the government was purchasing maize from neighbouring countries. Maize is the staple diet of this country and so essential, especially with the continuing drought in the north of the country. But I would be told more about that later in my trip. The city behind us, now traffic was far lighter, even that going the other way into Nairobi.

We would still pass many herdsmen on the verges of the road, grazing their sheep, goats and cattle, and presumably finding water for them somewhere, although it was not immediately obvious where. And then we passed into areas where farming looked more intensive. There were vast fields of pineapple plants and some coffee bushes, though it is mainly grown further up in the Central Highlands where the soil is more suitable and the climate more favourable. Coffee is one of Kenya's leading exports and world famous. But still everything seemed so dry and dusty, I was worried about it still being the rainy season when I was out here, but that had long passed this year. A phrase I would hear time and time again in my stay over here, global warming.

The pineapples, well I had heard of Del Monte and eaten their fruit from tins back home, and this was where some of their products were grown. Vast fields, rows of plants stretching back from the road as far as you could see, irrigated, good crops. These plantations would often be behind protected fences, sometimes with guards at the gates. Altogether it was a different type of farming from what I had witnessed so far on my journey.

We had already been driving for what seemed an eternity, but on we went, slowly gaining altitude and with that came more agriculture. The soil looked more fertile, cultivation looked better with a greater array of crops grown, but on a small scale from what presumably were smallholdings. There was maize, healthier and more forward than what we had witnessed coming out of Nairobi, rice and even green grass fields. We did even pass the occasional water hole and reservoir, though the contents often looked muddy and dirty.

Women worked the fields, weeding and hoeing between rows of their crops. There were stockades on these holdings to contain their livestock at night for protection. Still, we came across sleeping policemen from time to time, and as before, these were taken as opportunities to overtake lorries, especially buses that we had been following slowly up this gentle gradient towards the Highlands.

I would have to admit here that the effects of the long journey were starting to take their toll on me, reading the paper and chatting with Bilal would often be interrupted by the feeling that my eyes were closing again. But if I could manage to stay awake, then I wanted to do so. I could continue to find out more about this country from my driver, and he was very informative. I could sleep later when at the hotel.

Our journey would take us on through the towns of Sagana and Karatina. I suppose to a westerner these places look quite squalid. There was usually a garage or two, some shops and banks lining the main road but appearing very shabby. Often in old green paint, the buildings looked in need of some renovation. But more striking were the lines and lines of market stalls lining the road. They were probably no more than six feet wide, not much more in depth, wooden and looking as if they were about to fall. But again, manned by women, those that were stocked displayed fantastic looking tomatoes, water melons, bags of red onions, all sorts of fruit and veg, and all looked amazing quality.

What of the men? Well they were there, but just seemed to be sitting or standing around talking to each other. Others were grouped together under shelters sitting on their motorbikes. It seemed the women did the work and were also the breadwinners.

Off the main road, the roads of the town seemed to be largely untarmacked, earth in fact, dusty now and rutted. I would hate to see what they were like in the wet season. But worst of all was the litter, rubbish, garbage, whatever you want to call it, just lying there behind these stalls and in front of the shops. This would be deemed a severe health hazard back home, but as we drove on, it seemed to be the norm in these Kenyan towns. Was this a lack of a waste disposal system, or just sheer laziness? Someone had attempted to burn some of these piles of rubbish, others you would find cattle mooching through, looking for something to eat. Not good for food safety or hygiene. These did seem like mainly roadside conurbations, from what I could see through the earth streets, they didn't seem to stretch that far back from the main road. Housing was made up of rows of tin shacks. I would have to find out more about these houses later.

For the moment, I would continue to view the agriculture and crops; there were well developed maize crops that looked as if they would be worth harvesting, bananas, and one would have to admit, the livestock that we passed, well they did look healthy.

Bilal assured me we were making good progress. The five hours he had predicted, well, we would be a lot less. But I was thinking, surely if we were getting closer, shouldn't the second highest mountain in Africa be starting to become obvious? We passed a sign saying that we were entering the Aberdare National Park, and promptly took a right turn before entering the town of Kiganjo.

This was a more affluent looking town, bigger and with signs of a fair degree of industry, including milk processing plants, apparently owned by Uhuru Kenyatta, the Prime minister. To the west we could see the hills of the Aberdare Range stretching away, with peaks of more than 4,000 metres. The range was some 160 kilometres long, stretching from Kinangop (close to Lake Naivasha where I would visit later on my trip), up to the Laikipia escarpment. An area in colonial times known as the White Highlands due to the number of white settlers here. We were now in Laikipia County as all the posters advertising the forthcoming election were telling us, the candidates very much in your face. We were getting near.

We passed through roadworks, resurfacing, and again it was noticeable how many women formed these road working crews, if only directing the traffic. What looked like large livestock farms emerged to our left, huge fenced off fields, some containing cattle and sheep, some empty, and in the distance farm buildings. They did look well managed, Bilal said, almost certainly still farmed by European settlers, but again, striking for the absence of an abundance of grass, especially so soon after the rains.

On the sides of the road, outside these fenced areas, the nomadic Maasai herdsmen with their herds were trying to find suitable grazing and water for their stock. I had read of the conflict between white farmers and the Maasai, especially with the drought in the north of the country. The Maasai weren't going to let their stock starve, so had broken onto the white estates, and in some cases where there had been conflict, they had murdered white farmers.

Then, on our right, Bilal said: "There is the mountain". High in the clouds there was a faint, and it was faint, outline of Bation, one of the two highest peaks on Mount Kenya. She wasn't giving much away, you could barely see her even in this sunshine, and then she was soon gone. We were close.

The next town, Naro Moru, was where my hotel was, and where I would meet my guide and anyone else who would be doing the climb with me. A long journey, but the real journey was about to begin.

6

Naro Moru

NARO MORU IS one of several starting points for the climb of Mount Kenya, so I don't know what I really expected on arriving in this town. The descriptions in the couple of books I had read, and on Trip Advisor, had certainly suggested to me that it must be some sort of resort, a well-built centre for tourists, and a modicum of wealth as it capitalised on the asset it had standing over it. When we visited Moshi before and after climbing Kilimanjaro, it seemed like a town of reasonable resources thriving on the tourists' money, bringing climbers into the town too.

As we arrived at Naro Moru, my first thought had to be: "Is this really where I am staying?" It was a town yes, built along the roadside of this busy trunk road. On the mountainside of the highway there were the pasturelands we had just driven past, buildings, a town like the ones we had already driven through and loads of people going about their business, which in a lot of the men's cases looked like nothing. There were men on motorbikes hanging around the roadside, hoping to pick up a lift which would pay them a few shillings. Cattle, sheep and goats tried to find a blade of grass amongst the bare and dry earth. Rubbish was littered about everywhere. It was busy, dusty, and dare I say, poor!

There was the usual array of shops and garages, like those we had previously passed, but it was hard to imagine that somewhere here was the grand hotel that would act as my base for my climb.

We took a left turn midway through the town, passing the petrol station, then we took another right, running parallel to the main road. We were now driving on dirt, dry and dusty. People everywhere were going about their daily business, saying hi to Bilal, fellow townsmen of course. There was a variety of small, and I mean small (but this is Africa) shops selling all sorts of wares. I suppose they all made a living, just! I wondered how the supply chain for these shops worked - money up front and hope you sold?

Another left turn saw us running alongside a tarmac road, covered with boulders. This was the Kenyan way of stopping you driving on it as it was undergoing repair, or even being laid for the first time.

After the crossing point, there was a 'grazing' patch, with shacks on either side offering housing to the people of this town. There was a railway line across it, and youth attending their stock. A few children kicked a ball about, but as we drove across I was beginning to wonder where a posh hotel could be in this place!

The earth track, deeply rutted in places, after all the long rains had just finished, came to an end, and we had come to a gatehouse.

A female security guard opened the metal gates, emerging from her small hut to let us through. We had arrived at the entrance to the hotel, and as we passed through security, after a short drive through gardens and past a tennis court which looked as if it had seen better days, we pulled up outside a lodge.

The reception at Naro Moru River Lodge was a wooden, logged building amongst the trees, and to be fair if I have sounded a bit downbeat about the town so far, then in comparison this did look very welcoming.

Bilal stopped the vehicle and we got out. He unloaded my bags for me and took them into the reception, but I already had a greeting party in front of me. It was very welcoming as I was offered the hand of the manager.

"Welcome," he said, handing me a hot wet towel to freshen up from the journey, and a glass of refreshing mango juice from the receptionist who was a very attractive young Kenyan lady.

After my warm welcome, I signed in and gave my passport for

the hotel to copy, while everything about the place was explained to me, the location of the dining room and meal times etc. At some time in the afternoon, someone would come to explain about the climb, departure time and all other necessary details.

I was here at last after what seemed like an endless journey, but I had really enjoyed chatting to Bilal on the way and getting to know something about the country I was visiting. If the mountain had been a bit shy in showing herself to me, then so be it, it wouldn't be long before she would really be standing in front of me.

I was shown to my room, my lodge, Lodge 23, with my bags, and left to settle and unwind. I was tired. It was a long time since I had left home, a long flight then a long drive to the hotel, I was hot and sweaty. I took a quick shower before I unpacked a little and took myself off to explore some of the grounds.

The hotel was set in wooded grounds bordering the Naro Moru River, a large lawn surrounded by a variety of different trees in the garden. Across the river there was just forest (but how far it extended I didn't know). Flower borders fronted the length of the lodges set out along a footpath leading from reception.

It should have been the end of the rainy season, but it had finished some weeks back, so the river, which should have been in full flow, barely had any flow at all. It was just a series of pools linked by a slow trickle of water. But the gardens were pretty, aided by sprinklers feeding the hungry plants in their quest for water. An array of birdsong surrounded me as I walked through the grounds, though the only ones I saw were a pair of timid Ibis feeding on the lawns with their long bills.

I wandered around the grounds, shaded here from the now hot sun (and this was supposedly Kenya's coldest month) by the tree canopy above me. Finding the restaurant and bar, I returned to reception to check on meal times, and to find out when my guide would arrive. It had been such an early arrival that the morning had barely started. I would return to my room, do a little sorting and then take myself up to the swimming pool.

Armed with suntan lotion, if the travelling caught up with me and I fell asleep, then so be it. I also took with me *Out of Africa*, a notebook and a copy of *Kilimanjaro. My Story* to flick through, plus my camera. I found my way up to the pool area, only to find it all locked.

On my way back to reception I wandered through more well-manicured borders around and above the hotel entrance. I also found someone who would open the pool area for me. Again, surrounded by lodge style buildings, an accommodating bar, restaurant, games rooms and changing rooms, this area made for a pleasant place to relax, settle myself down in the sun and read. The pool looked inviting, but not yet.

I made myself comfortable in the sun and settled down to relax and unwind after the long journey. I had seen no other guest in the hotel. After a while, a waiter, Jamie, did appear offering me a drink. On Kili, we had the choice of Kilimanjaro beer, or Tusker. Unlike the others I preferred the Kili, but it transpired that it was Tanzanian beer. Tusker was more universal, brewed in Kenya, and that is what I would have. It was cool, it was long, and it was refreshing.

All was well with the world, other than a lack of internet signal to tell Jane I had arrived safely. She would be departing for Spain in the early hours of the following morning with Helen, her best friend. I read a little, I drank a little, I closed my eyes a little – peace, other than Jamie's frequent appearances to top up my glass. I was his only customer!

The morning passed into afternoon, it was hot, and I was relaxed. Another couple did appear and made use of the pool for an hour, but otherwise it was me and my own company. I ate a chicken and chips lunch here by the pool, and another beer from the Nelion poolside restaurant. As I flicked through my *Kili* book, fond memories of an experience that had changed my life returned.

Every now and again I would take a stroll around the pool, wondering if Mount Kenya would emerge from the clouds and show herself, just like Kili had on that first afternoon in the hotel grounds when she suddenly appeared looking down on us. No, she was going to hide until tomorrow. Swallows swooped over the pool and I tried to track down other birds from their song in the branches of the surrounding trees.

My peace was disturbed after lunch by the tour organiser finding me, introducing himself and, seeing my book, instantly deciding it was his, a gift from me. A 'famous' author, I instantly became 'Meester Rod', and there was a shaking of hands, as if my fame had spread before me.

He introduced me to my guide for the next five days on the mountain, a young-looking guy called Boniface. Being slightly deaf, it would take me a while to adjust to his accent, but he did speak English very well. He was shown my book, he too had climbed Kilimanjaro but by a different route, and then we were left to get to know each other and for him to explain the climb, the route and the camps to me.

I would be climbing by myself with a team of porters to assist, starting in the morning by driving to our starting point at Sirimon Gate. He plotted our course, the altitude we would finish at each day and an approximate walking time, which he hoped would see us succeed in reaching the summit before our descent down the other side of the mountain. We would then be picked up and returned to the hotel.

Boniface seemed very pleasant, we got on okay, and I hoped he would give me a further insight into his country, Kenya. I checked that a sleeping bag had been provided for me. It hadn't and so Boniface said he would find one for me. We agreed we would meet up at 8am the following morning to check what I would take with me and that I had everything that was essential before the trip got underway.

We stood, shook hands and parted. Until the morrow. There, I knew what I was doing now and would relax by the pool a while longer before laying my luggage out, separating that which I would take to climb with from that which I would safari with and leave at the hotel.

Later, back in my room, this was done, and apart from packing it again after Boniface's inspection, I was about ready to go. I took my book and sat on the veranda, reading and listening to the birds as the sun started to set. We were near the Equator, so by 6pm the light was fading; by 7pm it was dark, but still very pleasant to sit outside, and the birds weren't going to leave me by myself, singing merrily away.

Time for dinner, and after changing I took myself off through the gardens to the Kirinyaga restaurant to be greeted by Peter, my barman and waiter for the evening. I ordered another beer as I inspected the many pictures and maps of the mountain I would start to climb in the morning. Many t-shirts pinned to the ceiling were signed by previous climbers over the past three decades, one I noticed by a venerable old gentleman of 81 years. The manager popped by, showed me this shirt and said he had accompanied this man to the top. He would buy me a beer on my return in a few days, he said, and wished me luck.

I supped my beer and ordered my dinner, onion soup to start - as it would be on several occasions in the next few days - then lamb chops. I ate in solitude; the meal was pleasant, but the chops were rather overcooked. I had a sedate meal, finished my beer and retired for the evening. I would have to be up reasonably early, and in for breakfast as soon as the restaurant was open so I would be ready for Boniface's arrival at 8am sharp.

I arranged the mosquito net around the bed, hoping that at just under 2,000m above sea level I would be immune from attack, and settled down for the night. My adventure had begun. What will await me in the morning and over the next five days?

And still the birds sang, late into the night, they weren't going to stop. The joys of Africa.

7

To Judamaier

I SLEPT FITFULLY, tired from the journey the previous two days but in great anticipation of what was about to begin. The birds were singing when I went to sleep, and they were singing when I awoke. I guess somewhere along the line they too must have dozed off ready to fill the skies with song in the morning to come. There was only the solitary sound of a mosquito, waiting for silence in anticipation of the start of its attack, but none was forthcoming, the net was doing a good job. If the mosquito had inspected more closely, it would have found a hole or two, but I was lucky, and escaped the night unscathed.

So, at 6.30am I was up, with an hour to sort my things, arrange what I was going to take on the bed for inspection, shower and shave for the last time for a day or two (though I hoped I would be able to shave), and prepare to go to breakfast.

My journey was about to begin. Although it was cool before the sun rose high in the sky, I put my jumper on, and it was a comfortable temperature as I made my way to the restaurant again to eat my meal alone. I had a plate of fruit to start with; I could fall in love with these gorgeous fresh pineapples, and the watermelon, of which I have never been a great fan, but these were delicious.

Wilfred passed outside the window, still clutching my book, and popped his head around the door to wish me good luck: "Meester Rod!"

My cooked breakfast arrived, plus coffee which I rushed down as I didn't want to be late for Boniface's arrival at my lodge at 8am.

I finished and was back with a minute to spare while I waited for Boniface to appear. At 8.30am there was still no sign of him, so I wandered up to reception. Back at the lodge I waited, and just before 9am he arrived. Kenyan time, no such thing as hurry! We went through my clothes and equipment; my phone charger was of great interest to him. He was satisfied I had all I needed, it did seem a lot, but like Kili, the final ascent would be cold, and that last climb was where a lot of the clothing would be necessary. I packed energy bars, and my new-found love - packets of dried mangoes - useful for a snack on the way.

We packed it all into my holdall, other than that which I would carry with me in my rucksack. I carried the rucksack and the bag containing what I would leave at the hotel. Boniface took my trek bag and we made our way up to the reception to leave one bag and start our adventure.

Bilal waited with the van, along with three other men who would be my team for the next five days. They introduced themselves one by one, Tim who would be my cook, and Patrick and Johnson, the porters. They seemed friendly enough, and again spoke good English.

We were ready to go. No, we weren't!

They had provisions to collect and disappeared into the innards of the hotel. They were gone for some time. I wandered around the reception area and the grounds, watching birds, little black wren like birds with long beaks feeding on the buds on the trees, buzzards hovering overhead, an eagle, and a pair of Ibis now perched in a tree.

The crew at last returned and we started loading all our food, cooking utensils, a stove, and our personal luggage into the van. It was fast running out of room. At last it was just us left to get in and we really were ready to go. Boniface was surprised I could still remember all the team's names, but if they stayed as they were and kept their hats on, I had worked out a system to remember them by. Patrick was easy, but Tim and Johnson looked very similar - Tim had the hat!

We were off, back through the security gate, waved away by the hotel staff with their good luck cheers, and back through the town of Naro Moru. Here, all of us, bar me, were known, so there were several stops to chats to friends and acquaintances. Boniface had told me that there were many men in the town who earned their living by working as porters on the mountain, as in neighbouring towns and villages, but they must take turns to go up so that everyone had an equal opportunity to earn a living. Boniface couldn't go out and choose his favourites. Back through the dusty tracks towards the main road, we stopped briefly to fill up a couple of containers with fuel, which Tim would cook with when on the mountain. Then we continued out onto the main road and towards the next big town, Nanyuki.

The nomadic herdsmen were already out and about with their stock, eking out what little grazing they could find. Theme parks, other hotels offering accommodation for intrepid mountaineers like me, and the lines of market stalls lined the roads, selling what looked like amazingly good quality fruit and vegetables. One vegetable had a white cross section I did not recognise, but Tim told me it was arrowroot. There was a steady flow of traffic, but not over-rushed, as we approached the outskirts of Nanyuki.

We came to a halt and Boniface asked me to get out.

"Stand over there," he told me, pointing towards a sign, "and give me your camera".

I looked at the sign and did as he asked. The sign read, 'THE EQUATOR'. He wanted to take my picture standing on the Equator, and I was only too willing to oblige. I had crossed it in a plane on the way to and from Kilimanjaro, but now I was standing on it, and as strange as it seemed, I was only a few miles from a snow-capped mountain. How queer was that? I was standing there, more than a little hot in the cloudless sky, while somewhere over there was a mountain, at this time hidden in cloud, but with white stuff near its peak.

Back on our journey, we stopped at a supermarket to get some more torch batteries. I had two head torches with me, one of which

I had used for the final night climb five years ago, but Boniface thought I should get some spares in case I wanted to read at night, as well as for the final ascent before daybreak.

He wondered what I thought of their supermarket, but this one was on a par with any back home, clean, tidy and with amazing looking fruit and veg, fresh meat and well stocked shelves. The only real difference was that back in England we didn't have a man with a gun standing at the door!

We were back in the van, and back on our way, but no, we stopped again, going down a back street, this one tarmacked, unlike in Naro Moru.

A town of nearly 37,000 people, this bustling town has made its living from being a base for trekkers like me, acting as a gateway to the Laikipia plateau and all its wildlife, and for being the main base of the Kenyan Air Force. It also acted as a training facility for the British Army. It would in all honesty offer the passing traveller, me, more than my base of Naro Moru, where I would probably feel uncomfortable going out in the town by myself. I digress.

We pulled up outside what looked like the back of a store, and my crew all got out of the vehicle and disappeared inside. I was fascinated by the petrol station next door, doing a roaring trade filling up the tanks of motor bikes queuing to be refilled. Some were old, others new, some heavily laden with an assortment of goods, logs, planks, hay, all sorts which must have taken a good deal of skill to negotiate these busy roads with. In the short time we were parked there, I don't know how many came and went but it was a lot, and the petrol attendant's hands were filling up more and more with Kenyan Schillings.

Eventually my team returned, emerging out of the building with bags full of bread. This was obviously the back entrance to the local bakery, and we were now loaded up with five days' supply of bread.

Was that it? Were we finally ready to go to our start point at Sirimon Gate? By all accounts we were, but I was still fascinated by all these bikes, how could they afford them? Patrick told me that it was almost a status symbol to possess one of these bikes, many of the young men strived to get one, but once he had his own he would have to earn money to pay for it. He would give people lifts with their shopping back home, at 100 shillings a trip. The more trips, the more he could pay for the bike and the better model he could have. Some of my mates back home have bikes, and I know they cost a lot, so how could these people afford one? Patrick explained that these were Chinese imports, probably only costing $800, not a lot to you and me, but in Kenya this was expensive. Many paid chores would make them affordable. It was my first sign of the Chinese influence creeping into Kenya.

As we drove through Nanyuki, we did indeed pass the British Army Training Camp, the housing and large security gates. I had spoken to ex-army personnel back in Telford who had indeed climbed Mount Kenya as part of their training and had been posted here for a short time. I didn't realise this was the place, a place I had never heard of till now. We also passed the war graves, those fallen helping us fight in World Wars, a reminder of the Commonwealth, maybe even of bygone days of overseas British colonies.

Onward, we drove along the main road, watching women tending their crops, the hills in the distance to the north of us, and what looked like more productive farmland to our south, right! We passed government agricultural institutes with crop trials going on, then onto what were apparently white owned farms, taking farming to another level from what we had seen before. There were reservoirs for irrigation, large machinery, discs and cultivators which would take seconds to do what we had seen people in their fields doing by hand. Modern farming, rich, healthy soil and productive looking crops.

We reached a point where we were to turn off down a road, a track marked with big signs saying: 'sponsored by EU grants'. This road took us past good farmland with smallholdings on either side, people tending their stock and their crops and children playing by the side of the road. It looked a better standard of living; the crops looked healthy and more productive. We were starting to go uphill along this made-up road, steadily ascending more and more as we proceeded along for some four or five kilometres. Gradually it became more wooded, and then as we came upon a posh looking lodge and some nice bungalows on one side of the road, we had reached as far as we would drive. We had at last reached Sirimon Gate, the start of my climb up Mount Kenya.

Something, somewhere in my travel notes was a comment that we were going to use a little used route up Mount Kenya, approaching it from the north. As we drove towards the gate, this place was looking more than a little crowded. To the right of the road was a shaded area, bordered by housing, on the left it was more open, a grassed area, a large clearing and then bush. On the shaded side, there was a large group of teenagers being arranged in a line by their teachers or guardians, and two Europeans who looked like they were alone. On the grassy area were large numbers of porters being organised by a guide. I wasn't sure if they were there hoping to find work, or if they were assigned to the group of teenagers - I would later find it was the latter. The couple by themselves, were they part of this group, or climbing alone, and were they also waiting for porters?

The starting point was far busier than I had expected. I hoped this wouldn't make it too much of a procession up the footpaths we would no doubt encounter sooner or later. Time would tell. Sirimon Gate is not actually a gate, but the start of this route from the north. It's a newish looking building where you check in and register your climb, and a place to pay your climbing fees to get onto the mountain. Again, armed men were standing near the post where Boniface would take my passport and sign me in. We went through a similar process at Londorosi Gate at the start of our Kilimanjaro climb, and no doubt I would have to be checked off the mountain as well in five days' time.

While Boniface went through this process with the authorities (I had paid my fees when paying for the holiday - when that was passed onto the park attendants I didn't know), the rest of my crew: Tim, Patrick and Johnson unloaded our vehicle, laying everything out on the grass. Were we seriously taking all that? It looked enough to feed an army, more than enough to feed just me and them. Fruit, veg, including arrowroot (I would be trying it at some stage on the journey), tins of food, bread, fuel for the stove, potatoes, greens, meat, and of course the tents and our luggage. Where were we going to pack it all? I was now feeling a little guilty about the amount of clothing I had in my bag, which one of them would carry it for me? Boniface did say it was okay, and that was my only redemption.

The three of them busied themselves arranging, sorting and packing all this. All one could say was that the further we went and the more we ate, the less there would be to pack. All I could do was stand around and wait. This place had the last posh loos we would see for a few days - so use them Rod! I had some phone reception so sent what messages I could, while I could. Jane would no doubt be getting ready to fly, Helen would be round to the house soon. I messaged her while I could, wishing her a good holiday and told her I would see her soon - a wedding was coming up, ours! I reminded my son Richard to phone my parents to tell them I was okay when I had reached the top.

Now, at last, the clouds cleared and the summit was now in full view. Above the rainforest towered the multiple peaks of Mount Kenya, and to the left of those, the impressive sight of a billiard table like mountain with its sheer faces dropping away from the plateau on its top. I had seen pictures, but here it was for real. Time for a photo session, though no doubt the closer I got the better pictures I would take. Back home they wanted photos for the work Facebook page, so I got Bilal to take a couple and sent them back home. Lastly, I wanted pictures of us all, myself, Boniface, Johnson, Tim and Patrick standing in front of the building, below the sign saying Sirimon Gate at 2,700 metres above sea level.

We had already ascended some 700 metres by road, now it would be walking, walking to a height of 4,985 metres above sea level. We were ready to begin.

No, not quite. I helped Patrick squeeze my bag into his rucksack, guilt again. Having got it in he started putting more and more provisions on top of it and would then strap a tent on the top of it all. Boniface said we would make a start and the others would finish their packing and catch us up. We were given a packed lunch each, which we put in our rucksacks.

We were ready to start. Rucksack on my back, I took my first step forward. My climb was uphill right from the start, though this was only a very gentle gradient. Boniface and I were the first to be on the move, setting off side by side at a gentle pace across the grass and towards the made-up track in front of us. I wasn't expecting to be walking on a hard surface like this, a good concrete road similar to what I was used to driving up to farms at home when out and about on my rounds. But no matter, we were walking, and this is what I had trained for over the past few months. I felt good, even if those peaks in the distance looked more than a bit intimidating, even from this far off. It was slightly overcast as the clouds breezed across in front of us, sometimes hiding the sun, other times blue sky and hot in the direct sunlight. It wasn't a bad temperature to be walking in; I was in shorts and with a jumper on, we could review that later.

It wasn't very far before we were out of the clearing and into woodland, more factually rainforest, though on these northern slopes of the mountain, they looked rather dry. Still on the concrete path, lined either side by a trench which I presumed was to take the run-off water from the road after downpours, we were surrounded by tall trees that had bolted for any available light, so long and spindly but not the thick canopy I had expected overhead. Lichen and mosses hung from branches and there was a cacophony of birdsong. No, just these tall trees perched on valley sides, and as we progressed further, from what I could see there were deep gullies down to the valley floor. These were probably etched out by glaciation in the past, but over time had become wooded as they were now.

Midday, and the sun was shining now all the time. It was getting hot, the top of the forest was not dense enough to keep direct sunlight out, and I was glad I had thought to wear a cap and smother some factor 15 suntan lotion on before we started. It is rare for me to wear anything on my head!

The gradient was getting a little steeper, but at the pace we were walking it wasn't a great strain. I remembered 'pole, pole' from five years ago, how could I forget? Slow, slow, use the available oxygen as its concentration thinned the higher we got. We were not at altitude sickness heights yet, but better to get into the habit now so that in the coming days the changes in concentration wouldn't be too much of a strain to adjust to.

It was time to get to know each other, for the next five days it was just my walking companion and me. Side by side we walked the road, me realising I would have to speak up (what's new) so Boniface could understand me. If he spoke just a little slower so I could decipher his English through his accent and with my partial deafness, then we could communicate okay!

So where to start? I supposed I could tell him something about me, my job, my climbing experience, i.e. Snowden and Kilimanjaro five years ago, of which he knew a little because Wilfred had announced me as the great author and climber when he confiscated my book at the swimming pool less than 24 hours ago. Boniface had already told me that he had climbed Kilimanjaro, a few years ago now, and on a different route, but it gave us something in common to build our relationship up from. I didn't want five days of silence and without interaction from my 'helpers', they were part of my story, part of my climb. It had been a big regret not getting to know my porters five years ago, they were so helpful and so friendly, but I was a different person then from what I am today, I lacked self-confidence and felt bad about myself, so there was no way I was going to find it easy to get to know them. There were too many demons in my own head, which thankfully the climb had allowed me to rid myself from.

We were breaking the ice, with him telling me of his wish to be a tour leader one day, having his own company, just like Chunga on Kili. He told of how the designation of porters was made, so they could all in turn pick up some sort of wage, even if not as frequently as they wished. This was their winter, June their coldest month, and the climbing season was short and seasonal. The rains had finished early, but there hadn't been many parties go out before us earlier in the month. My empty hotel was a climber's hotel. If it wasn't for that large party behind us somewhere, the mountain would indeed be sparsely populated today.

But other than our talking, I was surprised how quiet the rainforest was. Not the constant chatter of birds that I had expected, but silence, silence only broken by the occasional chattering and squawking of what I thought were monkeys. No, Boniface informed me, these were birds hidden in the upper branches, singing cisticola. How big they were, I don't know, much as I peered up into the branches from where I thought the noise came from. Yes, I could hear noise, but never saw where it came from. I guessed they were relatively solitary birds, there was never a great conversation between them, just the occasional chatter.

Behind us, no one was in sight yet. We must have been walking a good hour, encouraged to drink now and again, but totally on our own. It was hot, and it had been a while since we had eaten. We stopped for lunch, giving us time to explore what was in those lunch packs. Finding the only two comfortable looking stones visible to sit on at the side of the gulley, we took our rucksacks off, found our lunches, and opened the mystery paper bag. Fruit juice, good, sandwich (double layered), couple of cakes, a chicken leg, and a couple of bananas. Carb packing, I suppose, but for me, not ideal. Fruit juice and bananas were fine, a meat and jam sandwich was not really my cup of tea and I have never been a great fan of chicken limbs, but I would eat what I could off it, and discard the rest. Oh, and lurking at the bottom of the bag was a hard-boiled egg. I had eaten a good breakfast so would survive on pickings from it. Boniface enjoyed my cakes, the rest, hopefully the wildlife would consume.

At last coming slowly up the hill another person was appearing - we hadn't seen anyone else since we had left Sirimon Gate.

As he got closer, we could see it was Tim, but he was alone, and behind him there was again no-one in sight. He joined us, but of course without the only two comfortable stones on the trek, he sat himself down on the bank, clearing away a few plants and I hoped not finding an ant's nest. Tim and Boniface chatted away in Swahili to each other and to be honest could have been talking about anything, including me. If the chat didn't contain 'pole, pole', asanti or karibu, then I was clueless about content.

Tim ate his lunch rapidly, then with Boniface saying: "Trende. Five minutes," we prepared to set off again on our walk.

Now there were three, Tim, Boniface and I, as we now walked three abreast up the concrete road. The evenness of the surface didn't make it hard walking, only the heat of the sun made our journey a tad laborious. I was surprised we hadn't seen anybody else yet, there were so many waiting to start their walk at the start, and the porters would walk far quicker than us trekkers (not trekkies!). But as we walked on, slowly but surely, there were signs of life behind us. The porters were off, walking fast, catching us up and saying: "Jambo" as they passed us, and having a laugh and a joke with Tim and Boniface if they knew them - and they seemed to know most of them.

What was obvious was that whereas I was warm too hot, they were not. It was their coldest month, and they were well wrapped up, with woolly hats as well, and what was surprising was the array of footwear they wore. I knew they wouldn't be rich, but some of the shoes and boots were struggling to stay together, looking on their last legs, and shoe laces were optional. If I had brought my other walking boots, I could have left them for one of the porters, but these ones I had on still had a lot of use in them for me.

The gradient was getting slightly steeper, but still I was comfortable and found the pace easy, almost having to put the brakes on to keep 'pole, pole'. But it was important to stop for a break every now and again, especially to drink. One had to be a bit of a contortionist to reach round and get a bottles from the back of my rucksack, so Boniface would often get it out and replace it after drinking.

It was on one of these breaks that the Scottish (the European pair) couple we had seen at the gate passed us, saying hello as they went. There was no porter in sight for them, just a couple of backpacks, a tent, cooking equipment, and a map dangling in a bag in front of them. An exchange of pleasantries, and they carried on up the road.

On we went, still no real change of scenery, just the rainforest, but other than the occasional, and it was occasional now, bird in song, with the odd sighting, all was very peaceful other than the sound of us walking. We would now and again pass a pile of faeces deposited on the road, buffalo in transit from one part of the forest to another, but no sign of monkeys or anything else. Disappointed? Perhaps I was a little as the books and brochures had eluded to there being far more likely sightings of wildlife than you would see on Kilimanjaro. Although a safari awaited, I still would have liked to see something on our way, as we walked.

We had been walking some two and a half hours, and now the forest was just starting to thin. The road changed from concrete to tarmac in different places, the gradient varied, and I thought just around the next bend it looked as if it was just evening out a little, maybe even slightly downhill; but as you took the turn, no, it was still uphill.

On one of our water breaks, as Boniface and Tim chatted to other teams, I went and had a chat with the Scottish couple who we had now caught up with. I introduced myself, and them to me. Adrian and Debbie, a married couple, she was temporarily based at Nanyuki at the British Army base. Adrian had flown over for a break from Scotland to join her briefly, and as she had taken a couple of days holiday, they would try and climb Mount Kenya over the weekend and in her time off. Adrian would stay a couple more days before returning home to Scotland. Married Army life, they saw each other when they could!

They were travelling by themselves, had set their target - an itinerary similar to ours - and would navigate themselves with map and compass. If they made it, then great, but if they didn't then at least they had had a chance to spend some time together before Adrian went home. Debbie was only on a short posting so would see him again soon.

It was nice talking to them, but time to get on our way again. Still no sign of Johnson and Patrick, but Boniface had spoken to them by phone. All these porters seemed to be on their mobiles all the time, a few blasting the forest with their music, but most just chatting to someone. Still the trail went on steadily uphill, perhaps even increasing in gradient, but on we would go.

There was the odd wisp of a cloud in the sky, it was one of those days where as we got higher I asked myself whether I should take my jumper off, unsure whether I would be too hot with it on or too cold if I took it off. Still the steady stream of porters walked past us, but there was no sign of any other walkers other than Adrian and Debbie in front of us. More signs of buffalo poo and the odd crow. Today it was a people's mountain. At last, Johnson and Patrick were in sight behind us, and we slowed to let them catch up. I guess there were rules for porters on how much they could carry, but they did look more laden than the rest of us. Patrick now looked older than I thought he was when we started the trip, and he was carrying my stuff!

Slowly but surely, we were emerging out of the rainforest and onto moorland, the trees either side of the road were replaced by bush and large heathers. It had taken a day and a half on Kili to reach this change in vegetation, but here we were on Mount Kenya after about three hours. And with the change in vegetation, our views changed as well. Far in front of us perched on top of a hill with the road, we could just see our destination for today, the path snaking up to Judamaier Camp. To our left we saw that billiard Table Mountain again that we had seen from Sirimon Gate, and the closer to it we came, the more impressive it looked. Steep, almost vertical stone cliffs rose high above us in the distance to what looked like a flat plateau on its top. Circular in formation from what we could see, I had seen pictures of this geological feature in books, and the views from it. I could only admire from a distance, perhaps one day I would try this mountain from a different route, exploring the different scenery found on different paths. For now, I would see, enjoy, and where there was a suitable gap in the bushes to take good pictures I would stop briefly for a few snaps.

Up and up we went, perhaps now taking more frequent breaks. The boys were carrying more than us, and for those last few strides, perhaps it was steeper now, perhaps we were tiring a little. But how encouraging it was to see the end point! Judamaier for a time seemed to be getting no closer, but then yes it was just there, just above us.

For a short while I did seem to tire dramatically, so close but so far. It was steep, the last bit, but I needed to call a break, and I think Patrick was quite grateful for my call. I had a drink of water and caught my breath. A nod from Boniface: "Trende". Yes, I was ready, and with a renewed vigour that tiredness of a few minutes before was gone, Boniface and I were striding towards the end of our walk. There was a clearing on the left of the road, about 300 yards before we reached the camp buildings, a well grassed area, surrounded by heathers. This is where Boniface had intended us to camp for the night, but those porters who had overtaken us had already earmarked this spot for themselves, well in fact for the large group of youngsters we had seen at Sirimon. Boniface would have to think again.

We continued up to the buildings to find a spot. Further on and to the left, another clearing, below one of the toilets and an area surrounded by some plastic netting. Well grassed but slightly sloping, it would do perfectly. It looked as if the local mole population also had a liking for this small lawn. Numerous logs with compass points marked on their cut end stood in a circle, something to sit on, and a large cut trunk which sat on a couple of other logs made a nice bench. We were there, camp one. We had walked uphill on a made-up road for the best part of four and a half hours including breaks.

Enough walking for today, first things first, Tim and Patrick used the shelter of the plastic netting to act as a kitchen. They found the stove and fuel, lit the stove and put some water on to boil. It was time for a cuppa. I don't, can't drink milk, so it was black coffee for me, served on my bench for me by Patrick: water, sugar, milk, coffee powder, and a mug.

"I don't drink milk thank you Patrick," I said. That would save one hand for him on future meals and breaks. The others, they enjoyed their tea, always drank it, I never saw them have a coffee on the whole trip.

I looked towards the mountain in front of us, peaks hidden in cloud. Just below us, their tent pitched, were Adrian and Debbie. We waved. I would go and have a chat with them later.

I was on the mountain at last, so were they. Their thoughts would be on the mountain ahead, as were mine - the real challenge was about to begin.

Naro Moru Lodge

The start. Sirimon Gate. 2700m

The author

Heathland, Mount Kenya

Mackinder Valley

Mt Kenya's peaks

81

Lobelia, Mackinder Valley

Dawn Shipton's Camp

The final climb, would have been

Lunchmates, Mara

African Savannah

Mara Elephants

Wife, only 12 cows

Zebra on the Mara

Cheetahs, Masai Mara

Baboons

8

First Night

THE COFFEE WAS much appreciated and thirst quenching, but it was time to get to work. We had two tents to erect, and it only seemed fair that I gave the lads a hand where I could, though they seemed very adept at putting them up. It was no time at all before I was putting the last pegs in for the guy ropes and putting my kit inside. Then, we quickly erected theirs, it was bigger and would sleep all four of them, but being seasoned climbers on the mountain they weren't carrying the amount of stuff I was. Our campsite was complete, Boniface told me to go and have a quick look round, to go to the buildings at the top of the hillock to see the rest rooms, wash rooms and toilets and just explore for a bit. It would get dark around 7pm, so we had around two hours of sunlight, then the temperature would drop rapidly.

I organised my tent, what I would need for the night, my book, torch, pills for the morning, and of course my eye drops. Even on the walk up to here, at the appropriate time I had stopped and done the necessary. Boniface had blown up my mattress for me and I found the sleeping bag. I was all ready for nightfall when it arrived an hour or two later. The lads were busy over the stove cooking supper, so I went for a short wander over our domain for the night. Behind the tent and through a gap in the heather, there was a small hummock from the top of which I had good views of all our surrounds. I wondered if we would get one of those memorable African sunsets as it drifted over the farmland and plastic covered crops we had seen earlier on our way to be dropped off, before dipping below the horizon

Towards the peaks of Mount Kenya, Adrian and Debbie were sitting on a rock carved like a garden bench. It looked very comfortable in the evening sun. I wandered down to see how they had settled in. Enjoying the warm evening sun, they had organised their tent, cooking stuff etc and were now enjoying a rest before cooking and then turning in for the night. We chatted about home, where they came from back in Scotland, Glasgow, and about Shropshire. They had walked a few of the Munroes back home, and so Mount Kenya was a short challenge for them. I explained why I was here, about depression and Kilimanjaro five years ago, and that now I was fulfilling a promise to myself. I told them about the book I had written, and the one I would be writing on this climb. They would now be characters in it. We enjoyed a pleasant 15 minutes or so chatting away, no doubt we may see each other in the morning, but it sounded as if after that our paths would diverge.

"Oh yes, do you know the election result?" I asked.

Debbie told me it had resulted in a hung parliament. Just what I had feared, the worse possible result at such an important time in the country's history with the Brexit negotiations fast approaching. Fingers crossed for our future, and for the Kenyan election in two months' time, I was hoping tribal tensions would not resurface again. Politics, even up here on the mountain.

I wandered back up to my tent and got *Out of Africa* out to read, that is until Patrick came down with the first course of my meal. It was chicken soup, which I ate sitting on my bench again. As the temperature was dropping fast, I had now put on over trousers and a fleece to keep warm; the soup was very welcome. Next there was a stew, veg and potatoes, followed by watermelon to finish. Then more coffee. It was good, though far too much. I took my coffee and went and sat on my hillock again.

There was lots of noise coming from the camp buildings above, the porters from the other group were in good voice, jollity and singing rang out across the airwaves. I looked towards the mountain.

The clouds that had been drifting across the sky earlier in the afternoon, obliterating the peaks from our sight, had now reversed and were drifting slowly westwards, the opposite way from earlier. With that, way across the moorland and the deep cut valleys you could just make out the higher slopes, the peaks were becoming more visible. Bastian and Lenana standing high above us, the clouds drifting slowly down their slopes, and then others following, casting a ghostly hew over the mountain tops, and then they were gone, lost in cloud as the night descended over them. I turned my attention to the sun in the opposite direction, but the cloud there was still high, and so all I got was the last rays shining above the cloud as the sun disappeared behind them and was gone. No spectacular sunset tonight, perhaps another night when on the mountain. It was 7.15pm as I made my way back to the tent. I checked with Boniface what time we would be up in the morning before retreating to the 'comfort' of my tent. The temperature was not far off freezing point, there was certainly a ground frost, and the ground now felt quite damp.

Having cleaned my teeth, I undressed a couple of layers before snuggling down inside the hired sleeping bag. On Kili I had been cold every night, so had kept layers on; here I would anticipate the same, especially not knowing said sleeping bag. By torchlight, I snuggled down inside and read for some 45 minutes. I wasn't cold, yet, but when I had decided enough was enough tonight with the book, I zipped the bag up around me, the hood wrapped around my head. Remember the amount of heat lost through your head I thought. I hoped for sleep. Certainly, the mattress seemed to make the ground far softer. Yes, I did feel quite comfortable.

But could I switch my mind off. No, I couldn't and so way after I heard the lads settle down in their tent just opposite me, I was still wide awake, my mind climbing mountains, writing books. Rod, please switch off. It could be a long night, 11 hours in the tent was a long time, way beyond my normal time in bed. If I looked out of the tent, I would see a star filled and clear sky above, so it even seemed quite light under canvas.

The hours ticked by, and still no joy. I think it was about midnight when having tried various positions without success, I started thinking that perhaps underneath was feeling a little harder. A quick squeeze of the mattress, yes, there was some air in there. It was getting harder underneath; another check and the mattress was flat.

Great!

I rustled around in the dark, finding the valve to blow it up again, puffed and puffed until fully inflated again, and once again comfortable, I tried to sleep. Another hour, the same thing, and I was repeating my actions of before, then settling down again. Another hour, and I was back in the same position again, doing the same, re-inflating my 'bed'. I would have to say at this stage, at least the bag was very warm and I was relieving myself of layers and my socks to cool down. Another hour, the same. It obviously had a puncture, and, alas no sleep for Rod. I lay there patiently waiting for daybreak, and at last Patrick arrived with a cup of coffee. Today, a long walk ahead on no sleep.

Why hadn't Boniface let me bring my own brand new Thermorest with me, which was now sitting in the store room of the Naro Moru River Lodge Hotel. At last light. Alas, no sleep. But with light, I could start packing clothes and putting books away ready for the upcoming day.

By the time Patrick did arrive at the tent entrance, I was there to greet him, open the flaps and gratefully accept the hot drink on offer. Even with my hearing I knew the others hadn't been up long, so breakfast may be a little while as Tim cooked again on his stove under the protection of the netting. It was in fact a crisp, clear morning; the moon was still evident above and there was a clear view to the flat-topped mountain and to Batian in the distance. There was still the hint of a frost, and to begin with I was in a fleece and hat, though okay in shorts, my legs warm enough. I took advantage of the facilities as they were so close, none of the hole in the ground toilets of Kili or having to worry about the flush having frozen overnight. Luxury, well almost.

I enjoyed the sunrise as it slowly glowed brighter behind flat-topped mountain, before finally rising above it and greeting us with warm rays. Gold shone around as the sun gradually rose higher and higher. We mustn't forget, the Equator is only a few miles away. Debbie passed by, it was her turn to use the facilities and I greeted her "Good Morning" as she walked by. By then, Tim had done the business as I sat on my bench again and was presented with a 'Full English', well not quite, but certainly a hearty cooked breakfast for me to start the day. Today was expected to be our longest walk. It went down well, followed by more coffee, fresh oranges and watermelon. Looks like they really don't want to carry food any further than they must.

Breakfast was done, it was good but it would soon be time to get on our way. Patrick took my plates and mug, I helped Boniface and Johnson take down the tents. These modern tents are remarkable for how quickly you can erect them, but with their collapsible support skeleton, I soon found there was an art in how you extracted them from the canvas. Having started well, I found if you could keep it in one piece it came out easily, but if you split the frame you were just pulling the elastic between each section and getting in a bit of a muddle. Boniface had to help me out, I hoped I was more a help than a hindrance, but I couldn't just stand by and watch them do everything. The tents were down and ready to be packed away, my rucksack was packed and other than giving Patrick a hand to put my kitbag back in his rucksack, I had thought of an easier way of doing it than we had done the previous day, we were about ready to start walking again. I had noted one pair of walkers setting off a few minutes before (no sign of the large party making tracks yet) following what looked like a narrow path, rather than following the wider track up towards the Met Station above us. Patrick brought over a packed lunch for Boniface and I. Oh good, it was the same brown paper bag as the day before, no doubt with the same contents.

Oh whoopee!

I was glad I had eaten well for breakfast because I wasn't going to fancy much of my lunch. Boniface ensured I was carrying enough water, and then: "Trende," we were ready to rock 'n' roll. The other three would catch us up later, when they had finished clearing the camp.

Our intention today was to walk to the Likki North Valley, a long and steady walk, of, yes you guessed, four to five hours. By now, I was getting well accustomed to Kenyan time, everything was four to five hours. This would take us through a beautiful valley below the subsidiary peaks of Telekei and Sendeyo, two ancient parasitic vents of the main peaks. We would end up at Likki camp where we would spend the night. But Boniface was wary of this large group behind us and didn't want to be walking hand in hand with them all the way to the summit. He decided we would take a different route, crossing the Likki Valley and into the Mackinder's Valley, walking to Shipton's Camp, which was our destination for our third night.

It was going to be a long walk, but yesterday I had found easy, so why should today be any different? At 7.30am we set off, the two of us at the normal pace of 'pole, pole'. As the sun rose higher over our left shoulders, the moon slowly disappeared. The chill was lifting from the air, the clouds were few and far between. It looked like it was going to be a hot day.

As we made our way back to the road we waved to Adrian and Debbie, and I wished them a safe trip if we didn't see them again. It had been nice meeting them and being able to talk to them the previous evening when I perhaps had felt a little isolated as my Kenyan guides gathered around the camp fire by themselves. Now I was on my own again but would make the effort to engage Boniface as much as I could, both for company and to find out as much as I could about his country, Kenya.

The road soon petered out as we made our way to the Met Station above us, which we were now walking towards, but it looked further away than when just observing from our campsite.

Though there was some sort of track for vehicles to get up to it, we were following the path of the walkers I had seen earlier, following a surprisingly narrow footpath for the number of people who must come this way and winding our way between the large heathers still making up the moorland landscape we were crossing. Rocky, uneven and very dry, it wasn't the easiest of walking, and loaded up with water for the day, army rucksack felt a lot heavier than it had when climbing yesterday. I had to look on the bright side, the further we went the more I would drink so my bag would get lighter. As we wound our way between the bushes, there did seem an abundance of flowers, either open or about to burst into bloom. But it was striking that considering this should be the end of the long rains, the ground seemed parched, and this became my first topic of conversation of the day with Boniface.

"The rains, when did they finish?" I asked.

It was over six weeks ago now, Kenya was struggling. It was my first of many conversations on the effects of global warming on a country right on the Equator. Like with Bilal on my journey to the hotel, Boniface was aware of the problems facing his country, a country they both seemed so proud of, but a country that needed water. We talked of the farms we had driven past when turning off the main road towards Sirimon Gate and of the plantations I could see covered in plastic when sitting on my hillock at the campsite we had just left. European farmers knew how to get water, or could afford to pay the price for conserving it so that they could irrigate their own lands. When the path allowed and we could walk abreast of each other, we chatted long on this subject. Other times, we would have to go in single file.

Looking behind, Adrian and Debbie were taking down their camp, otherwise all was quiet.

Slowly but surely the Met Station did get closer, surrounded by a wire fence. We reached it after about 45 minutes, and then turned east. We had been able to see the formidable peaks of Bation and Nelion up to this stage, but they would soon disappear behind the brow of the hill - the ridge we were now crossing. Yes, it was getting hot and we stopped for our first rest, mainly to make sure I drank. Boniface didn't seem to need to drink nearly as much as he expected me to. He had the experience, I didn't.

Our moorland now seemed even drier, if that was possible, with less flowers and dried grasses and heathers looking desperate for a drink. Bare roots crossed our narrow path, meaning we had to take more care with every stride forward, and 'pole, pole' they weren't large strides. We were, in places, having to climb as well, not a continuous haul like yesterday, just a few strides where I had to step up, making sure Boniface had moved forward before placing my feet where his had just been.

Behind us, we could see our Scottish companions now on the move, looking as if they were following the path we had taken.

On our original route, we would not have turned east when we did, but now we made our way towards the Orltulili Valley, up, down then across it before ascending gently the other side. I described Exmoor to Boniface, how similar it was to the scenery we were crossing now, other than the unexpected peat bog you would find, well hopefully wouldn't find, but would certainly be aware of if walking the moors back home. The woes of Carver Doone. But of course, with the footnote that we were a few feet - more than a few feet - higher here than we would be on Exmoor, an area I had loved so much when my parents had lived down there. One valley gone, another two to negotiate today. We were on top of a ridge, Orltulili behind us, and about to descend into the Likkii Valley. A different beast here, more of a rut than a wide gulley - the effects of more recent glaciers meaning the sides of the valley hadn't been eroded away so much, and therefore were far steeper. Our association with the Likkii Valley today would be little more than climbing down to the valley floor, and then going straight up the other side.

Debbie and Adrian were fast catching us up, but after starting to descend towards the valley floor, we soon lost sight of them. I thought I wouldn't see them again and that they must be taking a different route, they had certainly intimated to me that they would follow the route we were originally going to take.

Down we went, and if there was one thing to make me feel happy, despite the deep step downs on loose soil in places and the signs of ice particles in dips still not reached by the sun, it was the sight of a beautiful mountain stream running through the bottom of the valley - twisting and turning around rocks as it made its way down through the moorland and to the rich lands below, the other side of the rain forest. I took long steps down, treading carefully and then we were at the valley floor, grooved into the rock. There was a cut back on the path and then we reached a bridge crossing the stream before ascending the other side of the valley. I love streams. We were going to have to stop as I stood on the bridge, leaning over the rails watching the water tumbling down from higher up the valley. Around and over boulders the water flowed, clear, and probably very cold. But for all the dryness around us, here was a plentiful supply of water, mountain run off or springs, I didn't know.

I have a fascination with running water and was happy to stand here with Boniface and just watch it flow. He said we would stop for a rest here, so we made our way over the bridge where there was a strange looking structure, like a bike shelter with no stands in it. It was a shelter and if the weather was inclement, other than offering a roof over one's head, you would have been fully exposed to the elements.

We sat ourselves down close to it, finding a comfortable seat on the side of the bank. Water, yes, good idea. We were fully exposed to the sun now as it rose high in the sky. It was getting very warm and it was important that we kept the fluid levels up (and it would lighten my rucksack). It was also a good time for a snack and to see what we had in our lunch pack today. The same as yesterday. Instantly, we had company as Boniface tucked into a cake, me, well I tried the sandwich again but just couldn't be doing with this jam and salad combination.

From a distance to start with, but feeling ever braver, a little bird approached us. It stopped, and with its head held to one side looked quizzically towards us as if demanding food himself. A mountain whinchat, Boniface informed me. It was really a very friendly chap, or chat for that matter, as it hopped closer and closer to us. He knew what he wanted, and he knew we had it. I suppose up here there were no natural predators for him or his mates, so it held no fear. Walkers meant food, so it wasn't long before it was almost at my feet, with others now loitering a bit further away. I broke a bit of my sandwich off and offered it to the bird, and it was quite happy to come and take it from my hand. To appease his mates, I broke other bits off and threw them in their direction. They scrambled after the scraps and as they grabbed their bit, more and more would appear. It was lovely to watch them and to feed them, though I'm sure in their starter menu there was nothing about jam sandwiches mentioned.

That passed a few minutes, and in that time coming down the other side of the valley was Tim. He crossed the stream over the bridge and joined us, sitting down beside us. I didn't think I better give the birds any more in case he was upset, he may have made the sandwiches, but I knew at the first opportunity they were far more likely to enjoy further snacks of them than I would. They wouldn't touch my lips again. Wait for our next stop birdies! We were ready to go again, sad to leave our new friends, but a steep uphill climb beckoned.

Boniface and I did again have a brief discussion about this resource running through the valley and questioned whether better use could be made of it further down. A dam may be a better use of the EU money than the road we had walked the day before. I also asked him about the mountain and his tribe. To the Kikuyu, of which he was one member, Mount Kenya was a sacred mountain. But why did he worship it? No answer was forthcoming, he was a Christian, and other than agreeing that to the tribe it was sacred he wasn't going to say any more on it. Tribal history - I suppose the Kikuyu and the mountain had been there a lot longer than Christianity.

We were climbing again, and this was probably the steepest part of our climb today. Twisting up the other side of the valley, short step by short step we were getting higher. The heathers were getting shorter, the ground was again very dry and amongst the vegetation were some big boulders. Here you could see the true nature of what we were climbing, an extinct volcano.

Looking closely at these boulders, there was a combination of hard magma and softer rock that had trapped it, along with evidence of lava flows from the past, many thousands of years ago. There were blacks, browns and lighter shades of these rock formations as we made our way past them and further up to the rim of the valley. Like so many slopes, and like the top of the Barranco Wall five years ago on Kilimanjaro, just as you thought you could see the top, over that brow would be a bit further to climb. What I could say was that this was hard work in the direct sun we were in, but in fairness to Boniface, for me he had judged our pace just right. We were moving steadily, not out of breath, but again not so slow that it felt like we were stopping every step. Just a slow steady pace over - well I'm not sure how long we walked, but then we were at the top of the ridge and that was our walk in the Likkii Valley over. Literally in one side, cross the stream and climb out the other side. A ridge to our left going up the slope and again to our right going down the valley, more correctly, valleys as we stood above both the Likkii and the Mackinder's Valleys, the latter stretching away both ways as far as we could see.

But here was one impressive sight. Although the bottom of the Likkiii Valley was out of sight, as you looked in front of us and down below, again there was a valley with a large stream running through it, steep sided but with a larger valley floor than that we had just come out of. The older effects of glaciation had ripped out the valley floor, leaving it wider and more rounded. Directly opposite us, a huge cuboid-like boulder perched on top of the ridge adjacent - one wondered how stable that was! It had been a long haul out of the Likkii Valley, and as I have said, how long it took us I don't know, but Boniface thought it a good idea to stop again, eat again, and of course drink.

We sat ourselves down on two huge boulders perched near the edge of the valley ridge, four feet away was a drop - I wouldn't like to consider how far it was - but we were sheltered from the breeze up here and had a little respite from the sun. We could stretch our legs out, and even sitting on stone we were surprisingly comfortable. We were nearing that time of day when the weather would change every day. Now as we sat perched high on our rock, below us to the south we could see cloud starting to build up and slowly but surely make its way up the valley. It looked thick, and when it reached us it would surely block out the sun. We would have to wait and see, but this could drop the temperature considerably. For now, it drifted slowly up but was still some way away from us. Was it because it was a narrower valley that it could obscure our vision? It would ascend quicker than on Kili as we got to this stage of the day, which would just cloud over, but the cloud seemed to remain higher. I suppose the slopes up to the summit were more gradual, and you didn't get these deep valleys as high up as we were on Mt Kenya. As I sat eating my chicken leg and bananas, which were probably all I would take from the pack, other than the mango juice again, we started talking politics.

As I said earlier, Bilal had told me about the election approaching in just over a month, and the possible outcomes from it, but Boniface had no idea that we had just had an election back home either. Nor did he know of Brexit or our vote 12 months previously. Debbie, the night before at Judamaier, had told me the election result and I tried to explain to Boniface why Mrs May had called an election early to try and strengthen her hand in Brexit negotiations, and to get a Bill on it through Parliament. Now it all looked as if it had backfired, and I tried to give my interpretation of the pitfalls of negotiations that could now happen. The election result that I had feared had indeed happened. A great opportunity for our country may now be lost because she got greedy on how she read the opinion polls!

Tim re-joined us; the others, Patrick and Johnson were still some way back. Then from nowhere, Adrian and Debbie re-appeared but without stopping carried on into the MacKinder's Valley.

"Trende," said Boniface, and with a nod, I stood, put my rucksack again on my back, stepped carefully off our boulder and set off on the path lining the side of the valley. Boniface had taken the plastic bottle of fuel from Tim and carried that himself now, but he thought I should go in front so the fumes wouldn't affect me. No, I was happy where I was, following him. He knew where we were going; I didn't, though presumably it was just a case of following the path. But he was a far better judge of the pace we should walk at than me, and the direction of the wind coming from behind us meant the fumes would not trouble me anyway! This was a narrow windy path, it was hard to judge whether we were going up or downhill, but as our destination was high, I guess we were walking UP the valley. Still there were traces of ice particles, though they would soon be in the sun.

Strangely, the clouds crept up the valley, and then just as we thought we were to be immersed in them, they would disperse, and it would be clear again before the next lot started climbing the valley. Ever closer, then gone again. We could see Debbie and Adrian way ahead of us, disappearing behind a corner in the valley. They did look like they were below us, so we must be going downhill. Below us were streams, fast flowing waterfalls and rockpools, to me a gorgeous sight, so clean and so refreshing. Slowly we were making our way down on this narrow path to the valley floor, and closer to the water. If I thought this once, I thought it repeatedly - this could be the Barle Valley, the Exe Valley back home on Exmoor, but at a considerably higher altitude. Peace and quiet, away from the hum-drum of daily life. It was beautiful.

Out from the shade of the ridge we had walked down, we were now just above the stream, some 20 to 30 yards away to our right and now in the full sun again. The clouds had gone but appearing in front of us once more were the peaks we were heading towards,

Nelion and Point Lenana - now so close compared with where we had camped last night. Ever closer we were getting, this peak rising so abruptly out of the valley. We had been walking a long time now. How much further were we going today? No complaints, this was beautiful scenery, but maybe, just maybe I was starting to feel a little tired and seeing the end may just have given a little encouragement. Time for another break, and now a conversation about my job and agriculture back home.

On the way to Sirimon Gate we had passed many cattle grazing by the side of the road, on dry grass, bushes, some even wading through rubbish dumped on the side of the road. Now and again my crew would proudly announce a Holstein as we passed a black and white cow, but compared with back home, their condition was usually poor almost to the point of emaciation. They were trying, but I don't think this breed of cattle would survive well in these dry conditions. The native breeds, Brahmins and Zebu, herded about by the nomadic Maasai, looked far healthier and suited to the conditions.

Boniface was interested in my day-to-day routine as a farm vet, and I started to tell him how my life had changed over the past 40 years. From doing 15 to 20 calls a day in Devon back in the late 70s and early 80s, visiting neighbouring family farms where I may see one or two cows on each farm, to now where I may only do two or three calls a day but would see 20, 30, 50 cows on each visit. There was now far more preventive medicine than treating individual cows. I would spend a day doing a lot of driving between calls, though in terms of mileage, Shropshire was nothing compared to the expanse of country we were now in.

I explained about making silage to feed the cows, hay as they did in Kenya, but now less common in Britain and the size of the bales as modern machinery got bigger and bigger. I pointed out that some of the machinery we had passed on the European farms we had also passed on the way to the mountain, like what we had back home, but here it was probably only economically viable on the rich soils of the Central Highlands where irrigation took place and rich crops would be harvested. And maize, Kenya's staple diet, of which we had passed a lot on my journey from airport to mountain. It seemed harsh to tell Boniface that we used their staple diet as cattle fodder, a rich starch source for our Holstein cattle.

He was interested in how much milk they were given, 50 litres a day plus in some cases where maize would be a large part of their diet. The lower yields of cows on grass or organic systems still produced 4,500 to 5,000 litres per lactation, with the top herds averaging 12,000 plus.

Did I hear him right when he told me these cattle grazing besides the road, all 10 of them, may produce a kilogram of milk between them? Milk is essentially white water with a few bits and pieces in it. Without water, how could they produce milk? It was an interesting discussion, and although it was time to move on and continue walking, our conversation on farming in the two countries carried on.

The other striking feature was now the change in vegetation; gone were the heathers of the upland moorland as we now entered more alpine moorland, replaced by the lobelia and senecios that I had last witnessed on Kilimanjaro five years ago. They ranged from small ground level plants to the mature 'adults' towering above us, lining the path, and rooted in the screes above us towards the high valley sides.

Boniface would stop and point out the fluid that the lobelia collected in their centre, a syrupy liquid that provided sustenance to the plant, producing a chemical the plants would live on. I thought it would attract birds and insects, but apparently it didn't. At night as the temperature would drop, these leaves would close over the liquid and tender centre to protect it from the frosts that were so frequent. Nature's way of protection. Then as the plant matured, it would grow upwards; over five to six years it would be towering over me, the trunk rugged and dark where older leaves had died and fallen off, reaching up to the succulent greenery we had seen in younger plants at ground level. A flower would then emerge from the centre, a striking yellow, and the life cycle would continue once again.

Other wispy leaves flowed down from their growing point, upright but far narrower, and again standing way above my height gave a surreal view of the scenery around us. 'Soldiers' stood on the slopes of the valley, guarding all around. More birds, sparrow-like singing cisticola, magpie-like malachite and tufted malachite sun-birds with vivid green tail feathers flew around, singing, especially around the banks of the stream. And still our little whinchats fol-lowed us, hoping another jam sandwich may appear. We really were alone with nature here at this moment in time, Boniface, me and the Mackinder Valley. Other than the birds there was peace and quiet, lovely.

Another stop, more water and by now Boniface was happy enough to drink water straight out of the cool mountain stream, rather than the boiled water that I was drinking. We were now by a small bridge that crossed the stream as it moved from the centre of the valley to run more down the left side. We would now con-tinue down the centre. This spot was a lovely place to rest, sunny and quiet other than the flow of the stream a few feet away, and the re-emergence of whinchats looking for, or rather hoping for, a snack from us.

It seemed like we had been walking forever. I wondered how much further we had to go but didn't want to ask. We were well into the afternoon, and the four to five hour walk mark had seemed a long time ago. For now, we enjoyed the solitude, until in the distance we could see the others making their way along the path we had just followed. We waited for them to complete the days' walking together, however much longer that would be. A quick break for them, and we were back walking.

We were surrounded on three sides now by the high valley walls leading to and forming the numerous peaks that make up Mount Kenya, but with our goal of Point Lenana in front of us, standing aside the close peaks of Bation and Nelion. The closer we got, the more intimidating they looked - but there was my goal.

On we walked, further up the valley until at last we could see the green huts of Shipton's Camp in front of us, perched on a rocky ledge. We started to climb again up towards this ledge. After a brief stop to watch a little mouse, who seemed quite oblivious to us as he had a little snack on the rocky path, we stepped higher and higher. We were approaching some caves eating into the rock face, and these were known as Shipton's Caves, and would have offered shelter to humans thousands of years ago. Now?

It would have been good to have a closer look, but they didn't look that accessible to walkers, and I guess I wanted to get to the camp now as soon as possible. Some of the rock climbing here was hard, and for the first time today I really was starting to find it hard work. My heart rate had gone up significantly, but 'pole, pole', not much further to climb and then a more level walk to camp and we would be done for the day.

Puff, puff and we were nearly there. The top of the ledge opened out onto a green plateau, almost looking like a bog, but no, it did almost look fertile here at 14,000 feet. Camped near the stream at the far side, we could see the tent of Adrian and Debbie already set up, and the stove going, ready for a brew.

Another 300 - 400 yards over a rocky hillock accommodating the toilets and we had finally arrived at Shipton's Camp. With nine hours of walking it had been a long day, with only another couple of hours of light remaining before darkness would take over the shadows of the peaks all around.

A large expanse of flat rocky ground greeted us, bordered on the side we had just come from by green wooden huts. These was accommodation for porters and walkers alike, though most would sleep in a tent like me. I don't know how comfortable the beds in the hut were, but there was me sleeping under canvas while my four colleagues had the luxury of a night in the hut on beds.

But this sight had to be remembered for its location, beneath the remnants of the volcanic rim of this dormant volcano. The peaks of Bation and Point Lenana, now seemed almost within touching distance as they rose above the scree slopes in front of me. Vast rocky outcrops made up the second highest mountain in Africa, and from where I stood now, though considerably smaller than Kilimanjaro, the climb that was left looked much more daunting.

But that was for tomorrow. Now was a time to recuperate from our hard day and get the kettle on. Tim was at his stove in the kitchen of the huts; the others, before I could believe it, had already erected my tent, somehow managing to get some of the pegs into this hard, stony terrain. Home sweet home for another night. I could start unpacking again ready for the night. Looking at the ground I was concerned as to how I was to have a comfortable night in the absence of a mattress that would stay inflated for the duration.

My pitch was at the edge of the clearing, any further and one would be amongst lobelia and other shrubs. A few nearby birds sang out, the ever-friendly whinchats were close by again. It was a lovely spot, though I fancied when the sun went down, we would know about it - with a more than sudden drop in temperature.

There were a few other tents already erected, but the site looked generally very quiet, other than porters milling around the hut. Our brew was ready, so I went into the hut where there was a long line of tables and benches for us walkers to sit and eat from. For now, I was alone, alone with the coffee that Patrick had placed in front of me on the table. Then he brought out some cake and bread but strangely I really didn't feel hungry, though I wasn't that worried as it would be supper time soon. I enjoyed my coffee before returning outside to enjoy the late afternoon sunshine.

As I arrived back at my tent, Boniface had solved the problem of my bedding, he had managed to get a mattress from the huts that the warden said he could use. We managed to manoeuvre it into the tent, though it didn't leave a lot of free room. Boniface advised that I should try to keep any of my luggage from touching the sides of the tent, I probably had less than six inches either side of the mattress. But even if it looked as if it had had better days, it was soft and would protect my bony self from the stone below.

"Thank you, Boniface," I said.

Once organised, I found a nice rock to sit on and continue *Out of Africa*, I was finding it hard going, and occupied myself doing this until Johnson appeared to say my supper was ready.

I had bumped into Debbie again while I was reading. I said I had seen where they were camping, it looked a nice spot. She had just come up for a wash while Adrian had taken himself off to explore the lower slopes for the final part of their climb. They were trying for a day less ascent than me, they would be up very early in the morning, aiming to be awake by 3.30am and back down again soon after breakfast time. They felt fine in themselves so were ready for the final push. I wished her good luck and hoped I would see them again after their success as we continued our route up in the morning, just to see how they had got on.

With that I had to go and eat. What Tim managed to prepare on his stove was amazing. Two hot courses followed by fruit. Soup again, and bread, for which the couple of whinchats who had found their way into the dining area waited patiently for, in case any offerings were put their way. Then a casserole (with more arrow root, oh good), but despite the chips he had cooked as well, my appetite had nearly gone completely. I felt bad for the effort put into preparing all of this, but I really did not want it. I nibbled at the fruit that was to follow as Boniface came for a chat over another drink. He didn't like coffee, so while I drunk more of it, he had his tea.

He explained our route for tomorrow, told me we had done well today and that he was pleased with me. I seemed strong and we had walked a long way today - the best part of 12 kilometres in the heat of the day. The summit awaited us, but tomorrow we would ascend to Austrian Hut and spend the night. I too could sleep in the comfort of a hut tomorrow as he had booked our accommodation there. From there, the summit was a mere 40 - 50 minute walk the next day before we started our descent down through the Telekei Valley.

I was looking forward to the different scenery, tarns and

maybe proper rainforest. I had seen the slopes in front of us, below Point Lenana, and the last remains of a glacier peeking out from behind a rock in front of Bation. They were grey and dirty, nothing like the glaciers near the summit of Kilimanjaro five years ago. But then last time I also wrote about the receding glaciers. But what looked most daunting for tomorrow's climb was all the scree which we would need to walk on at the start of the walk. It was steep, and it would be hard work.

As I made my way back to the tent, it was hard to see exactly where our route was. Boniface said we would go up the scree then bear left, up and behind the ridge we could see. Somewhere back there was Austrian Hut. If I felt up to it, Boniface said that on the fourth day, after a short walk to the summit, we could walk off the mountain the same day. I wasn't keen, though another night in the tent with probably no sleep wouldn't be missed. I had gathered our route down was very beautiful, and I had wanted to enjoy as much of it as I could. And I wasn't sure if there would be a room at the hotel when we got back. I needn't worry about that now.

I bumped into Adrian who was coming back from his exploration. If I thought I had walked a lot, then he must have done a couple of hours extra, but he had sort of planned their summit walk for the morning and now needed to rest. He would be up and walking in just a few hours.

Back at the tent, Patrick brought me some hot water in a thermos for the night, and I enjoyed the last of the light, wrapping up warm as the temperature dropped. From somewhere, a mangy looking dog appeared, looking for any scraps it could find. To give him a bit of a hunt, I threw the rest of my packed lunch into the surrounding bushes for him to look for. He found what he was looking for, but on his return was ushered away from the camp by some porters.

I went back in under the canvas and thought about settling down for the night. I had been hot in bed the previous night so decided to wear what I had finished up in. The mattress should be warmer as well. The usual arrangement of torch, tablets and eye drops (still for the cataract) were laid out beside my inflatable pillow. I was really pleased with how I was getting on after the operation, not wearing glasses at all now when walking or looking into the distance. They were only necessary when I wanted to use my camera. Having said that, Boniface seemed to have fallen in love with my camera and had appointed himself as head photographer. I would just tell him what pictures I wanted.

A last look at my Fitbit, 28,217 steps today, 8.91 miles, and 4888 calories – there had to be a negative energy balance there. I had worked hard. Darkness fell, and it was surprising how many people I could now hear entering the campsite. Lights, talk, the erecting of tents and then quiet. Having settled down, I did want a drink at one stage. Sticking my head out of the tent, under the light of a full moon, I was surprised how many new pitches there were now. Looking up, 'starry, starry night' would have been a good and apt song to sing.

Sleep was the issue now - Rod try and get some - tomorrow would be a shorter walk but probably a lot harder. The mattress was soft, I was warm and probably felt a bit uncomfortable after my meal, all this stodge wasn't going down well and I had had a tiring day. Surely I must be tired. I lay there, found a comfortable position and waited for my eyes to close. They didn't want to do it by themselves, so I closed them and waited for sleep to arrive. It wouldn't, and with that my mind went into overdrive, and unlike at home when even if awake my mind would go blank, here it just kept churning things over and over. Minute after minute, hour after hour I struggled to sleep. But in the early hours of morning, alarm bells started ringing.

My breathing was quickening and more laboured. Then after a while, I noticed my heart was beating fast, really fast. My Fitbit counted 120 beats per minute, while my normal resting rate was 70. Was I anxious? Was I ill? Was this altitude sickness? I didn't know, but my heart rate wouldn't settle. This wasn't good. I lay there until daybreak, and I suppose worrying about it didn't help. I got up, got dressed and went to the toilets, climbing that short walk up to them perched on their little hillock. My heart rate went up to 130, what was going on? I would have to talk to Boniface when I saw him at breakfast. For the meantime, I drank the coffee Patrick had brought me at the tent, before making my way to the hut to eat.

I thought of Adrian and Debbie somewhere up above me, they should have summitted by now and be starting on their way down. And I thought of me, I wasn't good, but would I be worrying if I didn't have a Fitbit constantly telling me how I was if I cared to look? How many times had I looked already this morning, lying awake in my tent? Far too often, and at no stage had it given me the answer I was looking for - my heart rate and breathing easing. It wasn't changing.

I sat down at the table in the hut, a sole diner. My breakfast was brought for me, but I really didn't feel at all hungry. There must be something wrong with me, there was bacon on my plate and I wasn't that interested in it. Rod - the guy who would never refuse bacon. I managed to eat some, but not very much, and I had a little fruit too when it arrived. I felt terribly guilty about the effort Tim had put into this, but I just didn't want it. More coffee, yes, I could drink that.

Boniface came in and asked how I felt. I explained not good and why, showed him my Fitbit, and explained to him my resting heart rate. What it was now he could see for himself, and it wasn't changing.

"Do you have a headache?" he asked, concerned that I may have altitude sickness.

"No, I just don't feel like eating, I'm a bit breathless and my heart rate is high. No pain, nothing else, I don't feel sick, I was hot in the night but seemed okay," I replied.

We decided for now that I would rest and see how I felt later. We could leave at almost any time if we gave ourselves four to five hours to reach Austrian Hut.

I went back to the tent but knew in my heart that we wouldn't be going anywhere today, unless there was a sudden change in my condition. For all my veterinary and medical knowledge, and it wasn't long since I had done a First Aid course, all I could come up with was that I had tachycardia, but why, who knows? But, for the time being, I wouldn't be going anywhere. Back in the tent I just lay down on my back, closed my eyes and hoped, really hoped that it would pass quickly. I wanted this mountain, I wanted to see over the other side, the views of Bation and Nelion from the summit of Point Lenana. I wanted to walk through the Telekei Valley, see the tarns along the route, and hopefully see proper rainforest as we descended towards Naro Moru. Please don't let it end here!

I hoped I would doze. Lack of sleep had certainly been a problem the past few nights and I had none over the past 60 hours. Yesterday had been a long day, perhaps it was taking its toll on me now. Rest Rod, and hope.

It was getting on for 10.30am when I needed to go to the loo, to walk up to those delightful buildings again. Again, my heart was racing as I climbed that short way, I was feeling more than a little disconsolate. On the way back to the tent I found Debbie, she was rather red, but they had made it and were down again. She asked of me, and I could only tell it as it was, I didn't think we would be moving today, but fingers crossed we could go straight for the top in the morning after resting up. She told me of their climb, the early start and how cold it had been then, the scree was hard work, but it had all been worth it in the end as they reached the top soon after sunrise. I was envious but congratulated her.

What now for them?

They would now rest before starting to walk back the way they had came. It would be a long day for them, but they were so much younger than me. It was goodbye for now, it had been a pleasure meeting them and I wished them a safe trip back towards Judamaier later. "Oh and look out for the book!" I said.

We parted, and again I hoped that later, or tomorrow, I could also enjoy the thrill of being at the top. Back in the tent lying down, I continued to hope there would be some change - but as of yet there was none. I am not one who can lie around for a long time, I get very restless and soon want to be up and about and doing something. Not today though, all I could do was lie there and hope. I tried to switch off, that might help, but as I did something else would start racing through my mind.

I questioned what would happen if I didn't get back, I thought about Jane, the wedding, Richard and Lydia, my wife to be and my offspring. I also thought about the charities I was raising money for, Send a Cow and Severn Hospice. How would they get the money I had raised if I didn't return? How would they know who had donated and paid and who still had to? The kind people who had sponsored me, was I letting them down?

I was questioning my immortality; since I had changed so much since overcoming depression, I was facing failure for the first time. I didn't like the feeling. Boniface appeared to see how I was, no real change and I suppose at that moment I wasn't really in the mood for conversation. More coffee, more rest. He would see me at lunchtime. Okay, but I asked that he please warn Tim that I didn't feel that hungry, no offence, but I didn't. It was back to me alone in my tent, resting, thinking, worrying.

Enviously I thought of Adrian and Debbie now on their way back to base camp, and how they had managed to get to the summit in three days. I wanted to lie back and relax, but I couldn't, I just kept thinking of what I considered important things, Jane and the wedding in just over three weeks now. She would kill me if I didn't make it back! Work, the charity, the kids.

One very important consideration was, if I continued feeling like this and just walking to the loos were doing my heart rate no good, then what effect would walking 21 kilometres plus have on me? Because, as I could see it, the only way off the mountain was to walk off it. There was no phone reception, I suppose a helicopter could reach us in emergency, if we could get hold of any authorities to send one. It was a consideration.

Slowly the morning ground on. I kept checking my heart rate, tapping the face of the watch to first make the number of steps for today show up, then another tap and my heart rate would appear.

It looked like I had tapped it so much today in worry, in desperation that the ticker would slow, that I had even managed to crack the face of the thing slightly. What was certain was that I wasn't improving much, and almost certainly the worrying wasn't helping.

Eventually lunchtime came and Patrick came over to tell me it was ready, asking me how I felt as we made our way back towards the hut. By now, other than a few deserted tents where people had set off to scale the summit after breakfast, and would return later, the camp was starting to fill with the large group of teenagers we had seen over 24 hours ago at Judamaier.

This was the party we had tried to get ahead of by walking so far yesterday in order to have a quieter final ascent. Now they were with us again, so we had gained nothing. I sat down and Boniface joined me. I think he thought that we could still have a bash at getting to Austrian Hut today. I explained there was no change and on mentioning tachycardia, I think he realised we would be staying put here for another night. We would decide whether to go on in the morning.

At this stage, I could only agree and see how I felt but I guess I was not that optimistic. We ate together, but again I didn't want any food; I did pick but it was more out of politeness than wanting it. He asked me if I would like to go to hospital when we got down, we could stop in Nanyuki on the way back to Naro Moru. Again, I said we would think about it in the morning. Again, I thought if I walked down and managed to get that far, then I probably wouldn't need any attention. I could wait till my return to England and go and see Tom Underwood who I had faith in.

Another coffee, I wasn't that sure if all this coffee would be doing me that much good, and I wandered back to my tent. It did seem such a shame, such a waste of a day to be sitting here on such a gloriously sunny day with a mountain asking me to get to the top. After lying on my sleeping bag for a while, I was at last beginning to make some progress. I don't know whether it was me accepting that for today at least, my journey was over, and I was more relaxed, but we were now down to 110 beats per minute, occasionally below that. I tried to forget about it and to not keep tapping my Fitbit, so if I didn't know what the rate was then I would not worry about it. I guess to some extent it was working.

By now, Patrick had brought me over the coffee, sugar and hot water so I could drink it to my heart's content, but for the rest of the day I decided I would just drink hot water. I could hear more and more people arriving, the large group and a few small parties. I sat in the tent entrance and people watched, before deciding I would walk a little myself. I gently strolled across the campsite to the huts, to the loos, to the ground behind my tent covered with large Groundsels, and then I would do it all again. Sometimes I stopped to lean against a large boulder close to the tent.

One had to be enthralled by the landscape surrounding me. All around were the rocky rims of the volcanoes now making up the multiple peaks of Mount Kenya. Bation and Nelion on the right of the campsite, so close to each other, separated by the Valley of the Mists, then Point Lenana, and moving further around to the left, Sendeo and Terere. Then following the ridge down past the plateau where Adrian and Debbie had camped, back along the path we had followed yesterday with its rocky wall, was the MacKinder's Valley.

What must this have all looked like all those thousands of years ago when this was an active volcano? A simmering, angry peak, regularly spitting its contents out and down the valleys. Behind what I could see, there would be more smaller peaks and parasitic vents, but again, dormant now. It was a completely different mountain to Kilimanjaro.

The wonders of nature.

As I stood there, Johnson came to join me. We hadn't really spoken since we introduced ourselves outside the hotel a couple of days ago. He was always seemingly in the background, getting on with his jobs. But now he wanted to talk. I told him a little about me, but mostly we were on that subject again, global warming. Global warming and climate change - every Kenyan I had spoken to was so aware of this subject.

We were but a few miles away from the Equator, but one of the prominent points of both Mount Kenya and Kilimanjaro was that they both had snow on the top. Johnson pointed out that the remains of the glacier we could see, which I had already noted, was now a poor excuse of what it used to be. It was grey, dirty and disappearing. He said we would be able to see the Lewis Glacier from the top tomorrow, but that wasn't what it used to be either. I said I had expected to come at the end of the rains, but everything was so dry now.

"Six to eight weeks ago they finished," he said "but even then, they were not what they usually are."

He had heard of President Trump abandoning the Kiyoto agreement, but was pleased that China were sticking with it. One had to be impressed with their knowledge of such worldwide issues: Johnson, Boniface, Bilal, all of them but it was them who were being affected directly.

I told him that I had read about the drought in the north of the country reaching crisis point as crop after crop failed. Even when it had rained, the Government had advised against planting the maize because the forecast didn't give sufficient rain to sustain the crops and allow them to grow. Turkana was bone dry already.

I had read of the nomadic herdsmen, the Maasai taking their cattle, sheep and goats onto white farmers land, and about the murders of the white farmers if they raised any resistance. All this was very serious, but we couldn't blame Mr Trump for everything. That said, a major industrial nation abandoning the 'cause' didn't bode well for the future. Johnson talked very knowledgeably about the subject, and how it was affecting him back in his town of Naro Moru. I commented on how I had expected the river in the hotel grounds to be in full flow, not the trickle it was. I didn't know how the cattle were surviving with so little grazing on offer.

We followed on with a quick discussion on the upcoming election, and what effect that could have on his country. His wish was for stability, which meant that the status quo of the present set up would continue. If there was corruption (and there was), it would continue, but at least there wouldn't be warfare again like there had been after the 2007 election. The country couldn't afford to stop the influx of tourism if Nation States were advising their people not to travel to Kenya if it was too dangerous. Without tourism, Johnson's income would vanish. He had a lot on his mind, a lot to think about, a lot to worry about for his future. It had been great chatting to him under the warm sun about his hopes and fears. But he had to get on with his jobs. He asked if I needed any more water, but I was okay.

He wandered off, leaving me to contemplate our conversation, and relate it to what I had seen already in this fantastic but complex country, Kenya. This would be a subject that would crop up more than once in the rest of my stay. I wondered how I could honestly help next year, 2018, when I was due to return to this lovely country to help educate its people on dairy farming, through the charity Send a Cow. What could I do without that important commodity of water? What is milk if it is not mainly water, white water, and its deficiency would easily explain the poor yields compared with British cows. And would the political situation be stable enough for me to come anyway? I would have to wait and see, but I did feel a little demoralised. For now, I would continue my stroll around the campsite, enjoying the views but noticing it getting ever more crowded with the influx of teenagers and their porters.

The rest of the day was uneventful. I wasn't that interested in food again at supper but again I picked, and developed an ever-increasing dislike of arrowroot. It looked as if most of the youths were staying in the bunkhouse, otherwise Boniface said he would have found me a bed, but there were so many of them they were sleeping two to a bed anyway. Cosy! Until it got dark, one or two of them played football. I spoke to a German guy who was going up to Austrian Hut the next day. Then it was dark, and it was time for bed. I did wonder why it had never occurred to me before that I had a kitbag, and that if I filled it with spare clothing, it would make a very comfortable soft pillow. Perhaps with that, I would sleep tonight. I settled down, it did get briefly quite rowdy as the youngsters messed around in the dark. Then quiet, just me in my tent, the moon, and a very full bunkhouse.

What of tomorrow? My thoughts and dreams were of a mountain, a challenge. What would tomorrow bring?

9

A Big Decision

THE NEW PILLOW was an astounding success in terms of comfort, for the first time on either mountain, here and on Kili, I did feel comfortable and my head was supported without chasing a blow-up pillow all around the tent. I had bought one for this trip, and it did offer a degree of support, but it did have a habit of going walkabout too, especially when I was restless and the mattress had deflated. Did I sleep though? Silly question, no I didn't. I was comfortable but could not switch off again. My heart rate had come down just before bed to less than 100 bpm, it had at one stage dropped to between 50 – 60 bpm, but not for long. But it was settling down slowly and my breathing was getting better.

Yes, I thought, I would go for the summit in the morning, after all, that's what I came for. I would close my eyes and try and switch off, then I would think - what about Jane and the kids? If something went wrong how would they get me back? Would someone have to come over here to sort things out? The expense would be unfair on Jane or whoever it was. No, I must turn back.

By the early hours I had decided I would go for it, decision made, and I would stick with it. Did I doze then for a short time? I don't think so. I was just lying there with my eyes shut, and my new pillow had re-arranged itself internally. Some of the clothes had moved so it wasn't quite as supportive as it had been. It had worked well for a while but nights on the Equator were long.

At last it was first light. Patrick had left me the coffee and sugar and plenty of hot water the previous evening so I could make my own coffee. I started tidying up the tent ready for us to move off again. Outside the tent all was quiet for the moment, but the picture I saw was beautiful. The sun still wasn't high enough to shine on all of the valley, and the campsite was still in the shade of the peaks, but rays of light caught the mountain's highest points the other side of the valley, illuminating them in a ruddy orange hue. With a full moon still clearly visible above them, it made for a stunning picture. The air was cold, the sky clear. I could only stand back and admire this painting in front of me.

Back to tidying and packing, but it was dawning on me that I was developing a headache now. just when I was beginning to feel so much better. I walked to the loo, I felt okay in terms of breathing and heart rate, but not my head. More on the hoof diagnoses, was the pain coming from my neck because of my new pillow, the complete lack of sleep over the past few days, or was this altitude sickness showing itself properly now? Was this what yesterday had been building up to? I had but a few minutes now to decide whether to go up and conquer that inviting peak above me, or admit my journey was done and head back down again. Was it just the Wood stubbornness, a woeful family trait, that was driving me upwards?

Patrick came looking for me, breakfast was ready. It was a fry up, as best as Tim could manage on his stove, plus pancakes and bread. I sat down, having taken the coffee, sugar, and my mug with me from the tent, and helped myself to sausages and a lukewarm fried egg. Boniface sat down and asked how I felt this morning.

"A lot better," I said "but…"

I told him about my heart rate and breathing, how they were now reasonably settled and though I didn't want to eat the stodge in front of me, I did have enough of an appetite to eat some of the fry-up. I had one important question to ask, I had seen photographs of the top, the summit of Point Lenana, but what was the path up to it like? I was well aware now that if we went for the summit, then we would be going up with this large group of teenagers, still head to toe in their bunks, but when they too were on the summit it could be crowded. Boniface told me that it was about eight feet wide, the path up to the top was rocky and rough, with steep drops either side. The summit itself was a rocky crag. Do I go up, do I go down? Up for me, to reach the top, succeed in what I had come for – or down for Jane, our marriage, our future together.

In the end there were two things that made up my mind. Firstly, if we continued up, our exit route was up and over the other side, to the Telekei Valley, and to MacKinder's Camp. All I wanted to see, but if I went up and felt ill again, the porters would be coming with us, carrying far more weight than me. It would be unfair to go half way then say no, we are turning back. Secondly, the headache. What if we got to the top on this narrow path and I suddenly felt dizzy and lost my footing? The potential for a serious accident was real. Even more importantly, this headache, if it was altitude sickness and obviously Boniface was worried it could be, then it was a no-brainer, I couldn't go any further up, I had to go down. Go down for Jane, my health, and the life we had envisaged together. And this wasn't all I had come for, I had come back to Africa to see its wildlife, I was going on safari and that was still going to happen, my heart was set on it. It WOULD happen! The mountain was just an aside, something extra I would do while I was over here.

I had made my decision, one I think Boniface had already made as well, and any responsible leader surely would have called a halt to the climb then, if not yesterday. We would do it again another time he said, we would do it together and get to the summit next time. I hope one day I can keep him to his word. There was no point fretting about it now. I wandered back to the tent to finish packing and to start the descent the way we had come. I just busied myself with whatever I could think of. Shave, teeth, pack, and when Boniface came over I helped him take the tent down and pack it away. My kit bag was put into Patrick's rucksack once again, we were nearly ready to leave. Boniface scooped up my mattress of two days and returned it to the camp warden from whom he had got it from.

We were about ready, but when they felt my rucksack, they emptied it of all but my walking poles, still unused, and some water. Somehow, Boniface packed my waterproofs, warm jacket, camera, other water bottles, and more in his luggage. This did seem unfair, I protested they all had enough to carry, that I would manage fine, but they weren't going to allow it. We were done, so with one long last look round, Boniface and I were ready to go, ready to leave the mountain.

Strange, this beautiful setting under the mountain peaks was the longest place I had stayed on three trips to Africa. I'd spent nights in the same hotel, or on the cruise ship on the Nile, but it had been different mooring sights or different rooms. Here, I had stayed in the same place for two whole nights.

"Trende," said Boniface, and we were on our way, past the huts on our right, past the hillock with the loos on the top, and then downwards. The path was gentle to begin with, then there was the steeper part I had remembered from our entry into the camp, down the side of Shipton's Caves. I took one last look over my shoulder before the campsite was lost from my view, though the peaks behind and above us would remind me of what might have been for some time to come.

Did I feel a sense of failure? Not yet, but it had taken us nine hours to walk here so I had plenty of time to contemplate it if I so wished. For now, the sun was shining, and all I had to do was consider putting one foot in front of the other. After a while I would consider how I felt. How would the heart be, how would the breathing be? The entrances to the caves seemed far closer going down, with rocky ledges in front of them.

"What was that?" I asked. There was movement over there on one of the ledges.

"There," I said to Boniface as I pointed at it, yes, it was an animal.

I thought that the mouse we had seen not much further down from here when going to the campsite was a Rock Hyrax, indeed I thought Boniface had said it was. No, it was a mouse, for what we were now looking at was a Rock Hyrax. Whether he saw us I don't know, but he stopped in his tracks and was motionless for a little while. Boniface had my camera and tried to take a few pictures before this creature, of I guess some half a metre in length, got up and carried on his business, soon scuttling out of site. I was surprised to be told that these tail-less 'squirrels' are distant cousins of elephants, and if we were close enough to see the little fellow yawn, then we may have seen some tusks in his mouth. Without being rude about the mouse, this was real wildlife, if only briefly.

We carried on, and as we had stopped here for a few minutes watching, it wasn't long before the rest of the team had caught us up. Even with my poor appetite, they were having to carry far less food now than on the way. For the time being our conversation stopped as the Kenyans chatted away in their native tongue.

I wondered how they felt about the trip not working out according to plan. Would they just take their tip at the end of it and not worry? We were down the steep part of the descent now and walking back towards the stream that flowed down the MacKinder's Valley. With the sunshine in front of us it looked a fantastic sight, enough to not make me think of the summits behind us, now getting ever further away. As each stride was taken, the view was the same, but it was one you could not get bored with.

The valley fell away gently from us as we embarked on our descent off the mountain, the lobelias and the groundsel towering above us along the path as we followed the path stream down. We passed over that lovely little spot where we crossed the stream on the wooden bridge, where we had stopped less than 48 hours earlier, then climbed higher as the path left the stream to skirt the side of the valley higher up.

We were spoilt with the sight of a group of malachite songbirds playing by the side of the stream, amongst the small amount of rubbish that had collected on Mount Kenya. A big difference from the litter strewn sides of Kilimanjaro. We stopped again to try and photograph these. I don't know why, but when I got back to the hotel I found that most of the photos Boniface had taken were out of focus, which was a shame because he insisted on being the photographer. This was even more annoying as the expensive camera I had bought some months earlier had an automatic focus. At least it hadn't befallen the fate of my camera on Kili, falling down the drop-down toilet, and though retrieved, it was never the same again. The songbirds hopped in and out of the water, washing, splashing, a joy to watch.

Time to move on, and we were going at a reasonable pace. Frustratingly for me as Point Lenana got further and further behind, was how good I felt. I offered to take some of my baggage back in my rucksack, but the team would have none of it. I felt fine, really fine!

It was wonderful enjoying the sight of the valley in front of us, the vegetation, the sunshine. We would stop from time to time just to look at the different stages of development of these large Alpine plants, the scarred trunks of older groundsel where older leaves had fallen off, but with new growth at the top where in some we would see the flower emerging. The ostrich feather lobelia towered over us.

Just like when we climbed up the valley, by mid-morning the clouds were starting to form further down, impairing the wonderful views we had. Creeping up the side of the valley, getting higher little by little, on they came. We had made good progress and were starting to climb up the side of the valley now towards those large boulders where we had entered, leaving the Likkii Valley behind us. Now it would be the other way around, leaving MacKinder's into Likkii. On the uphill climb we were now being passed from time to time by porters from other groups, and we were soon at those boulders we had stopped at on the way. It was time for a break.

But today the clouds were relentless in their climb up the valley, not suddenly breaking up halfway along like we had seen the previous days, but now wafting up the valley, hiding the sun, and with that there was an obvious drop in temperature. It would improve when we left the valley I thought. We stopped for a break and a drink of water on the same rock Boniface and I had sat on two days earlier. But today it was now chilly. A grouse, just like the one on the 'Famous Grouse' whisky bottle, suddenly appeared from nowhere. It didn't seem overly bothered by us, probably hoping we may have one of those 'wonderful' sandwiches to spare. We didn't, but he was quite happy to enjoy our company until scared by other walkers coming from the opposite direction. There seemed to be a lot of Germans on the mountain and these were some of them!

The one thing Boniface did have to do as we had changed our plans was to arrange for us to be picked up at the start of the Sirimon Route, not at the start of the Naro Moru route which had been planned. Phone reception had been poor to non-existent in the MacKinder's Valley, so he had so far been unable to make the call. At last he had some reception, so he put Johnson in charge of the walk as he stopped to make his calls. We were off again, four of us now, Johnson leading. I was quite happy at the back just to follow. To our surprise, well mine anyway, the cloud in the Likkii Valley hadn't lifted either. I followed in the mist, not dense enough to lose anyone, but certainly enough to make it quite chilly, and I was pleased to be well wrapped up.

These were now the dry slopes we had climbed before, with no real grip, so for the first time I did get my poles out and use them as an aid to walk. I had remembered the valley to be steep, but as I followed Johnson I was surprised by our apparent lack of loss of altitude, thinking perhaps we had taken a different path. This was more like moorland now, but I was reassured when we passed those volcanic conglomerate rocks that I had remembered from going the other way. Passing those we entered the valley proper, now descending steeply back down to the stream.

Once across it, he asked if I wanted a break. No, I was fine. We climbed up the other side, surely it wouldn't be long now until we were back at Judamaier. But still no sign of Boniface. You couldn't see out of the valley now, it looked as if the cloud was here to stay for a good while. I couldn't remember it taking this long to reach the Orltulili Valley, but it was masked by cloud, whereas on the way we could see the camp in the distance, but not today. At last Boniface did catch us up, telling me he had arranged the transport to pick us up tomorrow where we had started, we needed to be down there at the gate at about 11am tomorrow morning. We stopped for a break, for a drink of water again. The porters went on leaving the two of us.

We must have chatted here for ages, about what Boniface wanted to do in the future, where he saw his future to be. He was in his mid-twenties and didn't want to settle down yet, he wanted secure employment but sadly thought he would have to leave his beloved Kenya to make any money. Perhaps he would spend a short time in Europe, in Britain. Though he loved his mountain, with a roster for the guides and porters so everyone had an equal opportunity to climb and earn, he was never going to make his fortune here.

He sounded ambitious and was looking for a way of escaping the poverty of much of Kenyan village life. He told me of the money that was poured into the approaching election, campaigns financed by huge amounts of money, far more than the salaries the politicians would receive if in office, the corruption in politics, and though the likes of him and my team were very interested in what would happen in the election, and the future of their country, sadly the gap between the haves and the have nots would not change one iota.

Had I heard this in Tanzania five years ago? I think I had. This was Africa and African politics; would it ever change? The election would be for the Government, county governors, female representatives and more. I had seen no end of posters everywhere, on buildings, bill boards, on peoples clothing, on vans and on trucks on my journey out of Nairobi and to the hotel. As Boniface had said, the bill for all this advertising must be phenomenal, money that if spent in a different direction could have improved the lives of many Kenyans. There were tribal differences, Boniface and most of his friends, Kikuyu, others, the nomadic Maasai, and other tribes all had their own agendas and differing tolerance of other tribes. It was a very complex situation, and all Boniface really hoped for was that there would be some stability after the election, not a return of the 2007 election where the result was questioned and led to inter-tribal fighting.

Despite a drought, Kenya was re-establishing itself. It badly needed the revenue generated by tourism and couldn't afford to have its borders closed by other nations, fearing for their nationals if visiting for their holidays. Money was much needed for regeneration, conservation and servicing existing debt. His future very much depended, as did so many others', on the result of an election and continuing peace.

With that in mind, we went on to discuss what the state would do for him. The Government were intent on supplying everyone with electricity and improving the road situation, but other than that, there was no State Benefit system like back home. I tried as best I could to explain to him the system back home, council housing, unemployment benefits, child care and the school system going onto further education. Much of this did not exist, although the education system did seem to have a good structure here.

He took it all in, and who knows, if this sort of benefit system that we had back home existed in Kenya, what a great change that would be for the Kenyan people. It could mean an end to poverty for many, but sadly, it will never happen, there will never be the money available to fund a state benefit system here. Also, would it encourage or discourage work if it did somehow happen in this developing country? I guess we will never find out.

We must have talked for over 20 minutes there, just sitting on the bank and with the cloud coming down, it wasn't getting any warmer. It was time to move on again, Boniface leading, me following him. At last we did reach a point where we could see our destination, Judamaier, in the distance and the path leading down towards it. The Met Station was nearly in front of us again, so we would soon join the track that went up to it, and walking side by side we were able to carry on our conversation. At crucial points we would stop just to be clear on what the other was saying, then we moved on again. I learnt so much about Kenya in that hour or so.

We were back amongst the tall heathers again, with other colourful flowers also coming into bloom, brightening the scene despite the background of thick cloud which showed no sign of lifting. As we chatted, more and more porters from other groups passed us, a lot carrying chairs with them. Had I missed a meeting somewhere? What one could see was that there was a camaraderie amongst them all.

To the sound of songbirds again, we soon reached our camp. We had covered the outward journey of nine hours in six, despite our chat stops. I felt surprisingly good, and that made me question whether I could have gone the other way, gone for the summit, and off the mountain the other side. It was too late to worry about it now. For a fleeting moment there was a sense of failure, I had only walked for two days before having to stop, but then I was so close to the top, another four or five hours and 'success'. It wasn't to be, and I was soon looking around to see where we would be staying tonight.

My tent, I saw, was pitched in just about the same place as it was on our last visit here, but there were no signs of the teams. Boniface told me they would be staying in the porter's hut again, a nice comfy bunk to sleep on. For me, it was the tent again, but I would eat in the canteen contained amongst the huts. He would speak to the warden and see if he could get me a mattress again, he was sure it would be alright. I hoped so! We now just had to remember that some of my baggage was with him, we would sort it all out in the morning.

"Can I borrow your phone charger? My battery has run right down sorting out the accommodation again and the lift tomorrow," he asked.

The only use of my own phone had been brief; a couple of hours earlier when I had managed to find some reception I had messaged my son to pass on to Mum and Dad that all was okay, I hadn't summited but had got down okay. Mum is a worrier!

Boniface disappeared to join the others; I was left in my solitary campsite contemplating what to do as it was more than chilly with the sun still hiding. It was too cold to read outside, and we still had a few hours until it would be dark and I could snuggle down in my sleeping bag. Patrick arrived with some coffee and said he would call me when lunch was ready.

"Thank you, just a little snack will be fine," I said.

"Okay," he replied.

Boniface reappeared now equipped with the mattress he had promised me, hopefully some comfort tonight then. He asked me how I felt, and again asked me if I wanted to stop at a hospital on the way back to the hotel tomorrow. I now did feel very good, and said that as things stood, I would return to England and see how I felt after the safari. I would then go and see my own doctor. At no time on the walk back so far had I felt in the least bit stressed, I had found it a relatively easy day's walking. He said lunch would be ready in about 15 minutes so if I wandered over, he would see me then. We manoeuvred the mattress into the tent and he was gone. For the few minutes I had to kill, I sorted out my bed, tablets and torch and then wandered up for my snack.

I had soup to start, very nice, and then some sort of vegetable casserole with the remains of the bread. This was no snack, this was going to be a three-course meal. I was joined in the canteen by a German couple, about to start their trek up the route I would have taken via Austrian Hut. I exchanged a few words with them about my attempt before their guide joined them and started briefing them, in English.

I sat eating, only a little as my appetite was still far from back to its normal gluttony, and by now I had given up on coffee to wash it all down in case it was the caffeine keeping me awake. I just drank hot water. I could see it becoming a drink for me in the future. Anyway, there was no way I could eat all that had been put in front of me, and apologetically when Patrick returned, I said that was all I could manage. My favourite arrowroot seemed to be in evidence again, at least after tonight I would not have to eat more of it.

I headed back down to my tent, leaving the ever-increasing number of porters to their 'party', they seemed in good voice with plenty of singing on the rocks behind the huts. Thankfully by now the cloud was starting to lift, there was blue sky interspersed with white fluffy cloud blowing across, and I could see the 'Billiard Table' and Batian again in the distance. Perhaps tonight after all I may get to see a sensational sunset before I left the mountain. I took my book down to the 'stone armchair' where I had been talking to Adrian and Debbie.

It now seemed so long ago, two days ago. I was well wrapped up for it as it still wasn't warm, and I sat there reading, keeping half an eye on the sun. It was early evening and it was starting to disappear behind cloud, high on the horizon. There were no vivid colours as it did so, I was going to be disappointed with the hope of a sunset. As the light faded, I was struggling to read in the half-light so I wandered back up to the tent to be greeted by Johnson this time who informed me that supper was ready.

What! We had only eaten just over an hour ago, I wasn't that hungry then so certainly wasn't now. Perhaps it would just be a snack.

Back in the canteen I sat down, with Boniface joining me this time, to face yet another three-course meal. There was no way I was going to manage this, though it did look more appetising than the arrowroot casserole. I did my best, and luckily Boniface was very hungry so most of it did get polished off. He was impressed with the battery charger; his phone was nearly fully charged now. He just wanted to check if I wanted to be picked up here in the van, or back down at Sirimon Gate. I was determined that having not made the summit, I was at least going to walk off the mountain.

We chatted for a while. He had promised me that he would let me know the going rates for tipping the porters, but for Tim he wouldn't say, just giving a rough scale. His tip was up to me. We would get together after breakfast in the morning before we started down and present each of them in turn with their dues. I said that I also had some clothes that I would leave them, clothes I thought I would need on the climb but hadn't used, jumpers, shirts and some work woolly hats. We would distribute those, sharing them out at the same time.

Overfull and equipped with more hot water to take down to the tent, I departed, finding my way down in the dark. It wasn't the quickest route, but I did find the tent eventually. There was now quite a dew and the temperature was plummeting. It was time to strip off as far as I was going to and snuggle down in my sleeping bag one last time on the mountain, and who knows, perhaps at last get some sleep.

It was a clear night now, it seemed quite light under canvas and in the moonlight. I made myself comfortable, but after having so much food put in front of me and feeling too full, I didn't think I would be sleeping for a while.

After a couple of hours, a call of nature was needed, and being alone in my glade, I knew it didn't matter too much how I was dressed to leave the tent briefly, so I went out to find some bushes. It was a beautiful clear night, I could make out the silhouettes of the peaks in the distance and so many stars in the night sky above. But there were already signs of a ground frost. Absolutely gorgeous.

Back in my tent, back in my sleeping bag with warm feet, and at last on the mountain, at last Rod did sleep, a little.

Tomorrow, time to move on!

10

Off The Mountain

IT WAS MORNING, my last day on the mountain, a sad day in that I
didn't get to the top of Mount Kenya, and the end of my compan-
ionship with Boniface, Tim, Johnson and Patrick, my guides, my
companions, my team. They were a happy crew who had worked
hard for me. On the plus side, I was able to sleep in a bed again
tonight and get some decent sleep. Yes, I had slept a little and as
I arose ready for the next day I felt fine, no headache, no aches or
pains anywhere else, I was good. I had my water to make my coffee
(a normal start to the day), before stepping out of the tent to find
a frost on the ground.

What was green last night was now white. But there was a
clear view over the mountain slopes, and now I was able to make
out clearly those valleys we had walked and crossed, stretching
over to the peaks of Bation and Point Lenana which had domi-
nated our view for so much of our journey. The sky was clear blue
as the sun rose slowly in the east, appearing from below the billiard table, becoming ever brighter the higher it rose. I did most of
my packing and also sorted out the clothes that I would distribute
amongst the crew. Some of these I was still wearing, but I would
let them have these items when we reached the bottom, like my
jumper which I needed on this crisp and frosty morning.

Boniface still had things of mine in his bag, and I mustn't
forget Jane's battery charger otherwise she would have killed me!
I was ready for breakfast when Boniface came down to get me. For
my last meal I was in for a treat, an English breakfast, bacon, sau-

sage and egg. More of this and my appetite may have been better earlier in the trip. But with more fresh coffee, this was a good start to the morning.

I went over the tips with Boniface again, and asked what we should do with the clothes we would give out. With that, I returned to my tent to clean my teeth and put the last things away, leaving the clothes out. Boniface came down and collected the mattress to return it back to the huts, and on his return we took down the tent between us and packed it away.

The others would be down in ten minutes, so I divided the clothes out into three equal piles, placing one pile each on a separate stump, those which I had used as seats. I gave a woolly hat and my fleece to Boniface as they were probably the only items large enough to fit him. We then wrote the numbers one, two and three on bits of paper twice, one of which was put on each pile of clothes, the other set folded so we couldn't see the number written on them, the 'draw tickets'. We also created a slip of paper with each of their names on, and how much I was giving them as a tip. I only had US dollars, but it was a common currency in Kenya.

The three of them came down with their equipment, rucksacks and what little was left of the food. We packed away my bag, the tent and were ready to depart.

But now it was payment time.

First Johnson and Patrick were called forward by Boniface and I gave them their 'porters' tip. Then Tim - a cook's tip is slightly higher, but usually a set amount. Lastly Boniface, and I had no scale of what to give him, but I had in my mind what that figure should be, remembering what we had given Chunga five years ago on Kili. For these guys, as I had said earlier, this could be their wage for the next four weeks unless they could get another climb soon.

Then the clothes. Boniface explained to the three of them about the piles, and told them he had three pieces of paper in his hand. Each must choose one, then find the number on the pile which corresponded with the number they had drawn. He also explained which pile my jumper and shirt belonged on. All was done, other than Boniface calling upon Johnson to say a few words, thanking me and telling me that he hoped I had enjoyed their mountain, and their country. He knew I was going on safari, so hoped I would enjoy that. Lastly, he hoped, they all hoped, that in the future I would come back to Kenya and visit them again, and even try the mountain again.

I replied with a very short speech and thanked them for all their efforts. I was disappointed not to reach the top, as I was sure they were too, but they had been great, and I could only wish them well for the future.

Speeches over, and it was time to start walking.

"Trende," said Boniface - it was the last time I would hear that, and yes, I was ready to go. We set off getting back on the concrete road again, walking five abreast as we headed down from our 3,300 metre altitude, down to 2,600 metres at Sirimon Gate. The frost had lifted, the sun was out, and it was getting warmer and warmer as we headed downhill. They chatted away to each other in Swahili as we walked. Me, well I was just looking around, taking in all my surrounds. This was my last look at the mountain.

"What was that?" I asked.

In front of us there was some movement on the road, something, well, quite a lot of scurrying as a herd of something disappeared into the bushes beside the road. Dik dik, small forest deer, and unusually there were more than two of them. Real animals, I had seen something other than hyrax and mice! Was this a taster of things to come when on safari? I hoped so.

Then buzzards flew high above us, catching the thermals developing as the sun warmed the air. Other songbirds started their morning chorus, this was nature at its best. We passed on down through the moorland and entered the rainforest again. There were piles of buffalo poo on the road again, fresh from their meandering the previous evening, but sadly no sight of them now.

In the rainforest, I looked around me at the trees. Young saplings reached for the sky, other mature trees had their roots cut into when making this road, but the most striking thing about it all was that it was so dry, and it was a rainforest. Some saplings were dying, some large trees had fallen, and one could see they had no root structure. When it had been wet, they had no need to sink deep roots to get their water, but now the supply had dried up and they were stranded and vulnerable to any windy storm that came along. It was the third week in June, and it was so dry. Where had the rains gone?

It was downhill, so we walked quickly, and it wasn't at all jarring on my ageing knees. I was very comfortable. We saw a bus coming up the hill towards us, it stopped and some hefty armed men stepped out of it. They were followed by a collection of other men and boys, armed with spades and machetes. I was worried this may be a group of prisoners, out as a work party under guard. But it was in fact a group who had come up to replant trees in the forest, an attempt at conservation to maintain the forest. It would help to preserve the climate, and the fauna and flora of the forest floor.

As usual - perhaps it is just that everyone is so friendly - they all seemed to know each other, and as the bus was going back down the hill when it had turned around, they asked: "Did you want a lift?"

Was I being a killjoy when I said I wanted to walk off the mountain, which meant that at least one of the others would have to walk as well? All but Patrick carried on with me. Patrick did look tired and did look older now than when we had started up only five days ago.

Down, down, on we continued but by now the bus had turned around and was making its way back down the road, minus the workers. A change of heart, and Tim and Johnson joined Patrick on the bus. I was still determined to finish the walk, so Boniface - leaving his rucksack on the bus – and I, continued by ourselves.

Today's topics of conversation was our pension system, the State Pension, private pensions, how they worked, especially with our life expectancy ever increasing. Boniface would have to rely on his family in his old age. Then we got on to the Kenyan school system, the four stages hopefully leading to some sort of apprenticeship or university at the end of it.

I explained our system, the different levels of state, grammar and private education, but it seemed to an outsider that the Kenyan system was quite similar. As long as children attended school from an early age, it sounded successful. English was taught to everybody, and from all the people I had spoken to, it was apparently taught very well. The only problem was, at the end of it all, where were the jobs? Here, the unemployment rate was 45%, and as I had seen on the journey to the hotel, the women worked and the men worked watching the women work.

No benefit system made for a hard existence, as I had already found out with my tip being what my team would have to live on for the next month unless climbs became more frequent. It was a hard life for them all, more of which I would find out later. How Boniface must have been envious of our system, a system of state aid and benefits for the needy - but he did love his country.

And that took us on to marriage again. Over the last five days I hadn't mentioned that I had a big day fast approaching, in three weeks in fact. He was surprised that I was marrying at my age, but having explained it was the second time around, about my first marriage, and my children, he understood better, especially as it is not an uncommon occurrence back home as I explained to him. Boniface was not ready yet, he wanted to be able to support a wife and a family properly before he entered into a marriage. Sound sentiments.

It was at this point that in the distance on the road, I could see specks moving around. As we got closer, I could recognise these specks as a troop of baboons, and a lot of them at that. They were mainly just sitting around, minding their own business. It was a family group as it happened, a coincidence considering what we had been talking about.

"Should we be worried?" I asked Boniface as we drew ever closer. I had heard of and read of how vicious and dangerous they can be. Baboons hunt down leopards, attack and maim with their dangerous teeth, but he assured me they would be fine. We proceeded to walk through the middle of them, some moving out of the way, some carrying on with their games, and others just watching us pass as they groomed each other. One or two I noticed were a bit lame, one had only three legs, with what looked - from my veterinary perspective - to be a perfect above the knee amputation. I wondered if this was a human intervention, or was indeed the power of nature and natural healing. It was my first sight of baboons in the wild, and these were not as large as I had expected baboons to be. I had been lucky in the amount of wildlife I had seen on our final day of descent.

We carried on talking, now onto the dry season and back onto global warming, a subject I will come back to later as the effects of climate change on a country on the equator became more and more obvious to me. If I keep repeating myself, the long rains should have been finishing about now. I asked Boniface if, when he was at school, the long rains were still going on in mid-June.

"Yes," he said "but now they are getting shorter and shorter, finishing in May." We could see how dry it was now.

He worried that in a few years, Mount Kenya and the National Park would become a desert; it was a real concern to him. We walked past massive cedars lining the road, bamboos and plants requiring much water, but water was getting scarce. Shorter rainy seasons, the effect that had on the natural vegetation and the greenhouse effect meant this was becoming a vicious circle. The less it rained, the less the gases were absorbed by the trees as they died, and so it went on. They were replanting, as we had seen, but how many of those trees and saplings would survive without water? They were also replanting on the lower slopes of the rainforest, taking its edge further down the slopes, but this wasn't true rainforest territory, and Boniface doubted if it would have the desired effect. This was also edging onto the richer agricultural land, where whites were farming and irrigating. It seemed an everlasting struggle in these countries between land development and forestation.

Kenya, Boniface explained, needed its mountain, vegetation and wildlife for its economic prosperity; Kenya needed tourism. Over the past few years it had been in fluctuation, following the troubles of the 2007 election, tribal warfare, over a thousand deaths and the displacement of many people. The tourism industry had suffered, suffered badly as international Governments had suggested their people should not travel to this troubled land. Now, Kenya was on the map again, but given those two black clouds of climate change and the up and coming election, only time would tell what effect it would have on its economy.

Gosh, we had been in some serious discussion this morning, and as we walked through the baboon troop I reckoned we had about another hour to go. As we turned the next corner, there, not very far off, was Sirimon Gate. Another five minutes, and our trek was over. Tim, Patrick and Johnson were waiting for us, and so was Bilal.

I wasn't expecting to see him, I had been told that someone else would do the return journey. I suppose the fact that we had finished at a different point from that planned had changed everything. I shook his hand and briefly explained to him all about my adventure, and why I had to turn back.

Boniface had to go through the formalities of a group leaving the mountain with the Park Authorities, and while he did that I put my bags into the vehicle, went to use the 'posh' facilities here again, and chatted further to Bilal. He had got hold of my book from Wilfred and was reading it himself, and really enjoying it. I said I was pleased, and that he would be a star in the book I had already started on this expedition. He was chuffed.

Boniface was finished and returned to join us, we finished loading up and were ready to depart. The boys seemed worried about getting the rest of their clothes, but I said I hadn't forgotten. I gave my jumper to Johnson as it was now very warm, and assured Tim he would have my shirt when we got back to the hotel.

The journey back, similar to the one on the way out, was through the rich farmlands on the lower slopes. We passed an agricultural institute, where heavy farm machinery cultivated the land, irrigation reservoirs and then headed slowly back to Nanyuki.

"Sure you don't want to stop at the hospital?" asked Boniface.

"No, I'm fine, thank you," I replied.

I looked at the new buildings held up by wooden scaffolding (all looked more than a little precarious), and the cattle grazing the verges, litter heaps and anything else they could find. There were marvellous looking vegetables and fruit on display at market stalls, while squalor lined the streets behind.

We passed the British Army base in town, and there I thought of Debbie, now back at work after her short weekend break with her husband. There were war graves, a remembrance of World Wars, and the support from our Commonwealth friends. African and British history intertwined, some good, some bad. I'm not an expert so I wouldn't even think about commenting.

We were about to leave town, but something was obviously troubling Bilal. He kept looking down out of the driver's window, but I seemed to remember him doing that when he picked me up a few days ago.

We had just passed Nanyuki airport - perhaps landing strip would be a better description - when he pulled over into a stony drive. We had a puncture, and in all honesty I think I had more idea what to do about it than anyone else. The jack took some finding, mainly because it was buried under the driver's seat, entangled in I don't know what, and it took more than a bit of extracting. But with many hands making light work, we got the wheel off eventually, found the rather dust covered spare under the rear of the vehicle, and then Boniface got on with putting the nuts back on the wheel and tightening them, to the extent that they may never come off again.

This little airstrip saw many planes take off and land in the short time we dealt with our puncture. It was busy, very busy, as private planes flew in and out for rich businessmen and tourists, far quicker than the trip by road.

We were done and back on the road, with the remainder of

the trip into Naro Moru seeming quite uneventful. We stopped at the garage again, and this was goodbye to Tim, Johnson and Patrick. I got out, thanked them all, shook hands and said my farewells. I hadn't forgotten to take my shirt off and gave it to Tim, all debts paid, though he would have to wash it.

Lastly, we headed back through the streets of the town, along the piece of road they were renovating (and the work was progressing well), and back onto the track towards the hotel. It was time to drop Boniface off by his home; we had exchanged e-mail addresses earlier and he had given me back what he was carrying of mine. He said he would be along to the hotel later, so we would catch up again. I said I would buy him a beer and see him later. Then we went back along the track, through the security gates of the hotel – where the dear female security guard was still in her isolation – and ended up back outside reception.

My journey was over. Today so far, my Fitbit told me I had walked 18,244 steps, or 5.75 miles, and burned 3,115 calories. Now at midday I was back in front of the Naro Moru River Lodge, just Bilal and myself. He stopped the engine and we both got out, grabbed my bags and took them into reception.

I wasn't expecting a welcome party, but there to shake my hand was the hotel manager Wilfred who had promised me a drink, the first drink, if I succeeded, and the very attractive young Kenyan receptionist. They were very excited, even when I told them I hadn't reached the summit. They wanted to know my tale, how I was and how I had found it, so while Bilal brought the rest of my stuff in and retrieved the luggage I had left at the hotel before we started the climb, I told them of my trip.

The young female receptionist returned to her position behind her counter and asked if I had taken lots of photographs. She was surprised when I said she could look at them now - the days of digital photography - and she was excited when I showed her how to use the camera so she could flick through my pictures at her own speed. She had never been near the mountain, so the scenes captured in Mackinder's Valley, and at the base of the last climb were all new to her. She loved them, as well as being able to play with technology. I was only too pleased to show her, while acknowledging the rest of my reception party.

Bilal had to go and deal with the tyre, so I said I hoped I would see him later, especially if it coincided with when Boniface came back up. They had equipment to sort out and return to the stores. Our young lady had finished going through the photos and gave me my camera back. The manager made sure that when ready, the first drink would still be on him, and I just had to tell the barman.

I said to the young lady that I smelled, and really needed a shower. These clothes had been on me for five days now, and I could tell. Politely, she said I was fine, but I would guarantee if we had been on a date, she would have told me I smelled - badly.

With the help of a porter, I took my bags to my new room. It wasn't quite as far as the one I had stayed in on arrival, and when he had gone I took my boots off (and wouldn't be using them again on this trip) and having switched the shower on to a suitable temperature, got in fully clothed.

Whatever the nice lady said, I did smell, and didn't want to carry that odour around Kenya with me, or on a plane to London. What setting was the shower on for my clothes? I guess it was the setting for whites! A long hot shower, and then while I dried, I unpacked my rucksack and kitbag, leaving things in tidy piles on the bed. I hung my wet clothes in the sun on the veranda, in his heat they should dry quickly, certainly by the time I needed to repack to head back to Nairobi.

Then I headed to the swimming pool for some relaxation, to condense my thoughts, reflect, and if my eyes closed, then doze. I was greeted by my friendly barman, and had no hesitation in ordering that beer the manager had promised me.

It wasn't quite the peace and quiet I wanted as there were some rather raucous Asian teenagers making a lot of noise the other side of the pool, but I could easily switch off and cast them out of my mind as I sipped my Tusker. Lovely! There must have been a hole in my glass because I soon had to order another, it was so soothing, so good to taste after all that coffee and hot water of the past five days.

I went through some of the notes I had written, firstly to make sure I hadn't forgotten anything I wanted to write, and secondly and more importantly, to make sure I could read it while it was still fresh in my mind. Then I laid back, enjoying the beer, watching the birds, enjoying the sunshine, and thinking it was time to pause and think of what I had seen.

A beautiful mountain, wonderful valleys and streams, but the overriding memory of the past five days had been one of water, or lack of it. I would wait and see what the rest of Kenya would be like. A mountain on the equator, and it still had snow on it. Well, it did at the moment!

I had written about the snows of Kilimanjaro five years earlier, the retreating glaciers, and wondered if they would survive the next 30 years. Here on Mount Kenya, Boniface had said that the place could soon become a desert. I saw a bit of a glacier poking out from behind a rock, but as Johnson had told me back up at Shipton's Camp, it wasn't nearly the size it was a couple of years earlier. I closed my eyes and thought of this, then dozed.

Awake again, I ordered a burger, which, when it arrived with some chips, had to be one of the best burgers I had ever had. I ordered a bottle of water to drink with it, I didn't want to be pissed when Boniface showed up for a couple of beers. I had a pleasant lunch and there was NO arrowroot. The rest of the afternoon passed peacefully, and I stayed by the pool for a while. In the end I thought I had been in the sun long enough and was having my doubts as to whether Boniface would appear.

Back to my room to finish unpacking, repacking for tomorrow, and then I just sat in the shade on the veranda, reading and listening to the birds. Extravagant I know, having talked so much about water, or the lack of it, but I did shower again before heading across the garden in the darkness of nightfall, following my shadow from the full moon.

First, I had a beer in the restaurant bar, and a re-acquaintance with my friendly barman of a couple of days ago. A short chat, then he was gone, he was off duty, and hoped one day he would see me again if I decided to try again. The noisy Asian teenagers of earlier came in and started playing pool. The eldest of them, it sounded as if everybody talked, approached me saying that he had heard I was an author.

"Yes, I have written a couple of books, but at the moment it's a hobby, I'm a full-time farm vet. I will be writing a book on this trip though," I told him.

He told me he wanted to become a doctor, but the courses were far cheaper in Eastern Europe - Hungary I think he said, so he would soon be going there.

I had ordered my meal with the waitress, and it was now ready. Onion soup of course, and I did treat myself to a glass of red with it, then pork chops. I ate alone, until the teenagers' fathers came into the room, sat down and had their soup. From then on, they decided to try and find fault with everything that was presented to them. Chicken legs, not enough, they wanted half a chicken each, and they wanted it now. They wanted to talk to the chef, who eventually came out.

They were spoiling my meal for me, so I gave pudding a miss, finished my wine and left them to it.

My bed, a proper bed, was a welcome sight for me, so I undressed and arranged the mosquito net around the bed. I was going to sleep, and I did.

Tomorrow was the start of my safari, a dream come true.

11

Return To Nairobi

I would be leaving the hotel at 9am, so there was no need to rush for a change. A leisurely start, the only reason not to lie in was that the birds were up far earlier than me, and in full voice. If I had started singing, they soon would have shut up and flown as far as they could. But it was lovely hearing them sing, even if I did want to catch up on all the sleep I missed out on the mountain. I forgave them! Now, listening to them, I could get on with packing so that after breakfast all I would need to do was to clean my teeth and pack my wash bag. I would be done.

Breakfast was next on the menu, the full English again, followed by more of their gorgeous pineapples and bananas, and coffee. The only shame was for all the acclaim of Kenyan coffee, everything I got tasted like it had come out of a Nescafe jar. The true taste of Kenyan coffee would have to wait, I hoped they hadn't exported it all so there was none for me!

Teeth, wash and a final scout around the room and I was ready to carry everything back to reception. I visited the tourist shop to get a couple of things for Jane, I was also hoping I might find a book on Kenyan birds, but no luck; they did have a book on trees though. I guess I hoped that Boniface would still show up, even if we only had time to say goodbye.

Back in reception I paid my bill and chatted to the lovely receptionist about my book on Kilimanjaro, and the book I would try and write on Kenya, which wasn't made any easier by not reaching the top. She told me about a German film-maker who had been there a couple of years previously, he had tried to climb the mountain, had got stuck on it and had needed to be rescued, but he returned the following year to make a film about the mountain. I would find a story somewhere! A lovely lady, and in fairness, everyone at the hotel had been so friendly, really welcoming and had made my stay a good one. I know there were not many guests in the hotel, but they made me feel special, and even Wilfred and the manager came to bid me farewell.

Bilal would drive me back to Nairobi. I was pleased about that as I had bonded well with him. My luggage was on board, and after checking if I wanted to sit in the front again, which I did so I could talk with him, we were ready to depart the hotel. There was a party outside to wave me off, the author was departing, we headed up the drive with the manager on board until the security gate where we dropped him off to chat with the lady who so patiently manned the gate. I thought she must be roasting in her hut and bored by the number of people who passed through. The season WOULD get busier!

We drove past the buildings where we had dropped Boniface off the previous day. Bilal guessed he probably would have been out last night having a beer or two with his mates. I was inquisitive about the housing, which seemed like one long hut but which was home to many. He explained to me that all these properties would be owned by a landlord. The landlord would rent out a couple of rooms or, more strictly, a length of the hut which the tenant would then divide up into rooms with cloth barriers and curtains to make a kitchen and bedrooms, although nowhere in our conversations did the presence of toilets come into the discussion. The rent was about $10 a month. With electricity (a promise from the Government to get a supply to everyone), and water, you could soon see the $50 I gave Patrick and Johnson disappearing. Food on top of that, and there wouldn't be very much left. You could see the need for them to climb as often as they could in the season to get some cash behind them for hard times, or to buy those little extras. For those who had bought themselves motorbikes, these would provide a little extra income as they would become the locals' taxis, taking people back with their shopping to their homes. It was amazing how much some of them managed to get on a small bike.

The issue was that if they couldn't pay their rent, they would be kicked out, and there was no welfare state.

If we had seen a lot of women working on the fields on all my trips so far, and a lot of men just standing around doing nothing, then today, Bilal told me, if there did seem a lot doing nothing, they were waiting for a load of sand that they would help shift. Many hands make light work, at minimal expense.

We were out of Naro Moru, and back on the main road to Nairobi. It would take about three hours, Bilal reckoned, hopefully the traffic wouldn't be as bad as on my arrival, and anyway, we weren't going so far into the city. We travelled back through the arid grasslands we passed through on the way, and like on that journey, the mountain didn't want to show herself to me. It was her chance to say goodbye, but no, I hadn't reached her summit, so she couldn't be bothered with me!

We talked about the life of a villager, how they would get water, whether from a communal pipe, or a tank - which would be more expensive. We also discussed the health system, their general health scheme, county scheme and lastly a private hospital scheme affordable to some but not to the many. The lower in the system you attended, then the level of negligence increased, perhaps I was now glad I had decided to wait to get back to see my own doctor for a check-up.

From time to time we would pass a police check point. We would always be called through, or if we were stopped, then when they saw Bilal had a tourist passenger we would be waved through. He told me corruption was rife, and lorries or locals in their trucks would often be given an on the spot fine, even for bald tyres, lights not working etc - even if everything was in perfect working order and legal. You didn't argue, you accepted it as day to day Kenyan life, it was one of those things.

Police were corrupt, but that was how they earned a living.

There was a strict 50 kph speed limit, and that was one thing you did stick to; the faster you were going if you were exceeding it, the higher the fine.

Bilal told me that he had been working at the hotel for a couple of months now, but really wanted to be driving a lorry. He had his licence, and come his vacation, that is what he probably would do to earn some extra cash. One day soon, he hoped he could get a job in Europe driving and make some real money before returning to Kenya and settling down. When we had driven to the hotel, I had been very tired for the second part of the journey, so between eyes open and dozing, I had missed some of the sights.

Being a farm vet, I was interested to pass a dairy milk processing plant, owned by the president, Kenyatta, and even more intrigued by the procession of trucks, mopeds and bikes, all carrying churns or other containers taking their milk to be processed. I would be going back to Kenya in 2018 to help the Send A Cow charity, helping people improve their husbandry so they could produce more milk to support themselves and their neighbours. Being told about how little their cows produced in the way of milk compared with our dairy cows, there was plenty of room for improvement. But again, how much of it came down to water? In this town there were two milk processing plants, so they must be doing something right. Kenya does import milk from New Zealand, Bilal told me.

Our journey continued and the closer to Nairobi we got, the more road blocks, the more sleeping policemen, and the more people we encountered as we slowed down - always trying to sell us something, especially water or bananas. Back through the fertile and irrigated lands where the plantations of pineapples, bananas, and maize were being grown, Nairobi got ever closer until we reached the outskirts and the traffic started building up. There were more herders by the side of the road, grazing their cattle, sheep and goats on seemingly nothing, watering them at pools of what seemed to be dirty water. There was more rubbish by the roadside, and some cattle sifting through this. Nairobi was a busy place, with plenty of people milling around. How many of them were doing anything, that was another story.

From our outward journey, Bilal had pointed out the Safari Park Hotel, so I knew it was not anywhere near the centre. My wish had been to go and visit the National Museum, which I had read was well worth a trip, but I had already decided that I wouldn't venture any further away from the hotel as I was travelling alone. A restaurant called *Carnivore* served barbequed meat until you were over full. They just kept coming round with more meat until you were defeated. That had been on my itinerary as well for my brief stay in the Kenyan capital, but no, I would stay put in the hotel, hoping I would find enough entertainment there, and rest. At last we were there, pulling up outside what we thought to be the main gate which was guarded by armed security again. We had to turn around and find another entrance in, just around the corner.

Again, through security, Bilal found the guest parking and escorted me and my luggage to the reception, an incredibly large area with a large model of an elephant in the centre, and the reception desk perched on the far wall behind it. I checked in, enquiring whether there had been any messages left for me about a connection tomorrow. I asked where or at what time I would join my safari. I had just been given a rather loose instruction that I would be informed at my destination, but there was nothing.

We were offered a drink to refresh us, and a hot towel to wash with. It was Ramadan, and Bilal is a Muslim, so he had to refuse. Nothing could pass his lips until evening.

We picked up my luggage and followed a porter on a long walk through the hotel gardens, passing several restaurants and a swimming pool. We reached a block of rooms, appropriately for me it was called the Elephant Block. We climbed the stairs, along a veranda, and there in room 859 was my bed for the night.

We were shown in, told how the lights worked, and left alone. It was now time to say goodbye. Bilal had been a great companion on these long drives and had told me a lot about his country and his goals. He was reading my book and enjoying it very much.

He hoped we would keep in contact, I had already given him my email address.

Finally, a tip for him, we shook hands, and he was gone.

I was left to explore my room, which looked like something from days gone by. It was very colonial in style, filled with antique furniture, a massive four poster bed with mosquito nets, plenty of storage room in dark wood draws, and a large ensuite. To top it off there was a lovely balcony overlooking a pond and hotel gardens.

I made myself a cup of coffee, opened the patio door onto the balcony and sat at the table enjoying my drink. Clatter, clatter.

What was that? I stood and looked along the wooden tiled roof below me. A monkey ran along it, stopped briefly to look at me, then continued on his way. Clatter, clatter - his mate was following him and did exactly the same thing, but they were too quick for me to be able to get my camera out.

I was unsure what to do now, presumably someone would contact me at some stage. Do I stay in my room and await a call, or go out and amuse myself around the hotel?

A couple passed walking below, very recognisable by their very cropped hair, otherwise the place seemed very quiet.

I thought I would take myself for a walk after the drive, so I stepped out of the room to find it raining. Nairobi did seem to have far more of a humid heat than out in the Aberdares, so I guess there were a lot more of these showers here.

It wasn't enough to put me off and I went to explore the restaurant area, now busy as it was lunchtime and it looked as though many conferences had poured out for fresh air and refreshment. There were five different restaurants, I would have to choose one later, ranging from a buffet restaurant (where breakfast would be in the morning), to Italian, Japanese, Indian and a barbeque place where there would also be some cabaret later.

At the shopping precinct close by, several empty units were looking for new tenants, but looking very up market. Next, I viewed the swimming pools, two of them, the first a conventional pool, the other ornate, with islands, rocky water shoots and surrounded by trees and bushes. Tempted? Yes I was.

For now, I would continue my stroll, having found a walk which was marked around the perimeter of the grounds. It was interesting due to the shrubs, some glorious blooms, many birds and the odd animal - mainly squirrels. It was a chance to try my camera out on wildlife before we set off tomorrow on safari, if anybody finally got around to contacting me.

By now the rain was steady, it was the sort of rain that made you damp, but with the heat you soon dried out, so I continued my walk around the grounds, practising with my camera, swapping zoom lens' to see what affect it had on the different scenery. I found a group of ibis on the lawn and then overhead a bird of prey, but I wasn't quick enough to get a picture. I stopped to watch a rather colourful bird outside one of the hotel entrances, bobbing up and down through the flower beds, then returned to my room.

There was a message on the room phone, well four of them in fact, but could I get the answer machine to work? No chance! With my fiddling, I even managed to connect to reception and rather embarrassingly said that I had just been trying to receive my voice messages, but as she could tell, without success. She said she would send someone along to help me and rang off. I waited patiently over another cup of coffee, decaff this time being aware of the effect it may have on my sleep patterns. But it was a no show on this one as well. How long should I wait?

Eventually I decided to wander up to reception and ask again, admiring more shrubs and trees as I went, especially what we came to know as a sausage tree. I didn't know what its proper name was, perhaps I should have bought that book about trees in the shop before leaving Naro Moru. As I entered reception, I wandered around for a while admiring the vista. The elephant in the middle was life size and there was a flight of stairs to the Hemingway bar, which opened early evening and doubled up as a piano bar. It may be worth a visit later.

I saw tourist shops, then out of the corner of my eye I noticed the large TV showing the Sky News channel and showing pictures of a large fire. It eventually dawned on me that this was back home in London, the Grenfell tower block fire. It was horrendous footage and there were early reports of large numbers of fatalities, but also tales of bravery and how everyone had come together to help a community in distress. This would be a news story for days to come - as it turned out it was actually news for weeks to come - and still going on as I write my tale.

I pulled myself away from the pictures of horror and went to reception to ask again. Nothing. She thought we were supposed to be leaving at 7am the following morning from what she had gathered from other people who were on the same trip. I wasn't going to be alone this time! She would ring through as soon as she heard something. How much longer must I wait? Back in the garden I watched the fish lazily swimming around in their large pond before returning to my room to read. At last the phone rang, and a gentleman informed me that we would be leaving at 7am as the lady had suggested. The buffet restaurant was open all night and that was where we would get breakfast, just over the way from Elephant Block.

I could relax, so it was time for a bath and a long soak. This is what I would really have liked coming off the mountain yesterday, but there was not one. I had a slight issue with the bath plug, but I did manage in the end to wedge it in, so my bath wouldn't be a frustrating one of diminishing water levels. I got dressed and then had the Tusker out of the mini bar and enjoyed a drink on the balcony.

As at Naro Moru, as it got dark, the birds were in full song. On the guttering just along from my room, there was one bird that was giving his all, not a large bird, but certainly a large voice. I watched him and the dramatic effect of the garden lights which were now switched on, giving amazing luminous patterns between the leaves and branches of the tall trees surrounding the pool.

I had to think about a menu for the evening, but although both the Italian and the Japanese sounded very tempting, the choice was easy. I hadn't made it to the Carnivore, but here in the hotel grounds was a restaurant which would do the same. An African style restaurant, the Nyama Choma Ranch, a barbeque with as much as you could eat, and a cabaret act from the infamous 'Safari Cats', who performed dance acts.

I wandered in that direction to find an open facade building, large with many tables and a large barbeque with several large joints cooking in the flames generated from the hot charcoal. I waited to be seated and was escorted to a table close to the front of the stage where the performance would take place later. It was very multi-national, with many Chinese, Japanese, African and Europeans seated around. Business meals I wondered?

A waiter came over and told me the format of the meal after taking a drinks order - more beer, and a Tusker please! After a starter of soup, I was back onto the onion soup again, I helped myself to salad from the buffet. The chefs came around with the barbequed meat and placed on my plate whatever I wanted. To the music of a small group playing and singing from the other end of the room, I had my soup, enjoyed my beer, got some salad, and expectantly waited for meat. A sizzling hot metal plate was placed on my table, which the meat would be placed on, continuing its grilling. Then, with a long sword, the chef cut me some small slices from a skewered leg of lamb. On the table were also placed a tray of condiments, mint sauce for lamb, horseradish for beef, mustard for pork.

Time to tuck in. There were hot vegetables and MAIZE STUFF: Ugali. The lamb was good. I had finished that when a joint of pork arrived on a sword, I had a slice of that, then the food came thick and fast. Chefs visited each table giving out a slice here and there for whoever needed more meat. There was turkey, followed by sausages, and then crocodile. Everything tasted good, except for the crocodile. I was told this white meat came from the legs of young crocs, the best I could say was that I think the crocodile would have enjoyed eating me a lot more than I was enjoying eating him. He was rather tough.

I think at barbeques you always seem to eat more than you really want, especially when it is served a bit at a time like it was here. I did want another sausage, and I did want another piece of turkey, then I was done. I was quite happy to turn down the croc next time it came around, that wasn't a snap decision!

A desert followed, another beer, and as the restaurant filled, the lights were dimmed and the stage lit up. An announcement told me it was time for the Safari Cats, which according to the brochure were Kenya's sleekest dance troupe.

To music they came on stage, dancing to the rhythm and beat with African dances. There were various sets, then acrobatics, shows of strength, dancing with fire, a long routine and a colourful routine which everyone was enjoying immensely.

The announcer said no photos, but that wasn't going to stop our Chinese delegation in front of me.

It was an amazing display of energy, dance and strength which kept us entertained many minutes, leading to the big finale - muscle strapped male and female dancers with prominent six packs, their athleticism was amazing.

They were finished. But those that wished could go up on stage and have a photo taken sitting in the middle of the troop. A much-deserved long applause followed before they finally left the stage.

My meal was done and I paid my bill before wandering back to the room in the pleasant evening temperature. I had a thoroughly enjoyable evening, it was a wise choice, although I was sorry that I wouldn't be able to sample the Japanese cuisine, my stay was for only one night. I bet on that menu there was no croc.

As I got to my room, the bird was still giving his all, but was now also in competition with a chorus of cicadas. I packed a few things, and that wonderful looking four poster bed awaited me. Tomorrow - safari here I come! African wildlife at last in the flesh, and my chance to see my elephants, another lifelong wish.

12

To The Mara

U P BRIGHT AND early, today was the day, I would finally go on safari and see African wildlife in the flesh as it were. Dressed and ready for breakfast, I made my way to Café Kigwa, guessing most other people there would be eating early to go on the same trip as me. A blonde lady walking from another block followed me down the path, just across the way from Elephant Block. Entering the café, I saw the couple I had seen the previous day, the ones with the cropped hairstyles. Inside were couples; a mother and daughter, a couple of older ladies and a German couple said good morning to me. One or two more looked as if they had just got in from partying the previous night.

I had a quick breakfast, a very good breakfast, fruit salad and then a traditional cooked one. I've never been one to refuse bacon if it was on offer. I had to be at reception at 7am to meet up with the safari party, so I went back to the room, cleaned my teeth, washed, collected my bags (which were now considerably lighter after my donations to my porters), and then took the pleasant walk up through the gardens back to the lobby.

There seemed to be a couple of groups forming as I was directed to put my bags with one group, only to find after paying my bill, and the arrival of a lady from Polman Tours, that I was with her, and had to move everything to the other side of this vast space.

Like everyone else, I was obliged to take a couple of photos of the life-sized jumbo in the centre of the area, then find out if I could glean any further information about the Grenfell fire on the lobby TV. An increasing death toll was about all I could find out. Horrific for all those involved.

A group was gathering, and it was those people who had breakfasted early. I started a conversation with the German couple, Mike and Ula. No point in making introductions yet as I would only forget everyone's names in the next couple of minutes. I would try and remember them all over the next few hours. I would associate each and every one of them with a name, a country, something. By the time half a dozen people had introduced themselves, I had soon forgotten every name but Mike, and that was probably because it didn't sound very German.

The tour lady came over and did a rollcall, there were 12 of us and we were all present and correct. She went through an itinerary of when and where people would be dropped off, some were going on to Mombasa and Zanzibar mid-way through the tour, some on to Tanzania, and that left two, the blonde lady and I. I told her that there were arrangements for me once back in Nairobi that I had sorted out and paid for through my tour operator. She had nothing, but she would look into it.

We were introduced to our drivers, Ibrahim and Abdullah, and then divided into two groups of six. The tour info had said no more than seven would ride in each Land Cruiser, we would be six plus our driver.

I was allotted to Ibrahim and his vehicle, along with the two older ladies I had seen at breakfast, the couple with the harsh haircuts, and the blonde.

We found our luggage and took it to the cruisers, loaded it into the back and seated ourselves down. We were ready to go. It was nearly 7.30am and it would take the best part of four and a half to five hours before we reached the Masai Mara.

I had heard so much about it, Kenya's Serengeti (but then they did run into each other) and now we were on our way.

Ibrahim was the more experienced guide, so would lead for the first part of the tour. Abdullah knew Amboseli better which would come later in the week. It seemed incredible that I had been in Kenya for a week now, I had lost all sense of time, on the mountain I didn't even know what day it was. But, for the next six days I was going to enjoy the 'greatest show on earth', I was excited and full of anticipation.

Out of the hotel grounds, again after going through security in which mirrors were passed under the chassis of the car - inspecting for bombs I guess - and we were on the road. It was a different journey out of Nairobi, Ibrahim told us, to miss some of the rush hour traffic, but it still seemed very busy. We passed new hotels and shopping and business centres in developing Nairobi, and then continued into some of the richer suburbs of the city. Large, posh houses and new estates catered for the wealthy in this bustling and developing city. There were a number of lorries on the roads - business in motion.

Our group of six would be together for the next few days, so introductions were made. The elder ladies, two Kiwis, Geraldine and Penny (who had already been on safari before, in the Okavango in Botswana), had left hubbies behind on the South Island and would be going on to Tanzania at the end of our trip. The couple with the cropped hair, two Belgians, Stephan and Vivian, were much travelled and sitting on the back seat, quiet to begin with. The blonde was Janet from London, over here for a week's safari following an International conference she had attended through her work. She had arrived at the Safari Park late the previous evening too and would now relax for a few days. As she was in Kenya, she thought she would extend her stay to do something she had always wanted to do.

Lastly there was me, a vet who had just tried to climb Mount Kenya, an author of a book about depression and Kilimanjaro, and someone who had wanted to see African wildlife ever since he was a boy.

Ibrahim, who we would get to know while on our travels, was there to be our guide and our friend if any troubles presented. He would answer any questions he could and was keen to learn about us and our countries. Freelance, and hired by Polmans when they wanted him, he was an experienced guide and very interested in conservation. He was there to look after us. He told us we would drive for an hour and a half, then stop briefly, then do the same again, and then finally we'd move on to our hotel for lunch followed by our first game drive. We started to chat generally amongst each other, with Ibrahim filling us in with any information we required, while trying to find out more about each of us. I got the impression we would all get on well. Geraldine, and especially Penny were fun, Janet was loud and fun, Stephan too. We would have a laugh.

We left the suburbs of Nairobi behind, and Ibrahim had explained about some of the housing laws so that people's inheritance could not be sold off by one money grabbing member of the family - real estate was becoming a valuable commodity, a way to make money. Families needed protection, and this was being put in place.

First there were houses, but the further we got out of the city, the more these were replaced by plantations and vast areas of green houses where young tea plants were being nurtured. They were very tender when young and so would be grown in these nurseries for the first three years of their life, offering protection from the elements. They would be uncovered from years three to five, from when they would be harvested, and their leaves picked to make the tea we know. They could live for up to 50 years but would generally be replaced every 20 years to maximise production.

More plantations, maize and coffee, although the main coffee growing area would be in the Central Highlands where I had been through on the way to the mountain. We joined an even busier road, one of the main trunk roads of Kenya, and I was to find out that there were not many of them. Congested with lorries of all sizes in both directions, we had little chance to overtake and travel faster. Even if we did, we would soon be stuck behind other lorries. The sides of the roads got more wooded and the plantations ceased; we started to descend gently downhill, before the gradient got more severe.

The trees stopped on our side of the road as the land dropped away steeply to the plains below. We were descending into Africa's Great Rift Valley. There was bush, plain, the odd settlement below us and in the distance, hills rising the other side of this great natural phenomenon. The clashing of tectonic plates thousands of years ago caused this natural cleavage, or fault, in the earth's crust, stretching through much of the length of East Africa and extending up as far as Syria. Mount Longonot was in front of us, rising to 2,776 metres above sea level and 1,000 metres above the valley floor.

It had been a while since I had drank a coffee, but now I could do with a stop as Ibrahim had promised. There were one or two pull-ins with a common denominator, a tourist shop in each one. We stopped and were immediately surrounded by African ladies trying to sell us cloth, carved elephants, beads, bangles and bracelets. But my major concern was for the toilets, which happened to be at the back of one of these shops.

Relief, then a passage back through the shop. There were tables and tables full of carved animals of various sizes. We would have to barter if we wanted anything, but so early in the trip, not yet!

I tried to look interested while making my way back to the entrance and escaping, only to be pestered by the women again. Eventually, I managed to get to the rail which overlooked the Rift Valley and take in the views. Janet and Penny joined me, and it transpired that Janet had already stopped at this same place on the way back from her conference to Nairobi. They asked me about the book, and my fundraising from my mountain climb. We went on to discuss the view in front of us, the Rift Valley, and I was able to answer Penny's questions on how it was formed. I knew I had written a little about it in the *Kili* book.

It looked like everyone had satisfied their wishes, and we were ready to travel again. Further down the hill we passed several places where logs were being burned to make charcoal, and one small chapel built by Italian prisoners of war during the Second World War.

Selling cooked corn on the cob by the side of the road also looked like a local trade. We reached the town of Kijabi, a flat terrain now, and met a major intersection. We turned south towards the Mara, leaving much of the traffic behind us as it continued on towards Naivashu.

On and on along a straight road, gently undulating, and again I was surprised at how dry it all looked. We started to pass more and more nomadic herdsmen, the Maasai, tending their stock, driving them to new pasture (dried out) and the odd dirty waterhole. Thorny scrub bushes popped up more and more, as did Acacia trees, but very small ones. Interspersed with this scrubland was farmland, barley crops in large fields, maize, some grass fields, and then more scrub and more Maasai herds.

How many rivers must we have crossed now, so soon after the big rain, and all of them dried out, other than the odd small puddle that remained. But this would not last for much longer now into the dry season!

It was overcast and even drizzled very briefly, but that wouldn't be enough to do any good in this parched landscape. Struggling up one or two hills, overtaking lorries so we wouldn't lose our power, we at last reached the town of Narok, the administrative centre of the Mara.

It was a town with an agricultural bias, despite its population of 800,000. We passed grain granaries, machinery depots and even in a town this large, plenty of cattle. I suppose they had to do their shopping as well. But it was time for a stop again, we had been travelling over an hour and a half again, so as you may have guessed, we pulled up outside another tourist shop, emptied out of the Land Cruisers and trooped back through to the back of the shop again for our constitutionals.

In fairness, some of the animal carvings were very nice as I walked past them on the way out, but did I really want to have in my possession a six-foot wooden giraffe to carry around southern Kenya, and then onto a plane and home? No! I went outside where the sun was now shining, found Ibrahim and Abdullah, and chatted to them until we were ready to go. We stood under a tree and looked up, there was an abundance of baskets hanging from branches. Colourful birds popped in and out, and around the base of the tree were weaver birds and their nests, and some rather colourful starlings.

Back in the vehicle we wound our way out the other side of town, so dusty now. We took a sharp turn left and the tarmac road suddenly stopped as it turned into a compacted dirt road. This was a road being developed at present, with the help of Chinese money, to offer a better route into one of Kenya's biggest assets: the Mara. There were two roads, parallel with each other, packed hard but still very dusty, and because we had left the main road, it didn't mean our two drivers were going to take their foot off the pedal. We sped down these tracks doing 50 - 60 miles an hour from what I could see from the speedo, one lost from view of the other in the dust.

Did we feel every bump!

Again we crossed arid scrub land, from time to time passing Maasai herdsmen and their flocks of sheep, goats and herds of cattle. Their young in tow, how did they survive these dry conditions? Ibrahim told us that these goats were browsers so would eat anything and would breed twice a year. The sheep were grazers and could breed three times a year. Far different animals from our native breeds back home.

Occasionally we slowed down when we met something coming the other way, otherwise on we went at speed, leaving a dust cloud behind us. We passed the odd Maasai village where school children waved to us as we flew through, standing outside their schools smartly dressed in their uniforms. We saw many stockades built from wood or thorn bushes to keep their cattle in at night. And then, out of the blue, or should I say, out of the dust, wildlife, real wildlife.

First, we saw a giraffe, grazing over the top of a tree, then further along, a few zebra, impala, and wildebeest. Yes, at long last I was seeing the real thing, although we were not slowing that much to view or photograph them. Brahim told us we would soon enter the Mara park, and then we would go on to the hotel, register, have lunch and then go on a game drive.

The road got narrower, we travelled over several concrete bridges which were badly in need of repair before the next rains. There were women doing their washing in the little dirty water that remained in so few of the rivulets. Then more buildings, a large herd of cattle, and gates, gates guarded by security men again at the entrance to the park.

The cattle were impounded by rangers for being allowed to stray onto the Mara parkland. What else was there for them to eat around here? Not a lot from what I had seen. We stopped at the gates while Ibrahim went through the paperwork with the guards, and were immediately surrounded by Maasai women with their beads, bangles, bracelets and wooden elephants yet again.

Without sounding mean, I shut the windows tight and didn't show any interest. We would have plenty of opportunities over the coming days to purchase some souvenirs. The gates were opened, we got through without buying anything, this time! A rough dust track took us up the side of a hill and to our hotel, the Mara Sopa. A game drive awaited us, I was excited now. The hotel, set in the hillside at 2,104 metres above sea level, was a stone building into which we descended some steps into a lodge style reception. A desk stood in one corner and straight ahead were more steps down into the bar, and the restaurant. There were porters everywhere, waiting to grab our bags which we had carried down ourselves.

There had been a debate about whether, as it was getting late, we should go straight to lunch and then sign in later and then find our rooms, or the other way around. Porter pressure in wanting to grab our bags and get a tip meant we would go for the latter. We experienced a typical welcome of a cool drink and a hot flannel to wash ourselves off with and to remove the dust from the journey. Our passports were collected and given to reception, and then one by one returned to us along with our allotted room key. The porters were happy, at last they could get some of our money. They already had bags in their hands, they then continued to find the owner and head off down further steps, past the swimming pool and to a series of lodges set in the hillside.

Each lodge contained two rooms with a large lounge in front of the two doors leading to the bedrooms. There were enough sofas in each to seat most of the hotel. I was sharing my lodge with Janet. It had a large bedroom, ensuite and a king-sized bed. It looked very comfortable. Janet's was next door, a mirror image of mine.

Lunch was very good - a hot buffet, interrupted briefly by a couple of monkeys coming in for their lunch as well, scurrying across the beams before being shooed back out again. We would meet at 4pm to go on our game drive. Until then, I went back to the room and unpacked.

There was time for a swim as well in that inviting pool, and when I got there I found that Janet had already enjoyed the waters. It was cool but bearable, the barman/pool attendant provided me with a towel and looked after my valuables. He was more than friendly, he seemed to have taken a shine to me. The brochure had mentioned him as one of the attractions of the hotel. As I swam up and down, moving to keep warm, it was nice to see young African children trying the water, playing, splashing, and in some cases trying to learn to swim. Here I was only too pleased to offer support and encouragement. Then it was time to get out, dry in the sun, and prepare to safari.

The Masai Mara National Reserve (the Masai Mara) is a large game reserve in Narok County, which joins the Serengeti in neighbouring Tanzania. The reserve is named after the inhabitants of the area, the Maasai nomadic tribesmen. of which we had already seen so much. Mara, meaning 'spotted' in their language describes the circles of trees, shrubs and cloud shadows that are so distinguishable in this area. Set up in 1961 as a wildlife sanctuary covering 520 sq. km, including the Mara triangle, it was later extended into an area over three times the size, managed by the Narok County Council.

In 1974, it obtained National Reserve status, with some of the land being returned to local communities. The area was further reduced in 1984, and in 1994, a new council - the Trans Mara County Council - was formed to look after the western part of the reserve, along with the Narok council. The non-profit making Mara Conservancy took over the management of the Mara triangle in 2001. Therefore, this was a reserve, not a National Park. There would be conflict between the Maasai tribesmen wanting to graze their stock on reserve land, and the needs of animal conservation, even more so when grazing was scarce. This was the situation at the gate as we passed through it, but how could the limited resources of the 'powers that be' enforce the non-grazing policy? They could confiscate stock, but what could they do with them other than hand them back to the people who had transgressed?

We got into our Land Cruisers and made our way back along the rough, rutted and dusty track we had entered on; as we approached the gate, the status quo persisted.

For now, our safari was about to begin, along with I don't know how many other jeeps laden with people like us. Some of them had equipment that big that if a man had been standing next to them in the loo, they would have been severely embarrassed by their own small, LENS, of course!

The dirt track opened out of scrub onto well conserved tracks of stone - we were on the Mara. The terrain of the reserve is mainly grassland with seasonal rivulets. The western border is the Siria Escarpment of the East Africa Rift, stretching for miles and miles. Along this escarpment there is probably the greatest concentration of wildlife, as the swampy grounds mean access to water is always good. The easternmost border, where we were, some 220 kilometres from Nairobi, is where most tourists visit and is also known for being the site of Maasai ranches. The plains ranged from 1,500 to 2,180 metres above sea level, and there was rolling savannah as far as we could see.

As we entered the reserve, the first thing that crossed my mind was how bare, so barren it all looked, with dried grassland and clumps of acacia trees scattered about. This should be the end of the long rains, but they had finished weeks ago. The good news for us was that the great migration, which should start from the Serengeti in early July, had already begun. The animals were on the move looking for fresh pastureland to fill their bellies. In convoy, we would soon see a group of impala, our first wildlife on the Mara, one male with his own hareem of many females. He wasn't going to give them up without a fight to any other young male thinking above his station.

Ibrahim had opened the roof of the Cruiser before picking us up, so there had been a scramble to get out our cameras and click away merrily at anything that may appear as a spot in the distance as we got closer and closer. Luckily these modern cameras have a delete button on them.

The biggest sign of the migration being underway was finding wildebeest. There weren't many yet but they were here, albeit quite solitary, then the odd group of 10 or more appeared. I suppose the surprise was that they weren't quite as large as I expected them to be, but they looked in good condition with shiny coats, and as they followed in the pursuit of the lush grasslands, their condition would continue to prosper. They would calve on the rich pastures of the Serengeti in February, before starting their migration in June/July, taking in a large loop clockwise before going further north and then returning to the Serengeti to calve again. Nature's cycle.

This has only been a recent phenomenon though, possibly since the 60s when previously Rinderpest, a serious disease of Ungulates, would have wiped vast numbers out. However, since its control and eradication the number of wildebeest has increased dramatically, hence their need to find fresh pastures. But why have they come here? I thought. There's nothing for them, just dried up grass.

Next we saw zebras in the flesh, and what magnificent animals they are, so clean, so smart with their stripes. It is the zebra that will lead the migration Ibrahim told us, and the wildebeest follow them. On these abundant (we hadn't seen it yet) grasslands, these migrating animals would rut and mate, and continue their journey through life. Of course, with that, the natural predators of the African plains would be following them.

The Mara is infamous for its prides of lion, the Marsh pride being especially famous for several TV series. It's also known for its cheetah and leopards who would feast royally on this migrating larder in front of us. But for now, more wildebeest - some restarting their rutting and the assertion of male dominance - zebra, impala, and the sleek looking Thompson's gazelle. We got so close to them and soon found those distant shots to be unnecessary. Emerging above the acacias was a giraffe, the Masai giraffe, not one but two, no three, no four. There were seven of them, what an amazing sight as they just loped sedately from tree to tree.

These were sights I had dreamed of, and now having seen them they would be memories for life. The convoy was spreading out; across the plains one could see a vehicle zooming off in one direction, another in the opposite direction and clouds of dust in the distance. Unlike other National Parks, here the vehicles were free to off road as much as they wanted. Radios kept them all in contact, if there was a good spot, then everyone would converge together again.

We passed a group of eland, Africa's largest antelope, though harder to get close to. Topi, like wildebeest but in their dark tan colours, were more handsome and distinguished, and usually seen together in pairs, certainly in groups of no more than half a dozen. Other than the zebra and wildebeest, our search for finding new animals was slowing down. We drove around looking for something different, finding that the further we went onto the Mara the vegetation was greening up a little, but still there was very little grass.

We drove slowly towards a green, tree-lined water hole, and there, right in front of us stretched out on the bank was, yes for real, our first big cat, a single lioness enjoying her slumber. We pulled up to within 30 feet of her, but was she bothered? No, not at all! Other than the occasional yawn and twitch of her ears to discourage flies, she just lay there. Supper was on the plains not far away. Whether she had companions or other members of a pride close at hand I don't know, we didn't see any more, and weren't prepared to get out to investigate. What we did see as the bush telegraph kicked into action was a swarm of other vehicles coming to view as well.

Our lioness was an amazing sight, in good condition and what massive paws she had. We tried to make little noises to see if she would raise her head, which in the end she did but so briefly we were lucky to get a picture of it. We watched for a good few minutes, and then were on our way again in search of other game.

Other than a few topi and wildebeest, the plains seemed to have gone quiet, and we drove for quite some time before we found more wildlife - a group of zebra, grazing and looking after their young. Again, so close to us, I could see what good condition they looked in, with glowing coats richly emblazoned with their individual stripes. Beautiful. Ibrahim took us to a tree, just like the ones I had seen in the gardens of the Safari Park Hotel, a sausage tree but with far bigger sausages. The sausage fruits, of no use to man nor beast Ibrahim told us, were used by some Kenyan men who would crush and ferment them to make some noxious alcoholic concoction which they could pickle their minds with.

In the distance on the slope of a hill we could see a herd of buffalo. We were heading their way when we turned a corner around some acacia scrub and suddenly came across the animal that I had really come all this way to see, an elephant. There in the bushes was an elephant calf exploring the local territory. On our arrival she decided she ought to find mum - a massive matriarch some 40 yards away grazing another tree. And now I wasn't looking at a mum and calf, but several elephants, all that surprised me was that they didn't seem as large as I had expected. But with mum now looking after calf, who was still a little way away from her, she was in protection mode, striding out a few paces with her large ears flapping out in a gentle warning. We weren't going to venture any closer. At a safe distance we could just watch and take many photos. Three of the big five down, though the buffalo was still only seen at a distance.

In a flurry of excitement, the elephants were forgotten by the drivers who had got wind of something very exciting, and we were all heading off towards the gentle slopes on the east of the Mara, with some deep scrubland in the distance. Ibrahim said there was something special we may see if we were lucky, I guessed it would be number four of the big five. Would I be right?

Vehicles screamed across the plain, all centred on one point with our vehicle almost in the lead. Ibrahim slowed the Cruiser down, then, coming to a halt, pointed. Some hundred or so yards away, just visible above the long grass was a pair of black rhino. Heads up, horns prominent, this rare animal was in front of us. We weren't going to get any closer, there were too many vehicles around and the rhinos were more than a little intimidated by them. Slowly but surely, they made sure that a good distance was kept between them and us, a distance they were comfortable with. Distant shots would be the best we would get, but at least we had seen this endangered species – it was only for a short while before they hid themselves in longer vegetation, but we had seen them. We would leave them alone, the evening was starting to draw in now and the sun was going down in the distance, getting lower towards the hills.

We started to make our way back towards the hotel; we had seen a lot on our first drive. On a little way and we did find the remnants of a water hole, now not much more than a mud pool, but much enjoyed by three wallowing buffalo bulls. These were old chaps who had seen better days but had now been exiled from the herd by younger, stronger bulls. They would spend their last days, which could still be considerable in number, together as a bachelor group, the *Last of the Summer Wine*. It almost seemed quite sad, but this was nature for real, and this is how it is. They would still be a formidable outfit in case of lion attack, huge powerful animals but not now as powerful as others.

Speaking of lions, there just over the way was another group, three lionesses resting before their search for food would continue after dark. Much smaller than the madam we had seen earlier, but just like her, they were reluctant to do anything other than occasionally raise their heads. Still, it was just fascinating to watch and we were parked some 20 feet away.

With the last of the sun, and as we made our way back towards the park gate, we got a final glimpse of the silhouettes of the Masai giraffes and a few solitary wildebeest. How many of them would see tomorrow? Which one would be supper for hungry lions?

Then we headed back along the rough track back towards the hotel, our first drive was over as we got out, wishing Ibrahim goodnight - we would see him in the morning. I had seen four of the big five already, plus many more animals, yet, there almost seemed a sense of anti-climax to me. I had wanted these sights for so long, but I guess the disappointment was the lack of interaction. There was a wildebeest here, a zebra over there, somewhere else a Tommy, an impala, even the elephants and giraffes. Individual species were dotted about by themselves, as if someone had just placed them there for us to see. It was nature, and it was what it was, I guess I just wanted a bit more action and interaction.

We agreed to meet up for dinner in the bar about three quarters of an hour after we had arrived back at the hotel. Until then, I had a short time to unwind and clean up. Fairly routine - or it should have been. I went back to my room, unpacked a little, and went for a shave and a shower. The shave turned out to be something out of *Psycho* as I managed to butcher my face over and over again. To say I was bleeding was an understatement, I had a cut under one eye and a couple on my chin. Would they stop bleeding? No way. In the end I decided I would have to shower and hope it would eventually stop.

On went the mixer taps and I stepped in, a long shower cubicle with a brim on the front of it; plenty of room I thought, so no need to pull the shower curtain shut. I felt the water and it felt about right so getting under the flow, blood still pouring from my face, I looked forward to a nice long shower. But it was getting hotter and hotter and hotter, and then trying to turn it down, the shower mixer handle fell off in my hand. Much more of this and I was going to be boiled alive.

After much fiddling, I did manage to get the handle back on, but it wasn't going to cool the water. I had to get the shampoo off so bent down on all fours to rinse it, hoping that being lower down, the water would feel cooler. It was marginally, but still far too hot to enjoy the good shower I had hoped for. I was going to resign myself to the fact that I would have to give up and just switch it off.

Then I looked at the rest of the bathroom floor; I should have pulled the curtain across; the floor was flooded. Back on my hands and knees I mopped it all up with a towel, hoping in the African heat it would dry quickly. And I was still bleeding. I managed to stick some tissue paper over the wounds and hope that would give the cuts a chance to clot. It did stem a lot of the flow; I may have even been able to present myself in a reasonable state for dinner, but no white shirt in case it started again. I managed to get to the bar intact, meeting up with the larger than life barman from the pool earlier who was only too keen to get me a beer, a Tusker of course.

Most of the group had already arrived; a couple had already gone through into the restaurant. We followed at the end of our beer. I would have to compliment the chef on a wonderful buffet, it was possibly the best of the whole trip: a wide variety of well-cooked food, from plain to curries. Very good.

A film afterwards showed some of the wildlife of the Mara, including that scene I always hate of the crocs catching so many wildebeest when they try to cross the river on continuation of their migration northwards. Nature, but I don't enjoy seeing that carnage, perhaps I just don't like crocs.

Nights, as I had found on Mount Kenya, but even at the altitude of the Mara Sopa Hotel perched on the slopes of the Oloolaimutia Hills, were chilly, and it was supposed to be the coldest month in Kenya. But in the mild of our summer it seemed strange to have a roaring log fire in the centre of the lounge area. It added a sense of warmth and homeliness to the surroundings as we sat after our meal and chatted about the day and the amazing sights we had seen. One or two did agree that it was not quite as dynamic as they had expected, but still wonderful to see African wildlife in the flesh as it were.

The ladies retired to their laptops and sent emails back home. Geraldine and I were having an ongoing conversation about the British Lions tour in her home of New Zealand, a little lively banter as our trip went on, the results, the prospects. Also, the Admirals Cup, but her team were winning that hands down, beating us as their chosen semi-final opponents before going on to give the American holders an even bigger hiding. She was the main source of results coming from back home as I couldn't get good enough reception on my phone to pick up the scores.

I left the ladies to it. There was another bar here which overlooked the bush where the cooks would throw meat out so that any hyenas, mongoose and honey badgers could have a meal at the hotel - and we could watch under the African night skies.

Over the balcony was yet more wildlife and bush. As we were about to sleep, who knew what stories were unfolding out there? It was time for big cats to hunt, time for them to search for their supper.

The migration would bring welcome extra chances to fill their bellies before the huge herds moved on again.

There was a gentle breeze, and high above, a beautiful star lit night. Africa is such an amazing place to be. I took in the air, breathed the Mara, finished my beer and it was time to retire for the night.

Back in my room, the maids had been in to prepare it for my slumbers. Embarrassingly for me, they had finished clearing up the bathroom after the great flood, replaced my wet towels and restored the room to how they had left it before my arrival. The bed was turned down and now behind a mosquito net that extended right across the room, enclosing the bed as if it were the theatre.

I was ready for bed, but had to remember that at this hotel, the generator would be switched off late in the evening until first light. A torch had been provided by the bedside. Just remember where it is Rod!

I climbed into bed, thinking of the day to come on the Mara, and fell asleep.

13

The Real Mara

We were to leave on today's drive at 7.30am. No one had taken up the option of going on an air balloon safari, on offer at great expense, although what we were to see later may have given one everlasting memory from above - the migration.

I was up at 6.15am, but it looked as if others had been about before me. I was well bitten by the local insect life, it didn't seem as if my mosquito net had been that effective, unless the little bastards had already been my side of the net when it was closed. Try not to rub them, I thought. The bites were mainly on my feet and hands, the exposed parts of me extruding from the sheets. It would be hard, and I had put some of that foul smelling DEET on as well. Oh well, wherever I go, the local insect life always seems to find me tasty.

Breakfast was again a lovely meal; I mixed with the others and was able to have bacon and sausage to give me a good start to the day (it was another packed lunch day of which I didn't have great hope or expectation). I filled my belly for a long day on safari, that was my plan. I ate fruit and coffee, and it did taste like proper coffee for the first time. Was this Kenyan coffee at last?

Sadly, when we congregated at reception to await Ibrahim's arrival (the guides slept at a hostel down the road), we found that Penny was ill. She had a bad tummy, sickness and stomach cramps, and would be staying in her room for the day. I told Ibrahim when he arrived, who went off to see her advising her there was a doctor in the hotel if she so required. She would rest, drink plenty, and as we found out later, did see the quack. A shame for her.

The five of us boarded our Land Cruiser, changing seats from yesterday so we would be able to chat to someone different while travelling around the Mara. Today I was opposite Janet. We headed off back down the dusty track towards the Mara, with Ibrahim pointing out the damage elephants had caused to the bush: broken branches and smaller trees uprooted as these large and magnificent animals had feasted, scouring the vegetation for a ready meal. Next, we caught a brief view of a pair of dik dik, shy animals that disappeared quickly out of sight when they heard our presence nearby. They were a loyal pair who would stay together once they had bonded and mated, remaining companions then on for life. Ibrahim told us that when one died, the other would be so stressed and heartbroken, that it would starve to death, if it wasn't caught by a predator first.

Ibrahim did seem very clued up on his wildlife, and talking to the others in our second Cruiser, it sounded as if we had got the better deal for information.

We were near the entrance gate to the Mara again, and were greeted by a group of small monkeys sitting beside the track. Adults were grooming each other while babies chased each other around playing.

The cattle had gone this morning. They'd probably returned to their herdsmen who no doubt would transgress back onto the reserve again, and so it would go on.

We journeyed back to the arid Mara we had seen before. It was a similar scene, a few wildebeest and zebra, some impala and a mixed group of Thompson's and Grant's gazelles, differentiated by their different stripe patterns (and the Grant being slightly larger), trying to find what grass they could. We seemed to have lost the procession of vehicles leaving the hotel temporarily as we headed off in the direction we had come back from the previous evening.

There were a group of warthogs, who from thence onwards

would always be known as Pumba (from The Lion King), a family, with well-grown offspring. Ibrahim told us that these ugly creatures with their large tusks sticking out from the sides of their mouths, were very forgetful, and had a very short memory. Often, if they were being chased by lions, they would suddenly forget why they were running, and just stop. True or false?

On the other side of the track was a pack of jackals, there must have been over 20 of them, but they were very timid animals, soon retreating away from us. If they were about, there must be a kill nearby, Ibrahim told us. This was the only pack we would see on the whole safari, a fleeting glimpse of their rear ends as they ran to hide from us. Then came the group of giraffes we had seen the day before. How many? Six, seven, our giraffe counting was not very good as these Masai giraffes blended in with the acacias they were grazing from. Ibrahim said that from the look of them, three of the females looked pregnant, and must have been somewhere through their 14-month gestation period. We stopped and admired these for several minutes before continuing our journey across the Mara.

It seemed quieter today, there were fewer animals about though it was still relatively early in the day, but we were told that they may be on the move – the animals of the migration were in search of better feeding.

This was yellow grassland, short and bleached in the sun. The odd carcass, or rather skeleton, was white, and again bleached. One wondered who had survived the night, and whether the lions, leopards and the hyenas had now satisfied their appetites, and were resting up again as the day got hotter, waiting for nightfall and their next meal.

I thought we were heading in the same direction again as yesterday – I usually having very good bearings of where I am - but the landscape gradually looked different. We passed a waterhole which we hadn't seen yesterday, a couple of big bull buffaloes were wallowing in this welcome swamp, submerged up to their briskets in mud and water but with their ever-present friends in close attendance. Egrets and oxpeckers were searching their coats for parasites to gorge on.

What was yellow was just beginning to seem a tinge green. The others agreed with my comment. There were few animals, other than the mixed species of gazelle and the Tommies, with their black stripes along their flanks and their tails flickering to ward off the flies. Their heads were down, grazing, but always alert for any danger that may be close at hand.

It was getting greener, there was more grass about and it was longer, a better bite to eat - this is what the herds were coming for. Although not in vast numbers, we started to see more and more wildebeest, larger groups of zebra, more topi, and a new animal for the day, the hartebeest. Again, it was like the wildebeest but larger. A tan, brown colour and in smaller groups.

In the distance to our right were a herd of elephants on the move, walking through long grass in a line, possibly 15 of them. But we didn't head off in their direction to take a closer look. I suppose I was a little disappointed. But time soon passes on safari, and those early morning cups of coffee were starting to have their effect. We would need a stop soon, and the bush was not a good place, especially for the ladies to be caught with their trousers down in mid-flow, only to be interrupted by a sleepy lion!

We were heading for an airstrip which had proper toilets, if you can call a couple of brick cubicles in the middle of nowhere proper facilities. As we drew closer, we spotted everyone else in their vehicles who we hadn't seen since entering the reserve. One by one, we used the facilities. On emerging, staring into the distance on a ridge of a far-off hill, was an incredible sight.

A line as far as you could see, the migration for real. Zebra to the fore, and behind them, wildebeest on the march. There was a marked change in vegetation, now rich grassland, tall grasses, their seed heads blowing gently in the breeze, waves of movement as they moved in unison. This is what they were coming for, from the Serengeti, the hills of which we could see in the distance.

Hundreds and hundreds of them moved in single file, almost

at the promised land where they would stay grazing and breed until it was time to move on to pastures new. Their ever-ongoing cycle in the search for food, and their continuing life cycle. Time for us to move on; we left the sight of the migration behind us as all the vehicles now seemed to be heading off in different directions.

Now sticking more to tracks than we did yesterday, the tall grasses of the plains were now extending as far as the eye could see. Food was in abundance for the returning herds. It was a wonderful habitat for birds as well, the seed eaters and the insect eaters who could feast on the vast number of prey living, hiding on the grassland. We seemed to be looking for something, I'm not sure what, but we soon pulled up close to a pair of solitary trees, along with another couple of vehicles.

"There, there," pointed Ibrahim, "up in the tree, at the fork of the branches, see it?"

We could, for up there was a leopard, sleeping alone on his branch, resting from his nocturnal activities. I wondered if he had killed? Again, like the first lioness we had seen yesterday, he was going to live his own life, catch up on sleep and not be worried by us – we were just another load of tourists who had come to take his picture. He did grace us every now and again by raising his head, yawning, and if we were lucky taking a brief look in our direction. That was the photo opportunity we all wanted, and Stephan showed us a wonderful picture he had taken zoomed in, having blown the photo up so the leopard's face filled most of the frame. What a shame Penny was missing this, for it was a leopard that she had really wanted to see. On her previous safari to the Okavango she had missed out, and again today, we had found one, but she was ill and was not with us.

Another one of the big five - that had completed the set for us. We stayed and watched her for some time, by which, as the bush telegraph was obviously working well, we now probably had every vehicle on the Mara surrounding the tree. Luckily, we probably had the best view of all, others were over 50 yards away. It just meant we couldn't go until someone gave us some space. Apparently on the Mara there is a rule that no more than five vehicles should be watching one animal in a scene like this at any one time, clearly this wasn't being obeyed today.

We had enjoyed a wonderful viewing session and now a space had cleared, and we were able to get out - it was time to move on. Up a small hillock and turning left away from our leopard, on a huge rock we saw two basking lionesses who did raise their heads slightly to acknowledge our presence. Otherwise, like yesterday, they were more intent on their slumbers. They were lying parallel with each other, face to face, paws slightly entwined, a lasting picture in one's mind.

Just below us on another rock were more, but they weren't that easy to see or photograph. We still hadn't seen a Lion King though, there must have been a male somewhere, but where eluded us. We continued, it seemed as if we were going back on ourselves, but we weren't and next we came across a small group of elephants. There was a matriarch female, with baby taking most of our attention, but there were others around in the long grass.

Further on we crossed a road where there were more zebra on the move, large numbers now. I thought they may be part of the procession we had seen earlier from the airstrip. In the sky, enjoying riding the thermals, was one of the five uglies, or our first sight of a maribou stork, though from a distance they didn't look quite so bad. We watched a couple of them before heading onto a small but lush copse, the other side of it was a swamp with very tall grasses and reeds growing from it. Not far away was another line of elephants making their way towards the side of this wet area, but on getting there they were diverting to the front of it, some 30 yards away from us, to enjoy the water, a drink and for the baby, a little playtime.

On our other side, emerging from the copse were more of these magnificent creatures, feeding on the trees' foliage. There seemed no effort for the two herds to come together, or even acknowledge each other, they were just getting on with their own business. The only disturbance was a lone hyena asleep in the grass in front of us, now wary of danger around and keeping low but alert to the presence of the herd no more than four or five yards from him.

As we pulled away from the herd, leaving them to their peace and quiet until the next tourists arrived, which probably wouldn't have been very long, we passed a small group of water-buck grazing just to the side of the swamp. Beautiful animals with majestic horns.

Then we seemed to be back onto the shorter, yellow grass of yesterday, but again Ibrahim seemed to know where he was going as we passed several ostriches, clumsy in their running action. They retreated until they considered themselves to be far enough away from us.

Ibrahim told us it was a large group, and that all the females would lay their eggs, but an alpha male and female would then tend all of them until they were hatched and they would all be reared together. A co-operative but run by seniors. We admired them, stopping only briefly, for this wasn't what Ibrahim was looking for.

But then we found it, going slower and slower until we stopped, as first one cheetah appeared from behind some bushes, followed by another, then another. Mum and her two kittens - although these two were very well grown and nearly as big as mum. But she was still looking after them. We were told these would be about 18 months old now and would soon have to be capable to fend for themselves. Mum would soon find another mate and breed again. Their time for breeding would be coming soon as well. Mum walked slowly and gracefully, before lying down in front of a bush not many feet in front of us, almost ignoring our presence. The kittens followed behind, playing a little game with each other before they too threw themselves down besides mum, stretched out and groomed each other with their tongues.

Surprise, surprise, as other vehicles arrived surrounding the cheetah's bush, but they weren't in the least concerned. They lifted their heads sometimes, but otherwise continued resting.

From time to time they sat up and sniffed the air, just in case lunch may be nearby.

It was lovely to watch them for several minutes, but then they got wind of something and were up and looking to move on. With their astute senses, Ibrahim guessed they must have got wind of some tommies close by and were off for a kill. They stalked around our vehicle, I could have leant out of the window and touched one if I had felt so foolish. I had seen stories of them getting into vehicles, but today we weren't lunch. They inspected us, gave us a tremendous experience, and were then off in their search of a meal. They moved fast over a short distance, but only a short distance as they only had a small heart - we didn't get to see them in full flight but knew from TV what graceful and agile cats they could be when running.

We would now head off towards the Mara river, the scene of these great migration river crossings shown so often on nature programmes. The day was getting on, we would go there, see the river and find a spot for a picnic before returning to the gate and an appointment with a local Maasai village to see their homes. First, having passed another small herd of zebra, we saw our first signs of a recent kill, the striped hide of a zebra stretched over what remained of its carcass and skeleton. The cruel side of nature, but everything must eat sometime.

Vivian asked if we could find a happy bush. I was a little mystified as to what she was talking about, but Ibrahim understood perfectly. She needed a pee, and out on the vast savannah, there weren't too many toilets. A happy bush, yes, something to squat behind, in the knowledge there wouldn't be any lions, leopards or anything else lurking hidden there as well. So, a suitable bush found, men in front, ladies behind, and the happy bush served its purpose before we set off again.

We passed another waterhole where zebras were enjoying the coolness offered, wading flank deep into the muddy wet, some of them playing like kids. Then, another sign of a kill, with vultures feasting on the remains, the last pickings on the bones of a dead wildebeest. Three types appeared, the large lappet-faced vulture feeding while the smaller Ruppell's griffon and African white-backed vultures waited for their chance of an easy meal. Zebra were now present in large numbers on the plains, gorging themselves on this abundant supply of grass. A few warthog were wallowing in muddy furrows alongside the track, and then, a scarcity of animals, they hadn't made it this far yet, but they would.

I chatted with Janet about my history of depression and how this and Kilimanjaro had been the trigger for overcoming it. Then we spoke about her job as a CEO for a care for the elderly charity, how it had all become so real to her the previous year when her mother had died and her father had needed to go into a care home for a short while as he adjusted to the loss of his partner. It had made the need to find suitable standards for care clearer to her. She found some of the homes she visited totally inadequate in the level of care she wanted for him. We spoke of my parents and their move away from the countryside into a busy town for the first time in their lives, and how they weren't coping with it, and how I might help them adjust to a new environment.

Then we were suddenly aware of the loneliness of this landscape, our group and the other vehicle behind us, travelling across the vastness of these great plains.

One lonely tree stood in all of this, alone but surrounded by the tall grasses of this yet un-grazed savannah. A picturesque scene. This could possibly be the cover picture for this book. We had to stop quickly for a photograph.

On towards the river, there were no animals but many birds fed amongst the grasses, some very brightly coloured. A small clearing in the grass and an earth mound saw a group of mongooses standing on their hind legs to watch us go past. The occasional lizard basked on rocks, enjoying the warmth offered by the sun. Butterflies fluttered above the grass; other insects were floating in the wind, going about their business.

We drove towards the top of a hill to admire the views around. The Mara river was a couple of miles in front of us, with hills rolling up the other side of the bank. The hills of the Serengeti were far away in the distance and the grasslands we had just crossed were behind us. These acted as forage for the migrating herds coming behind us on their annual trek. They were everywhere we could see now.

And of course, as we could get out of our vehicles, there were happy bushes!

Down to the river there were high banks above the water on either side. Some acted as places where the migrating herds could get down into the river before crossing to pastures on the other side, allowing them to proceed on their great cyclical trek. But where was the water? It wasn't the river I had seen on TV with hundreds of crocs waiting in the deep waters that the migration would have to cross. No, it was half empty and quiet, all we could see were the tops of a few large boulders sticking above the surface of the river, and a few hippos basking on the sandbanks left by the absence of water. For me I guess, my first thought was that the herds may be able to cross easier, this wasn't good croc hunting territory. Where were they anyway?

I guess I was a bit surprised when some of the boulders started to move. The five hippos on the banks were in fact part of a large school already in the river, spending their time submerged and asleep. They were huge animals, and I was seeing them in the flesh as more and more boulders turned into hippos. These schools of hippos were bathing now, but they were also grazing for food, needing large quantities of forage to fill their stomachs. Greyish pink in colour, with a special chemical that their skin produced to protect them from the ever-beating sun, they basked in peace, unworried by a few more tourists gazing down on them.

We drove further along the bank looking for anything else, nothing. Further along, we at last saw a crocodile, it was quite small and lying on the edge of the water with another swimming just behind him. But where were the others? They should be congregating, waiting for their meal to arrive on the hoof. Just one more we saw, on the bank the other side of the river, and he (or she) was massive, even from this distance it was a frightening sight. There was no time to let him know that it was only a couple of days ago that I had eaten croc meat, even if I didn't enjoy it. There were three of them, that was it.

We stopped for a picnic under the trees in a small clearing on higher ground. It was lunchtime as Ibrahim and Abdullah found us blankets in the back of the Cruisers and an enormous pile of 12 boxes containing our lunches. The vegetarian option Viv had was a lot more appetising than our meat version, which wasn't very different from what I had on the mountain, plus a bag of crisps. Stephan devoured his as well as most of Viv's vegetarian one, how he ate so much and kept so thin I don't know. I was glad I had a big breakfast, like most of the others, my lunch was reboxed and returned to the back of the Cruiser.

We had a long drive back to the reserve gate, we had to be at the Maasai village for about 4pm and had travelled quite some distance over to the Mara river.

We boarded the Cruisers and got back on the track only to meet a white Skoda coming in the opposite direction. Not quite the vehicle that is expected out here, it was a small family saloon. It pulled up beside us and the driver wound his window down, asking Ibrahim for directions. He and his passengers had been told that the migration was happening and was now crossing the river; they wanted to know which way they should go to see this spectacular event.

Someone had conned them and rented them a totally unsuitable car to go and see something that wasn't happening, not in the near future anyway! One could see a sad side to this, but also a funny side. All Ibrahim could do was give directions to the river, and more importantly, directions for how to get back to civilisation.

We set off, watching them gingerly negotiating the paths we had just come from in that hardy Skoda.

We followed a similar route back to the one we had taken down to the river, with fleeting sights of more mongooses, colourful birds, lizards, and the open plains. Eventually we met up with the herds of zebra, progressing ever further onto the grasslands. In the distance I could see smoke in the direction of the Serengeti, and asked Ibrahim if they burnt the grasslands on purpose from time to time to regenerate growth.

"Yes," he replied, "but also as a deterrent for the tsetse flies, and what is more likely happening now is that the Tanzanian Rangers are creating smoke and fire to slow down the migration off the Serengeti, they have a tourist trade to think about as well."

Now on a different path, a more direct route off the reserve, we had to negotiate crossing one stream/waterhole. This took a bit of planning before Ibrahim decided which was the best way to negotiate it, but we got through okay and were now amongst an enormous herd of zebra. Along with the million plus wildebeest on the migration, there would be some 400,000 zebras leading the way. As we drove on, there seemed to be a common purpose in them all in which way they were heading. There was plenty of grass for all.

It surprised me how many school buses we passed on our route, and the number of infants we saw. I suppose there were Maasai villages out here, we had certainly seen schools but not an actual village. And if there was, were the cattle and sheep allowed to graze these reserve grasslands?

We were getting closer to the barer pastures of the eastern side of the reserve, from where we had entered. We had a real close-up view of an eland bull on a bank, and a huge baboon feasting himself below a tree, his mates some way off. Back past our six, seven or was it eight giraffes, and we were at the reserve gate.

We stopped and had to show our papers, which once again gave the waiting Maasai women a chance to surround us and try and sell again. The one window we had open, Geraldine couldn't manage to close, but I managed it for her just in time to prevent all those arms coming in.

We were heading to the nearby village now, past a school and over bare and littered ground towards a settlement. We had to make a quick detour to find the other party, before arriving back to be greeted by the chief's son. He was 27 or 28 years old, with a wife and three children, and had been away to be educated and one day would take over the role of chief.

He, along with his mates, welcomed us, first with a song and then a dance. This ended up with the infamous jumping straight up in the air which they were renowned for. There were 11 of us, four men amongst us, as they continued to jump. The fitter ones just kept going. We were beckoned forward to join in, first the two men from the other vehicle - one of which was very good - and then me. I hoped I may be excused on the grounds of age - Stephan seemed to have got out of it - but no, one of the blankets they wore was placed over my shoulders, and I had to bounce.

We were told that a standard dowry when bartering for your wife-to-be was 20 cows gifted to the family. The higher you could jump, the lower this figure would be. It was three weeks until my wedding day; I guessed that on my performance, which wasn't bad for an oldie, that Jane (my wife-to-be) would have cost me 12, maybe 13 cows.

We were led into the stockade in the village where a circle of 12 huts, with 12 entrances - one for each herd of stock - all encircled by cut bushes kept out unwanted guests at night when the stock would all be brought inside. We were led in and there was a familiar smell for me, cow dung, all over the inside of the enclosure. It was dried now, but I dreaded to think what it was like in the wet season. Well, I could think of one of our farmers whose buildings were always a shithole, if you'll excuse my language.

We were followed everywhere by the rest of the men folk from the village. First we visited one of the animal pens where I was presented with a goat kid to hold. Luckily he didn't know my profession, though the chief's son was informed I was a vet.

Then there was a demonstration of fire lighting from a couple of twigs, the secret being the speed you could rotate one on the other to generate enough sparks to light the thin tinder wood, and then build your fire up from that.

Next, we were shown one of their huts. I thought we would

be split into two groups and have a quick look, but they split us up into pairs, and as we were Penny-less, that left one on their own, me!

I was left in the company of a young Maasai tribesman, Michael, who spoke English very well. He led me off to his hut, along with two other tribesmen in tow, and described how the huts were built and how they were sometimes left when the village moved to another site. Made from branches covered in straw and mud, the inside was divided into a kitchen area, a hearth from where they cooked, a bedroom for the man and wife, and another small bedroom for the children. It was very cramped, very dark and with a persistent smoky smell.

"What did you think?" he asked.

I was too polite to give my honest opinion, but it was their lifestyle and not for me to criticise. I changed the subject to talk about their cattle, asking them how they reared them and what happened to them when ready to kill. There was an abattoir nearby, and then they could market their meat in Narok, the Maasai capital as it were. They would also slaughter a beast for any family ceremony, or village festivity.

And they would bleed cows daily from their jugular, so they could drink their blood, a tradition amongst the males to give them strength and vitality. I would ask about this later.

Then the bit I had suspected would be coming, I noticed the other two men now guarding the door. Of course, they needed money to be able to exist - Would I like to look at some of their jewellery? I got the feeling I wasn't going to leave until I had bought something, I did feel quite intimidated now, especially being by myself. A couple of bracelets were produced, and I knew I would have to buy one of them, but with haggling got down to my starting price which I did not budge from. I said I needed to go outside to see my money, to give him his dues. I was let out but felt very uncomfortable, it was a horrid experience and I headed back to the others as soon as I could. To be honest, I had lost interest in the Maasai and anything to do with them now.

Our trip was done, other than listening to the young women sing for us, and of course try and sell us some goodies again. Not interested. Any last questions? Yes, I was interested in their nomadic lifestyle and of the tales of them obtaining their manhood. The chief's son would boast about how far he could walk, he even said he could walk to his relations on the Serengeti in a day, 70 miles! True or bravado? After circumcision, did they still have to kill a lion to obtain manhood? He said they did, although they would go out as a group to hunt, but he would have to kill by himself with a spear or dagger to achieve his goal. How did this fit in with conservation I wondered, would the rangers let this happen? He assured us this was still part of their tradition, it still happened. Again, I wondered if it did, Ibrahim would certainly contradict his story on another day.

The other tradition we heard of was of drinking cow's blood. The Maasai believe that drinking cow's blood makes the body stronger and warmer and is good for children and the elderly to build up their strength. It is often drunk mixed with the milk of the cow. An arrow is shot at close range to puncture the jugular vein, and the blood pouring out will be collected in a vessel until full. The Maasai are skilled cattle handlers and have perfected this technique to the extent that their cattle don't get stressed about the procedure at all, it's something that happens to them on a regular basis, with no apparent ill effects.

That was it, our trip was finished, and I headed back to the hotel for a well-earned swim in the cool pool, avoiding the Maasai sales ladies below. Once again I was enjoying the company of my larger than life barman, who always seemed pleased to see me, even more so if I was using his pool.

Like yesterday, the other occupants of the pool were African children, trying to swim, and they were doing very well at it. They were thoroughly enjoying the water, which even for me was still on the chilly side.

By dinner, Penny was feeling better and joined us for a light meal. She was worried that she had picked something up from the fruit, washed under the tap, like guardia - a nasty little proto-zoan infection. We were told not to drink from the tap unless first boiled as tap water was a common cause of food poisoning, or more strictly upset tummies. But now she was quite perky.

I drank a Tusker, and we ate, again feasting on a lovely buffet. While we had been on safari earlier, I had told Janet I was getting married in three weeks' time, and this was announced by her to the whole of our party, and a toast to Jane and I was made. A lovely thought by her, but what was I doing here by myself?

A final act of freedom? No, just something I had promised myself five years ago. It was just a pity that I couldn't send her a message as the phone reception was so poor. The last message I had from her said that she was enjoying Spain, but I knew by now she would be back at home and back at work.

After the meal we retreated into the bar and lounge; the ladies were back on the internet, emailing home. This evening's entertainment was Maasai dancing, no, I didn't believe it. I had felt, and still feel quite upset about my experience earlier, though I hadn't told Ibrahim. The others thought I should, in fact a couple of them had already complained about the trip. I would consider it, but wasn't happy, and there was no way I was going to watch them again. I returned to my room to shower and then went to bed. This time, I did pull the shower curtain across, but again the handle fell off.

I did find an ant by the bed, so whether he was the guilty party for my previous bites, or whether it was mossies' I didn't know, but this time I went to bed well Deeted, reading more of *Out of Africa*, before settling down.

Our last night on the Mara gave me time to reflect on my first experience of safari. Seeing lions, leopards and cheetah so close, and seeing the lines of migrating animals in the distance was amazing. At first I had thought the Mara looked barren, but today I saw these vast grasslands stretching as far as one could see, soon to be grazed by these huge herds. I saw the variety of wildlife, which was a reminder of why I had fallen in love with the idea of Africa, more specifically East Africa and its Rift Valley all those years ago as a kid. I was finally here.

Another dream fulfilled and still two more Game Parks to visit. Seeing the Mara river for real, and that huge croc put into perspective those TV films of the migration crossing the river and the steep banks they had to scramble down to, and then swim for their lives to the other side while a hoard of crocs saw their annual meal arriving. Please cross quickly while the water is so low, and you should escape the waiting crocs. Lovely memories to dream about.

But what of the future of the Mara? As the cattle disease, rinderpest, was eradicated in the mid-20th century - a disease that had spread from cattle to the wild herds of wildebeest - there was a great proliferation of their numbers. Even as recently as the 70s there were not the vast number of grazing herds on the Mara. Then, the Mara was just a brief stopping off point for tourists returning from the Ngorongoro Crater and the Serengeti. But this massive increase in the size of herds and the need for grass led the great migration to begin. The Mara became important as grazing land and a place the animals could find water during the dry season. And so, this great spectacle began, and with it came the tourists. So along with the explosion of the wildebeest population, there was also an explosion of tented camps and lodges spreading across this undiscovered landscape. Many attempts to create a management plan that would protect the environment and regulate tourism at sustainable levels were instigated, but none were properly implemented. Was there the political will? Without this it would be impossible for any plan to succeed.

A great show, now being in danger of being upstaged. Thousands of tourists descend on the Mara each year to witness the migration. The resident human population increases, lodges proliferate, and rampant corruption means money is not filtering down to the Maasai population, who are increasingly turning to charcoal and arable farming to make ends meet. Fences around lodges have been erected, shanty towns are developing fast. There are too many cows and not enough land, as we witnessed the intrusion of Maasai herds into the park when we entered it. Human waste was being dumped or buried. Man is mismanaging this environment.

We witnessed the number of vehicles racing across the savannah, and if an animal was spotted by one of them, like our cheetahs or leopard, then it was not long before rather than just a few watching the animal, there would be 20 to 30 vehicles converging on it. This was bound to affect the animal's natural behaviour, and it was hardly likely to hunt with a cavalry of vehicles in pursuit. Its victim may have little idea it's coming. The tourist industry here brings in millions in revenue each year, but could it be that its popularity is its worst enemy?

Back in 2008, a Maasai Mara Management Plan was instigated to try and push through the Narok Governor's vision of the Mara until 2018, but it was rejected by the Narok County Council. The plan was to be revised and updated as a matter of urgency. It needed the support of the African Wildlife Foundation and the Conservation Development Centre, but most importantly the leadership of the Narok County Government. But the plan was already seen as a key factor in the county's future, and with it a robust basis for the future of the Mara to rebound. There at last seemed a will from the Governor and his County Executives to drive the process through, and this was announced to a meeting in the Mara, spelling out priorities such as how the Maasai community would benefit more from tourist revenues.

The Maasai want to graze their stock, but don't want their lands turning into wheat fields. With wildlife on what they may consider their land, comes the risk to their personal safety, loss of grazing, disease and death of livestock, and they believe this should be compensated. They believe that money from the tourist industry should in part go to them, and as a result they would then be encouraged to look after the valuable resource they have on their doorstep.

We pay a lot of attention to the poaching of elephant and rhinos, but lions and hyenas are disappearing quickly too, and this is their natural habitat. Their future needs to be protected as well, to the mutual benefit of themselves and the community which benefits from their presence. The need for wildlife and humans to live in harmony is something which will crop up again and again.

Now is the time for change and challenge, and for those with vested interests – Kenyans - to engage and confront common national and local challenges. It will sustain a viable Masai Mara Reserve for all and for future generations to enjoy.

May it continue for the sight of the migration, those vast grazing lands, the oat grass moving in waves in the breeze, a diversity of wildlife, birds, reptiles. 'The greatest show on Earth'. It is in our hands to let it continue as that spectacle, but in saying 'our', it is for the locals and the Governors to have the will for it to survive and not to become over-developed.

We saw the road being built towards it with Chinese investment; what effect will that have in making the Mara even more accessible? Only time will tell, along with a management plan and local integration of the Maasai to support it.

14

Farewell To The Mara

O UR HOTEL, JUST over 2,100 feet above sea level, and 206 miles
south of the Equator, was perched on the hillside overlooking
this vast wildlife ecosystem. It was time to leave and move further
up the country to Nakuru.

Again I had a surplus of clothes, so I left a couple of items for
the maid, and I was ready, packed and off to make the early start
required. Breakfast had been brought forward for us so we could
be gone by 7am. I thought if I got out of my room early, then I
could escape the attention of the porters waiting to grab my bags
for the very short walk to reception, and even shorter walk up the
steps to our vehicle. No such luck, they were waiting outside each
room - there was no way they were going to miss out on their tip.
It wasn't the tip I begrudged, it was the second tip taking the bags
just up the steps. When arriving in reception, they were put in
such a place that they had full control on their next passage, and it
cost another dollar for the 10-yard walk.

I ate breakfast, checked out (though I did have problems
with the card machine and its connection), and we were all ready
to go. Ibrahim was there to greet us and it sounded like he had
had a far more exciting night than we had. Hungry elephants had
invaded their compound in the night, creating mayhem, and there
was more than a pound or two of elephant shit which would need
clearing up. No major damage was done, other than a job that
would need doing on the gates, and a big pile to get rid of. What to

do with a couple of 100lbs of jumbo poo on your yard, answers on a postcard please!

We were 270km from Nairobi and 105km from Narok and the main road. First, we took the bumpy, rutted road to the gate, and I could see the ravines created by torrents of water when the rains had been around. These roads would have been impassable at times in the wet season, but now they were parched and dusty. We sighted a couple of dik dik again, then we were at the gates and the Maasai salesladies obviously hadn't got up yet. We escaped them. We passed their school, their village and then we were back on the dusty road, speeding along, trying to anticipate the bumps, seeing some wildlife: zebras, giraffes, impala, tommies, and again the barren grasslands of this part of the Mara. This was not reserve land and so the local villagers could graze here as much as they liked, their only limitation being the availability of water.

Today was cloudy, which with the dust gave a very dull atmosphere. We took the opportunity to chat to each other more and get to know each other better, although our evenings so far had been jolly in each other's company. Our Kiwi ladies, Penny and Geraldine, were travelling without their other halves. It was the first time they had travelled together, and they'd planned three weeks in Africa and Asia, so they hoped they could bear each other's company; it was working out okay so far. Geraldine told us how they had bought a plot of land at a premium rate on the basis it would have some sort of agriculture on the 20 acres. They had a few sheep on their plot, and that was what their husbands were doing, looking after them and doing some of the husbandry jobs that needed doing.

Sheep are born with long tails, which are usually docked to a shorter length when young so that they won't be soiled by their own faeces, attracting flies, getting fly strike and being infected with maggots. The area around the tail, the perineum, is also clipped for the same purpose, dagging.

Janet and I were interested in what her husband was up to, and when Geraldine said he had been out dogging, we said nothing, we just looked at each other and let her carry on telling us about him.

We stopped for another break at another souvenir shop where we could fulfil our needs of nature, and the owners would hopefully make a couple of sales. They did.

I was chatting to Mike, our German in the other Cruiser, who had finally got around to tackling me about Brexit.

"What's it all about?" he asked. Janet was pro-Europe and gave her arguments, I was a leaver and explained what I thought would be a great opportunity for Britain to establish itself again, if these chances were grasped.

From a German perspective, he wanted a Federal Europe, just one big country. I questioned how they would get on if Germany could no longer beat England at football if both no longer existed.

Back to Geraldine and our earlier conversation, Janet asked her what dogging meant as it had a completely different meaning back home. She explained.

"Dagging," said Geraldine, "dagging!"

It had caused us much amusement.

Back on the road and even on a Sunday the workers were hard at it. A lot of Chinese investments had gone into this road to make the Mara more accessible to tourists. How long would Kenya be paying for it, we wondered. But as well as Chinese money and expertise, although some of the work force would be Chinese, it also brought work to the local community. A dual carriageway (for that is what it looked like it would be) to the Mara, would also bring in extra revenue by making it so much more accessible. For now, everyone would have to endure the dusty, bumpy ride we were enjoying, but I bet it wouldn't have been too long ago that it would have been worse than this.

Our journey continued onto Narok, and proper tarmacked roads. It wouldn't be long until we would be there, and then we'd travel by main road to Nakuru, our next safari stop.

You may have guessed; our journey would take four to five hours - Kenyan time!

15

The Road To Nakuru

IT CONTINUED TO be a cloudy day, though it seemed like we had been up for ages, it was barely past a respectable breakfast time. Narok would soon be with us. We'd driven here down through the corn fields of the Mara, and through the barren grasslands still being scoured by hungry Maasai herds. I wondered what it must have looked like a couple of months ago in the rains, flush with grass, and with plenty of food and water for all.

It was a Sunday, and as we passed through the town we could see all the children dressed in their Sunday best for church and family get togethers. We were surprised to find out that Kenya was nearly 85% Christian and only 11% Muslim - we thought there would be far more Muslims than this. All of our close associates seemed to be celebrating Ramadan, so this gave us the impression that Islam was the main religion.

It gave the town a bit of a buzz. Away from the street markets there was the look of a community coming together.

Soon Narok would be behind us, passing the souvenir shop we had stopped at a couple of days ago, already with its next lot of Mara visitors stopping there for a comfort break, and for the proprietors, hopefully sales.

We would follow the route we had come on until we joined the main road from Mombasa to Uganda, Kenya's landlocked neighbour at the town of Kijabi again. If we turned right here we would have started ascending the hill from where we got our first views of the great Rift Valley on the return route back to Nairobi. But we were following the procession of lorries west, towards Uganda, through Naivashu and then onto Nakuru - more specifically, Lake Nakuru National Park.

As we turned west, the most striking feature was that of Mount Longonot and its National park. Although everything seemed so dry here, bare pastures and dust, surprisingly we still saw the odd zebra. The mountain itself is a volcano, another example of how the Rift Valley was formed, with the disruption of the Earth's tectonic plates. If there was time, which there wasn't, we would have walked around the crater rim, apparently it is a very nice walk up there. Another day maybe. I already knew I would like to come back to this country.

We did stop for another comfort break, obviously another souvenir shop, but what was nice here was that they had a couple of coffee plants outside the entrance, and one of the locals did come and explain about coffee bean harvesting, extracting the coffee bean from the plants fruit, and then how the coffee bean was prepared. His was ornamental and the few beans on it were quite bitter, but if we had gone to the rich lands not far away, yes, we were close to the Central Highlands and the Aberdares again, then we would have seen the plantations which had given Kenyan coffee its good name.

This road was very busy again, even on a Sunday. Lorry after lorry after lorry in both directions and of all sizes carrying essential supplies to and from the coast to inland Africa. With such heavy traffic, opportunities to overtake were few and far between, and we wouldn't have gained a lot anyway other than getting stuck behind another lorry. Towns caused a bigger bottleneck, and the next major town we would hit would be Naivashu, a very much up and coming town in Kenya and a centre for the very financially rewarding horticulture trade. If you were to buy a bunch of flowers in a supermarket in England, the likelihood was that it would have originated here, before being flown over to the UK.

Janet recognised this place as where she had been for her conference the previous week, and roughly where the posh hotel she had stayed in was. The ladies were very keen to see all the plants for sale from the nurseries on the side of the roads, on rich soil running up the banks of the hill to the forest. Here we were close to the Hell's Gate National Park, and on the other side of the road, further down the slope was a large lake - Lake Naivashu, which we would be visiting tomorrow. For now, Ibrahim told us, its fame used to be for the vast numbers of flamingo which lined its shores. However, the water had now lost its salinity, and being fresh water, it didn't support the algae which the birds would feed on.

Other than Nairobi, this did seem like the most developed town I had seen in Kenya, with smart apartment blocks, a developing infrastructure, new petrol stations, and in terms of tourism, with the lake and the proximity of National Parks, it had a promising future.

We passed through the town, surrounded by the vast Delamere Estates. It was a name that was familiar to me from my present reading of *Out of Africa*, and to both Janet and I from the film *White Mischief*.

In the colonial days of Kenya and the British Empire, Lord Delamere was a powerful figure in the British community, and in the running of the country.

Now, all that remained were the vast estates we were driving through, a step up in agriculture from what I had seen before. There was a vast acreage, enclosed in a high wire mesh fence along with a large dairy enterprise. This training facility would go a long way in helping other dairy farmers in the country. Irrigation, zero grazing, and the sight of black and white cows – it was another plane up in farming. I guess it showed what could be achieved if water was utilised more efficiently.

The estate, Ibrahim told us, was also actively involved in conservation, looking after the wildlife of the country, and as we would find out tomorrow, had its own Game Park on the shores of Lake Naivashu. From my veterinary point of view, it would have been nice to have seen more of the estate, a guided tour even.

But our journey must go on. As we left the surrounds of the

estate, we headed into more open country where we saw no end of baboons lining the road, some big brutes as well, far larger than I had seen on Mount Kenya. I don't think I would have been so keen to walk amongst these ones. The ladies really wanted to get a photo of one of them sitting on the posts lining the road, I'm not sure if they ever did succeed, either we would be overtaking a lorry at the wrong time or something was overtaking us. Where Abdullah was during all this I'm not sure. Ibrahim kept in regular contact with him by radio, a device which had seemed somewhat temperamental at times and often required a smack to remind it to work.

We passed Lake Elementeita, another soda lake, before finally arriving in the large town of Nakuru. We were nearly there and Ibrahim explained to us how we could climb into the National Park and reach what he considered to be the best hotel he did on tour, perched overlooking the lake.

He knew a shortcut through the back streets of the town. We turned down a narrow earth track and past an agricultural engineer before re-joining another main road, running parallel to the road we had just come from but taking us back on ourselves. Ibrahim was worried that Abdullah would not find this short cut, as it wasn't easy to see from the main road, so the radio was in much use. We travelled along a couple of miles before turning off down a good dirt track and arriving at the gates of the National Park, Lake Nakuru N.P. Armed guards from the Kenyan Army patrolled the entrance as Ibrahim went to sign us in, while looking out for the other vehicle. At last they joined us and we were able to enter the park.

This looked a completely different ecosystem from what we had experienced on the Mara.

White rhino and calf, Nakuru N.P

Sunset Lake Nakuru

Hippo water party, Lake Naivasha

Impala

Giraffe and Kilimanjaro

Matriarch elephant herd

197

Sacred Ibis

Sole hyena, Amboseli

Life in the swamp

Three generations

Swamp...

...and drought, Amboseli

Time for a dip

Monkey deterrent, Amboseli

The Giraffe centre

Adieu to Kilimanjaro

16

Lake Nakuru National Park

WE HAD HOPED to be at the hotel for lunch, after which we would go on a game drive again. It would be a 15-minute drive from the gate to the hotel, we shouldn't be long. We drove steadily along the dirt track, passing some ranger huts before turning up the long track to the hotel. Unlike the Mara, in this park one had to keep to the proper tracks, and there were stone signs giving directions to spots of note, like the lake or the falls.

We were thinking of lunch, but as we went along the way, Stephan and I stood to get a better view of this different scenery. Unlike the Mara that we saw, this was very wooded, far greener, more like a National Trust Park back home. There were flowers, bushes, different trees and then open pastureland between. As I said, it could have been England and there was no sign of any animals – that was until we entered an opening from the woodland, and there in front of us stood a tower of giraffes, not six, not seven this time, but lots of them on either side of the road. I would count, and it wasn't easy as they merged with the trees, there were over 20 of them. They were not the Masai giraffe we had seen on the Mara, but the rarer Rothschild giraffe, introduced here as it was the chosen ecosystem for them when they became endangered in their native homeland of Uganda in the times of civil war.

Food had become sparse for the fighters and a giraffe made an easy meal. They were easy to hunt down and shoot, providing the troops with plenty of meat. Their numbers plummeted drastically, to the extent that some were rescued and a suitable environment found for them to return to the wild. Lake Nakuru N.P was that chosen spot. We really enjoyed watching this large tower (there's one to remember for the pub quiz) of giraffes. We spent some time watching them and another dazzle of zebra close by, before eventually moving on towards the hotel.

Keen eyed Stephan, what had he spotted? I had been told of the Nakuru tree lions, but it didn't do much more than just register in my memory banks, but he had seen them. There by the side of the road he saw a pride resting below a large tree.

"Look up," I said. There were three, four lionesses lying on branches some 10 to 12 feet up the tree. How lucky were we to see this? Stephan was a hero, we could easily have driven past and missed them all. A good spot.

We seemed to be finding so much more than the other group to look at, and again we seemed to have lost them - they may well have been watching the giraffe we had already seen.

We watched our tree lions for a quarter of an hour, fascinated with the group. Again there were no males, but we watched the cubs play with each other at the base of the tree while the lionesses rested, sprawled out like every other adult we had seen so far. The younger females were up on the branches, occasionally taking a little notice of us, but otherwise in a world of their own.

The others did eventually catch up with us, but we were ready to go on then and continued up the track towards the hotel, through the tree and bush-lined passageway, completely different from the Mara.

We emerged from the woods, up a bank and towards our hotel, with guinea fowl scattering as we ascended the last part of the route to reach what looked like a spanking new hotel. This hotel was perched on a range of hills that form the western border of the Great Rift Valley. Even as we got out of the Cruiser in front of reception we could appreciate the spectacular views over Africa, the lake, and in the distance the Aberdares.

Ibrahim had already told us that of all the hotels we would

visit, this was his favourite, and as we entered reception we were all wishing we were staying here longer than one night. Clean, smart, tidy and wonderfully friendly staff, we were checked in and directed into the dining room for our lunch. We were directed to a table for six on the balcony, outside, in front of the lake and with the park below us. An incredibly beautiful spot.

A menu to match, though although we were being offered a three-course meal here, were we that hungry? I think most of us had the fish and chips and ice cream for dessert, other than Viv who of course had the vegetarian option. It was lovely, washed down with another Tusker of course, but again we had the luxury of the balcony and all its views - the other six had a table inside behind us. Again, how lucky were we! As if all this wasn't heaven enough, when we had finished we were shown to our rooms. The hotel had a series of lodges built into the hillside, two rows - one above the other - but with their views unspoilt.

A buggy took me and my bags to my room, while others struggled along the path with theirs. My door was opened for me, and on entering I thought this room was heaven. There was a king-sized bed, a massive room with large windows in a semi-circle and a balcony outside giving full value to the views beyond. The bathroom, all tiled out in a granite looking tile, had a massive shower cubicle and double basins and mirrors for Mr and Mrs (sadly Jane was not here to share), an incredible facility.

Unfortunately, our stay here would be brief, but even after an hour I think most of us shared Ibrahim's opinion of the place. Our stay was going to be that brief it wasn't even worth unpacking that much, so it was just a case of gathering my camera and heading back up to the hotel reception to wait for everyone to meet up and start our next game drive.

I wandered around, taking in the views and managing a sneak look at what was behind the hill the other side; the hill descended again to rich farmland. This part of the country was rich in resources, both natural and from agriculture.

We were ready to go, ready to explore this park described

as a wooded and bushy grassland with a wide ecological diversity and characteristic habitats that ranged from the lake waters to the escarpment and ridges.

We headed down the track we came up on and back through the narrow track bordered by bush and tree. It was very dense here, but we were told this was rhino country, so Stephan and I stood as lookouts watching through the raised roof for any movement which would suggest this member of the big five was about.

Further down the track, there in front of us was a member of the big five, not a rhino, but a huge lioness just biding her time walking down the centre of the road. Would she let us past? No way. She was going at her own pace and would get out of the way when she felt like it, which wasn't now. We followed her for a few minutes, again the other six missed out because she was in front of us so they couldn't see her. How lucky again were we!

She did eventually move off the track, turning right into the bush then stopping to turn and look at us.

"How dare we disturb her!" I said.

She got lost in the undergrowth as we continued down to where our tree lions had been earlier. They had moved on. We did too, past our giraffes, before heading further into the park.

As we drove along the road, our next sight was two fighting male zebra, trying to assert dominance over each other and trying to decide who would get the prize of being top dog stallion for the mating season coming up. Gallop, there was a cloud of dust as they grappled with each other, kicking, biting, then another cloud of dust as they galloped further and then did the same again.

As much as Stephan and I tried to find other animals for the others to see, there seemed little activity. We drove to the Makalia Falls, but even this was nothing more than a trickle of water descending from high above, and I don't think it would have got us very wet even if we had stood directly below it. The small pool at the bottom was more like a puddle, and that was it. It wasn't the spectacular sight we were expecting to see, and we could not continue along this path any further, it was closed.

We did an about turn and followed another track, stopping to see a far more diverse picture than on the Mara. On this bushy grassland now in front of us, a whole host of different animals were intermingling, not taking any notice of each other, just going about their own business. Directly in front of us was a group of buffalo, some grazing, others lying, enjoying the afternoon sun. They had their own little eco-system, an example of symbiosis as they grazed or lay, then in close attendance, preening their coats for them was a red-billed oxpecker. This bird had a characteristic tseee-tseee call, and would feed off the ticks that were parasitizing the buffalo, their mouth parts plunged through the hide – it was easy pickings for the birds who fed on them.

Following the Buffalo everywhere were white egrets; they waited for the Buffalo to defecate and found their sustenance there. They weren't actually helping the buffalo as the oxpecker does but surviving by living alongside them. Symbiosis! Behind the buffalo, a dazzle of zebra and a troop of baboons were grazing, playing or just ambling across the grassland. The baboons were bigger than those we had seen on the Mara, and far bigger than the ones I had walked through on Mount Kenya. Gazelle as well, all were happily mixing on this pastureland.

There was a peace, a tranquillity about the scene in front of us; the wildlife were content to fill their bellies, with no obvious sign of predators about (wait until nightfall comes), and no danger that they could see. This was the Africa I had wanted to see, green, lush and with wildlife in abundance. We could watch this scene forever.

But what was that just in front of us, moving slowly through the grass? It was another of the five, this time not the big five but the little five. For each of the lion, elephant, rhino, buffalo and leopard, there is a little equivalent, and here we saw a leopard tortoise - though as tortoises go, this chap was quite large. He walked slowly along, before nearing the buffalo and retreating into his shell. Did he have a mate nearby? We couldn't see another.

We drove on, briefly stopping to see another pride of lions

resting almost hidden in the long grass, our tree lion pride, possibly? Again, there was a noticeable absence of a male present. Would we get to see one?

Then we continued on towards the lake, along a road lined with tall trees; on the other side, green pastureland ran to the shore line.

I could see a silhouette over there, and then Stephan saw it as well - that had to be a rhino. As we turned through the trees onto the lakeside pastures, we could see that - yes, it definitely was a rhino, with a calf at foot. Amazing, what a truly amazing site.

Not unexpectedly, there were numerous other vehicles in close attendance. Nakuru has rhino, how many I don't know, but for the time being we were quite happy to see one.

We parked up on the side of the track, watching her, her baby and numerous zebra and their foals close by. The baby zebra were quite playful with their brown tinged stripes - the colour would change to a more distinctive black as they lost their baby coats. They were interesting to watch, but not this time as interesting as mum and baby rhino, who seemed to take no notice of us whatsoever. Mum was nose down, grazing on what she could find. The baby, Ibrahim said, would probably be about 18 months old; it was mooching along beside her, the occasional suckle, and otherwise like mum, grazing.

What a spectacular horn she had, it must have been getting on for two-foot-long, finishing with a sharp looking point (I had read of a farm in South Africa where they rear rhinos and harvest their horns, cutting them off to try and reduce poaching, and to supply the Vietnamese market rightly or wrongly so they wouldn't need to poach them). They were slowly walking away from the shore, and closer and closer to us, taking no notice as more and more vehicles stopped to admire them. They got so close to us as they crossed the path in front of us.

Once, as they passed a large tuft of grass, we saw the little head of a juvenile jackal raise itself, then hide again. Abandoned by mum, or just awaiting her return, he was obviously feeling a little peckish as he raised himself again, sniffing the air, and getting a bit above his station, fancying a bit of rhino for dinner. He got up, circled around them at some distance, came a little closer and circled again, licking his lips. Again, another circle, and then sitting down he decided this was more than he could take on by himself, and so retreated into some long grass to hide. We must have watched these amazing creatures for some twenty minutes before moving on towards the shore.

In the distance we could see two figures emerging from the skeleton forest near the shore. The trees, presumably killed by the high salt content of the lake as it had risen, were now leafless and dead. As we got closer we saw that both were carrying guns – they were rangers whose sole job was to guard these rhinos 24/7 from poachers.

Poaching is a word I haven't used yet, but with conservation in mind it's something that has increasingly alarmed me - like so many others - as we lose so many beautiful animals to poaching, and to Far Eastern traditions that see rhino horns made into some sort of magic potion. A horn, the likes of which we had just seen, was worth a fortune to the right people. Thankfully, the ivory trade to China gets more publicity, and we may be starting to get somewhere trying to stop it, I don't know, but I will return to it later. But the mass slaughter of wildlife goes on as the poachers get more intricate ways of getting their fare: mass poisoning and killing more than just their intended targets. These rangers, part of the on-going battle, were two men who would watch over mum and baby in 12-hour shifts, before swopping over with another set of rangers. I do wish them luck, and more importantly, success in what they are trying to achieve - preserving these endangered species, rhinos especially, as their numbers shrink ever dangerously lower.

We made our way towards the lake shore, deeming it safe to get out of our vehicle some 50 yards from the shore, the only animals being some buffalo in the distance. It was 6pm now and the sun was starting to go down, giving a slight yellow/orange tinge to the sky. The soil below our feet, no doubt in the big rains under water, was now bare but dried mud, with some white near the water's edge from the high salt content of the lake. There was an abundance of water birds for us to see, but it was the flamingos that had drawn us here.

A muddy promontory divided the beach, stretching out into the lake; the area was inhabited by several maribou storks. Even from this distance one could understand why they were included in the ugly five. On the shoreline, many sandpipers flitted about looking for their food in these muddy areas. In front of us was the lesser flamingo, smaller in size than the greater flamingo and with a deeper pink plumage. There were many of these birds feeding on the surface of the lake. Unlike the greater flamingo which filters food from the bottom mud in shallow waters, they were filtering their food from the top few centimetres of the water. These birds, Ibrahim told us, live almost exclusively on these soda lakes where the water is alkaline, allowing their food source, a type of algae, to flourish.

I walked along the water's edge towards the skeleton forest bordering the lake further in front of us, trying to get as close to these birds as I could without disturbing them. We took photographs and just watched them wade through the water, feeding, looking and the odd one flying to another spot. The sun was now getting lower behind a little cloud, and the sky really was an orange colour now, offering a beautiful backdrop to any photo – especially one with a maribou stork flying across the lake some seven or eight feet above the surface.

In the distance were some greater flamingos, but to see them we would have had to risk the wrath of the buffalo. It was a perfect end to the day, watching the sun set over the lake, with these beautiful birds silhouetted in front of us. Dusk, and the park would soon be going to sleep.

As we grouped together for a vehicle photo, we watched as from out of the distance a solitary hyena emerged from the forest behind us, cautiously making its way across the mud flats in the direction we had left the zebra and rhinos. That was another picture that stuck in the mind.

Other wildlife were now becoming more active. They had to feed. It was time we returned to our hotel; the light was fading fast as we made our way back across the mudflats, past the ever-vigilant rangers, and back towards the hotel, taking a different route from that on which we had come.

Back in the wooded grasslands we disturbed a group of reedbuck, still grazing, but now aware that the predators would soon be active again, and they would have to be ever alert. Further on we could see the pride of lions we had seen earlier, still resting but sure in the fact their evening would be due to start soon. By the time we reached the hotel, it was dark.

Time for a quick shower, and I unpacked the little I needed to, changed, and then made my way back to the dining room where Stephan and Viv were already enjoying a beer at our table. I did likewise, and this was the first time I had really had a chance to talk to them. He was keen to find out about my job as a farm vet, the differences in welfare standards throughout Europe, and to tell me what he had seen of farming back home in Belgium. His job was beyond me, he was a very clever computer expert, and Viv, she worked in insurance. Stephan was also a very funny man, our sense of humour worked in harmony together to keep the troops laughing.

The others joined us and we started our meal, a buffet again, and here I had to try the Ugali. I had sampled it on the mountain and at the Safari Park, it was some concoction made from maize flour - here I would try it again. I am told that a meal wouldn't be a meal in Kenya without ugali, made from grains that are boiled into a thick porridge until it sets hard. It is then served, as it was in front of me now, in rather hard slabs. It can be eaten as a finger food and dipped into sauces, but only briefly in case it falls apart. I placed one slab on my plate and took it back to our table. The others were intrigued by it but did not themselves venture to try some. It passed my lips. What did I think? On the mountain it had seemed another of those heavy, stodgy foods that were given to me, and I didn't enjoy it as it lay in my stomach for what seemed an eternity. Now, in the restaurant, it was more passable as food, a little lighter, but totally tasteless. The others declined my offer for them to try it, and to be honest, it was unlikely that I would be trying it again. At least I had made the effort, but I did politely have to fend off questions from Ibrahim when I saw him later as he asked my opinion of it.

Our topic of conversation was travel, though I had to sit back and listen - my travels were nothing to those of any of the others, especially Stephan and Viv who seemed to be some sort of adventure freaks, preferring this to having a family. Where hadn't they been? What hadn't they done? They'd tried diving, caving, climbing, and led a very exciting life as they told of some of their adventures and close shaves.

Janet too had travelled extensively throughout the world and would soon be taking her children to the States for their summer holidays - a chance to see the Grand Canyon and other sights. Penny and Geraldine told us about living in New Zealand on the Pacific rim, and the continual earthquakes that they experienced back home. I knew of the Christchurch quake of a few years back, but didn't realise that smaller quakes were an almost daily occurrence. We had a very interesting conversation about the world we live in and my colleagues' experiences of it. They would also, as they had done in transit here, tell us of the Pacific Islanders trying to get to New Zealand for work, and how lazy they thought the Maoris were.

There was an interlude to get a sweet, and there was a large cake the chef had made. It was Father's Day, I had forgotten. It had been a most informative meal, and we knew each other a lot better because of it. For the first time on the trip, Ibrahim and Abdullah joined us late in the restaurant for their meal. It was still Ramadan, but it had passed the said hour and they were now allowed a meal. If we had known, we could have waited for them and had them join us for our meal. We would see them in the morning.

We retreated to the outside seating area above the pool to enjoy a drink in the tranquil surrounds, a nice glass of red wine. The ladies were back on their email back home, this was the one place they could connect.

The evening was drawing on and as I retired to my room, walking back in front of the other lodges, I let myself in and knew that I had to take advantage of the balcony and night-time view of the lake and Nakuru beyond. There were coffee facilities, and there was decaf. I made myself a cup and took it outside, sat at my balcony table and enjoyed the evening air and the view beyond, staring into the night. A clear night sky sitting beneath the stars - it was a lovely end to the day. I would take home with me the sight of the rhino and her baby, the lone hyena emerging from the forest, the tree lions and especially the sunset over the lake.

A quick look at my phone to see if there were any messages.

"HAPPY FATHERS DAY," Richard.

That was a lovely surprise.

Time for sleep.

17

N, N, N.
Nakuru, Naivashu And Nairobi

TODAY WOULD BE a long day, we had to drive back to Nairobi for lunch, then on to the airport before heading south towards the Tanzanian border. I had an old friend to visit, so it would be another early start. I wondered what a lie in is like in Kenya? The shame was that we were in this beautiful hotel for such a short length of time, unable to use all the facilities other than the dining room and a glass of wine the previous evening with the ladies in an outside bar. A wonderful looking swimming pool was set in the side of the hill below the dining room, and it had looked so inviting, but alas there was no time. In the gift shop was a gorgeous bronze elephant head, much nicer than all of the wooden ornaments we had seen, whether offered by Maasai women at the side of our vehicle, or in the several souvenir shops we had stopped at for comfort breaks. This, despite the fact it would have been expensive, I would have bought as a memory of my trip, but sadly the time we had spent in the hotel, the shop had been closed.

I was up at first light, making myself a cup of coffee, and opening the curtains to drink it on the balcony again.

Sunrise over Lake Nakuru. A blue sky interspersed with pink as the sun rose on this peaceful African morning. The soda lake was in front, at just over 1,754 metres above sea level, the hills behind it - the Aberdares, some of which reach 10,000 metres high. Behind them but out of sight was Mount Kenya. For now, all was quiet. In the distance, on the edge of the lake were the lights of Nakuru itself, a large town and the fourth largest in Kenya with a population of 300,000 plus.

Founded in 1904 it has continued to grow as a cosmopolitan city, basing its economy on small scale agriculture, manufacturing and tourism. Its name is derived from the Maasai for 'dusty'; it has a fairly constant climate throughout the year, described as neither hot nor cold, neither wet nor dry, although the big rains of April and May are frequently the wettest months. There are also sites of archaeological interest here, such as at Hyrax Hill.

For us, other than passing through the outskirts, I could enjoy the view, but the city itself we would glance at in transit to and from the National Park.

Over an early cup of coffee, it was just a lovely sight. It was Africa as I think it should be seen, the vastness, the peace, the scenery. I took a pleasant stroll to breakfast to meet up with the others, went back to clean my teeth and then caught a lift on the hotel buggy with my luggage to find Ibrahim waiting by our vehicle, ready to leave. I was ahead of the others, so I could chat with him and another of the drivers from a different tour about Kilimanjaro, my old friend.

If our trip was to be long today, that didn't stop us from stopping from time to time as we made our way out of the park. Groups of waterbuck lined the track, and the groups of monkeys up in the trees were happy just to stare back at us. Finally, a large troop of baboons appeared, sitting by the side of the track, of all sizes, some mothers with their offspring sitting on their backs, not independent enough to go by themselves. Who was going to turn down a free ride!

Mum would carry her young for the first two months, then they would sit on her back until they were five months old, then they would have to walk. It was lovely to watch them, the innocence of youth, but like us all they would have to grow up to face the harsh realities of life in order to find food, and a partner with which to breed. Being omnivores, they would eat both the vegetation and any wildlife they could catch; at times they were vicious hunters.

We reached the park gate and had to sign ourselves out, so while our drivers took care of this and others used the toilet facilities, I was interested to know what was keeping the interest of a couple of the soldiers, pointing into the distance and staring through their binoculars. I made a polite enquiry, they let me look too - a white rhino on the far horizon. The National Park, fenced to protect these rhinos, is the home of a couple of dozen black rhinos and more than 70 white rhinos - we had seen three of them, but at least we had seen them, and one keeps one's fingers crossed for their continuing survival, and the hard work of the rangers who look after them.

That was Lake Nakuru National Park, and I loved it. It had the diversity of nature between the wooded savannah and the shores of the lake, and the comfort and luxury of a fantastic hotel. Now we were back on the road again, driving through the outskirts of Nakuru, waving to children as we passed, their Sunday best now swapped for school uniforms. Back on the busy road back to Naivasha, we re-joined the convoys of lorries heading to and from the coast. At Naivasha we were due to stop to go on a boat trip on the lake, we had a crowded schedule today. The town itself was slightly higher than Nakuru at 2,086 metres above sea level, but it was a rich developing market town based on floriculture as I have already mentioned, and with a large Dutch influence.

Other popular tourist destinations are Hell's Gate N.P (featured a lot in The Lion King), Longonot and the lake itself. The site of some posh hotels and a golf course, this town has a population of just under half of that of Nakuru and is a growing town with a healthy future. Our route would take us through town, then down to the shores of the lake where we would board two boats, six of us in each. We pulled up in an area occupied by many Maribou storks, standing lazily on the shores of the lake. We took a comfort break to the toilet block before boarding and crossing the first line of ants that I had seen on this trip.

We hadn't been walking for very long on Kilimanjaro before our path was crossed by thousands of them in a single cause, nature working together as one.

"Don't get bitten," said Chunga, "it's very painful and you will feel it for a long time."

The skiffs were narrow, white boats with a blue rim, and would probably have seated another couple if all the seats were in a state of repair that allowed it. Joseph, our skipper, pulled the rope on the outboard motor, and with some hesitation the engine stuttered into life and we left the rickety quay.

Naivasha is a freshwater lake, deriving its name from the Maasai 'Nai'posha', meaning 'rough water', from the sudden storms which can arise.

Today, all seemed tranquil, at least for the moment. The lake is at the highest elevation of the Kenyan Rift Valley at 1,884 metres, in a complex geological combination of volcanic and sedimentary rocks, being fed by the Malewa and Gilgil rivers but with no visible outlet. Being freshwater would suggest that there is some underground outflow. It covers some 140 sq. km in surface area, and has an average depth of six metres, but a maximum depth of 30 metres; it is surrounded by swamp in some places, but the nature trails that used to exist around the lake have been greatly disrupted by the floriculturists and their rose nurseries. Now the unregulated use of lake water for irrigation has caused some concern to the authorities; the level dropped to as little as 2.25 metres in 1945 and nearly dried up as far back as the 1890's. Now, since 1968, it has been far more consistent at about six metres.

Our boat trip was to see the vast amount of birdlife on the lake, no flamingos this time, it was freshwater rather than the alkaline soda waters of Nakuru, and Elementeita meant the algae they thrive on could not exist here.

We nudged out onto the waters of the lake, though the outboard did seem just a little reluctant to transport us.

If we had started with the many maribou and herons lining the shores, it was not long before we were seeing cormorants flying, perching on dead trees in the water or diving for fish. How many times had I wanted to see a kingfisher back home? Here, they were in abundance. The pied kingfisher was hovering over the water before diving after its prey.

By one group of these wading trees we saw a group, a crash, (remember for the pub quiz again!) of hippos basking in the cool waters. There was the occasional sight of a head, but generally they were submerged with only their nostrils sticking out of the water. Happy hippos! But getting this close to them one realised what large and bulky animals they were. They could be temperamental as well, and listening to our coughing engine, I hoped this wouldn't be the time it packed up on us.

We crossed the lake to a promontory of land, having run aground a couple of times on the other shoreline. It was shallow in places and we observed a couple of fish eagles sitting aloft in yet another dead tree. With their distinctive black and white colouring, and their loud yelping call, you couldn't miss them - nor would you want to, for they were a joy to see. Others we would see high in the sky. These wonderful birds were feeding entirely on fish and we saw several more before landing again.

This promontory was called Crescent Island, it wasn't a true island as it did have a small land bridge, but it was the habitat of several grazers: giraffe, zebra, wildebeest, but no predators. It was a reserve managed by owners that were keen on conservation. We watched from across the waters as one young giraffe explored its habitat, with mum hidden away behind the trees a little distance away - a ploy, Joseph told us, to protect the young. If there were dangers present, a predator would see her rather than her offspring.

Just along the shore from here, we saw two varieties of pelican with their distinctive pouches on their bills. There was the pink-backed pelican, and its larger relation the great white pelican - their juvenile birds were brown in colour. It was time to head back to shore to continue our journey to Amboseli. This was a rich haven for birds, and from the ones we had seen, it offered plenty of fish for them to eat.

I wondered if there was a fishing industry on the lake as well, and asked Joseph about it. No sooner had I asked him, I noticed white floats bobbing up and down in the water and we ground to a halt. My question had been answered as we were caught up in someone's net. Our sister boat was now disappearing into the distance towards shore. We were stranded, unable to reach the propeller easily from within our own boat. Luckily another tourist boat appeared, and we were able to hail them down to try and rescue us.

I was beginning to think I would have to get into the water to try and untangle us, but luckily the other skipper with the minutest pair of scissors eventually managed to free us. We arrived back at shore nearly half an hour after the others. They hadn't realised they had lost us, and there was some concern starting up amongst them on our non-appearance, but in the end, we were all back safe and sound to tell our tale. An enjoyable excursion, and I hoped Joseph would fix his engine. For now, we were behind time.

Leaving the shore and Naivasha behind us we continued our journey back to Nairobi. It was uneventful and saw us joining the lines of lorries again, climbing that steep escarpment back out of the Rift Valley we had gone down and stopping on the way to the Mara. Continuing our discussion on the care for the elderly with Janet, who was so knowledgeable about it, we then asked Ibrahim about his family and his life in Nairobi. He had left school and gone to college to study business management and nature conservation, and he was now enjoying his job as a guide on these safaris. The downside? It was so seasonal, and he would be called in from an agency for his work with Pohlman's, our tour operator. He had four children of which he was very proud, producing photos of them for the ladies to see.

"We could stop off in Nairobi and meet them if you wish," he said.

If we'd have had time it would have been nice. We were back

in Nairobi, catching a glimpse of a rare monkey. Where? Sitting beside the busy motorway into the capital.

We made our way through the traffic to a hotel for lunch, the Black Café in a large hotel. We entered through security who were checking the underneath of the vehicles with mirrors on poles, before we went through another security check to enter the hotel. That seemed a bit silly as just along the corridor there was another double door which anyone could have walked through. We sat down together, as it turned out, for the last time. I sat opposite Christine and her daughter – they were the pair from Australia and we chatted about their country and spiders! In the dunny. We spoke of the heat, the nasty little creatures that inhabit their homeland and about their continuing tour of Africa. She had holi-dayed a lot with her daughter.

"Didn't hubby want to come?" I thought to myself.

It was a slow process when we didn't have a lot of time - there were 12 orders, three courses, and hopefully coffee afterwards. Our meals did eventually arrive, though Penny's chips took a bit of procuring, and Christine's coffee a lot more, but having myself asked the waiter several times for food to come, at last it did - about two minutes before we were due to get underway again.

To the airport now, through heavy traffic as we made our way through Nairobi. We were to lose two people, the other vehicle would lose two as well. Our six would soon become four. Stephan and Viv were leaving us and flying down to Mombasa for a week on the beach, although from what they had said over the past few days, I'm sure they would be doing something far more extreme than just sunbathing. The young couple from London who I had only had the chance to have a brief chat with at breakfast on the Mara, were also leaving to head to Zanzibar for a few days of total relaxation.

On the way to the airport we passed Nairobi National Park, yes, there is a National Park in the country's capital, it's 80% enclosed by the city, but with one passageway out for the ani-mals to reach other territories. At 117 sq. km , it's one of Africa's smallest parks. With a backdrop of the city's skyscrapers and the constant ins and outs of planes, the animals seem unperturbed by being in the only National Park on earth that borders a capital city.

It is the home to the world's densest population of black rhinos, over 50, although only four years ago even being so close to Kenya's largest city couldn't prevent one of them being killed by poachers. Lions and hyena were common, along with the occasional sighting of a leopard or a cheetah. Gazelle, warthog, zebra, giraffe, buffalo and ostrich were also regularly seen, but as we passed by, nothing obvious was in view. It does create some conflict though as the corridor left open for animals to migrate gets smaller and smaller as the city continues to expand. A lot of the park is fenced to keep animals out of the city, but what happens in the future with migratory animals following the rains, we can only wait and see. It was another story of conflict between humans and wildlife - something which we had already seen on the Mara and would see in Amboseli.

At last we reached the airport, we were behind schedule on our trip, but Stephan and Viv weren't worried as they had some time to wait for their connection and killing a bit of time in our company was a bonus for them, otherwise they would have been sitting around the airport lounges. First though we had to go through security just to enter the airport. We all had to get out of the jeep, passport in hand, go through a check point and then re-join our drivers and vehicles when they had got through their check. The check was so fleeting, it all seemed a little pointless.

Then we were outside the terminal and it was time to say goodbye. They had been good fun, especially Stephan with his sense of humour and insatiable appetite that would destroy anything put in front of him, and what Viv didn't eat. A shake of the hand, a hug, and they were gone. We would continue south.

18

The Road To Amboseli

STEPHAN AND VIV were gone, now there were the four of us to continue our journey onto Amboseli, close to the Tanzanian border and Kilimanjaro. There was a sense of anticipation within me, that object, that mountain which had such a dramatic effect on my life over the past five years, I would see her again. We made our way back out of the airport, through more security checks and people having to pay their parking charges - it was slow progress to get out, and I guess any hope of visiting Ibrahim's family had long gone; all was taking too much time. We still had a journey of, you guessed it, four to five hours to get to our hotel for the night.

A journey of nearly 250 kilometres, and we had to get out of Nairobi, travelling on the main road to Mombasa for some distance. It was heaving, lorry after lorry was queuing on the dual carriageway out of the city. There was a dirt ditch between the two highways and we saw trucks deciding to drive along the bumps and ruts of this to try and speed their journey up. Grazing herds stood along the side of the road, or again in the area between the highways - it was chaos.

Further south towards the edge of the city, where there was a lot of work being done on the infrastructure of Nairobi, Ibrahim pointed out the new railway line being built from here to Mombasa. A high-speed network, again being built with Chinese expertise and money. The Chinese were investing heavily in this country, it was an opportunity to get a foothold in one of Africa's potentially richest and fastest developing countries, if it could stay politically stable. At the end of the day, with a far better rail and road system in the country, it could only benefit the Kenyan economy.

As we drove down the main Mombasa route, this new line ran parallel to us; impressive new stations were being built, the only question as ever in Africa would be: When would it be finished?

At last we were out of the city, still in a convoy of lorries, but probably not as bad as that going into Nairobi. We would get past a few, then get slow down as we entered another village when all the traffic would concertina back up again. Then we would speed up again, pass a few more before reaching another village and slow again. But at least we were progressing now.

Immediately out of Nairobi we were back to the arid plains we had already seen so much of on the way down to the Mara, then rolling highlands around Salana, looking lusher, and with what looked like large cattle ranches with fences stretching into the distance to keep in the grazing herds. But through all this, we still passed the occasional nomadic Maasai herdsman tending his animals, moving them onto the next pasture to find the next watering place. The interaction between old and new farming methods was there in front of us.

Further down the road we passed mango plantations, trees festooned with weaver bird nests, and then an increasing sight on the landscape, eucalyptus trees. In the past these trees had been planted in vast numbers as with their insatiable thirst, they were used to try and drain the swamps, but as they had successfully done this, the people were now complaining they were taking all the water.

They were used to make telegraph poles, but now with progress these were being replaced with concrete.

Plantations, cattle fields, corn, desert - we were seeing a great diversity of scenery. What we had seen before was much more arid, but we were enjoying this great diversity in scenery on our route to Amboseli.

We drove through one town which was surrounded by the usual salesmen of water, fruit and papers, when suddenly Ibrahim stopped and got out of our vehicle, gesticulating at some teenage kid. We weren't sure what was going on. Had he tried to damage the Cruiser? Whatever it was, it had annoyed Ibrahim a great deal. The boy had run off across the road, checking behind him where our driver was before disappearing into the crowd. Ibrahim came back and got back in.

"What was that all about?" I asked.

He explained the boy had come over and spat at us. It was impolite to visiting tourists, which the African economy very much depended on. How would tourists respect Africans if they did that sort of thing?

It would soon be time for a comfort break. A different crop we were seeing now in the fields was a type of bean. Ibrahim was unsure, but thought they were French beans, they didn't look like that to me. We stopped, and as the ladies wandered through the shop I left the compound and went to find one of these plants and to pick a pod or two. I found Ibrahim with them, splitting them open to find a pea, these were cow peas, and were quite tasty even raw.

On we drove, now through red, fertile volcanic soils. Then in the middle of this different landscape, in the middle of nowhere, we turned off about an hour or so away from the hotel.

A little further, and there in front of us, in front of me, was my old friend. Emerging as a faint outline in the distance, almost merging with the clouds was the 5,895 metre-high peak of Kilimanjaro, looking over all of Africa below. I felt quite emotional, I said one day I would return, and there she was.

It was difficult to see the outline at this distance, but she was there and the first obvious thing to me was the lack of snow. There was a covering on the top, but not the snow that I had seen even five years ago. We were at the end of the big rain - take that as snow at that altitude - so this is when there should be more snow than other time of year. It was receding - was this more evidence of global warming? The experts thought that by 2030 it would all be gone. Ibrahim tried telling the others a little of the mountain, but here I knew a lot more than he, so I took over explaining the height, some of the facts about this free-standing mountain, and as we got closer and could see more, her sister peaks: Mawenzi and Meru, from this side they were out of sight. Ibrahim said he hoped we would get a clearer sight of the mountain in the morning, depending on the cloud. I assured them that we would, at breakfast she would be there in all her glory, but by 11am the cloud would be coming in and we would probably lose sight of the peak until early evening.

The others knew how much this mountain meant to me, what an influence it had on my life, and were intrigued to know how I felt. It was hard to put into words. How a mountain could evoke these feelings in one I don't know, but for me she had done. Was it a sense of being grateful, pride at reaching the top, a special bond? It was very hard to say but explaining where I was before and where in my life I am now, they could understand my emotion.

Dusk was falling, and with the mountain getting ever closer we entered a village which did look a lively place to be on a Monday night in downtown Kenya. There were cafes, bars and even a club, but we would now turn off the tarmacked road onto another dirt track, and eventually amongst the bush we would take another right turn into our hotel compound.

Pulling up outside a massive lodge we were greeted by the most enormous African I had seen in the past few days, we unloaded and went to check in and for a brief explanation of the hotel from the receptionist, before being allocated our rooms. We then wandered off into the darkness to find them, following a porter in search of his tip.

Each room was a circular lodge, set in and amongst the gardens of the hotel. Very comfortable looking. Having tipped the porter and now alone, I unpacked a little before changing and heading off back through the darkness to reception, the bar and a Tusker.

There was an instant rapport with the barman as I greeted him in Swahili. He brought my beer over in a chilled glass for me to enjoy and we shared another joke about my fluent grasp of his language. It had seemed a forever day, so now it was time to relax and enjoy a drink.

Janet joined me before we decided to go to the restaurant, where Penny and Geraldine had already arrived and were tucking into their buffet. On route, a glass of red wine was ordered, which my friend the barman would bring into the restaurant for me. I sat opposite Geraldine and had a long chat with her about depression, which her son had also suffered from and was still being treated for, and the importance of self-realisation, in that the only person who could really sort oneself out was oneself.

From the menu it was obvious that they had a thing about beetroot here, it even featured in the desserts. It was a long day, and time to rest, so I headed back through the dark to my room, and bed would soon follow. Like on the Mara, this was another hotel with a generator that would be switched off at midnight, so having a torch by the bed was important.

My phone was plugged in, there was even some reception. What was that noise? My phone? Jane? She was trying to message me, but the noise wouldn't go, she was trying to ring me on Messenger, but with my technophobe abilities, I didn't know how to answer her.

Somehow I got to speak to her. We talked about how I felt after the climb, the Game Parks, and about seeing Kili again.

She was back at work after her Spanish vacation, which she had enjoyed very much - and then the line was fading. Time to say goodbye, though again I didn't really know how to switch it off, I wasn't even sure if it was off. But with that, off went the phone and out went the lights. The generator had been switched off.

Back under the shadow of my friend, Kilimanjaro, I slept. Tomorrow, Amboseli and its elephants awaited me.

19

Amboseli

Today, Tuesday, was probably the day I had been looking forward to the most. When I was given the itinerary all those months ago and when it changed to visiting Kenya, then Amboseli was the one park I really wanted to visit. Why? Because it was nestled in the foothills of Kilimanjaro, and I so wanted to see my mountain again, and secondly because there would be some serious numbers of elephants. By all accounts, some big tuskers as well.

With this in mind I was up early, showered and dressed ready to be outside as soon as it was light enough. The power was back on, so getting ready to go out was easy as I could use the lights again and get my rucksack ready for the day - although all I would really need was suntan lotion, my camera and water. I shut the door behind me and hurried off towards reception and the dining room. The air was cool as the sun was slowly rising, but there, next to our eating place, through an open space before going into bush, slowly emerging through the mist, was what I had come to see.

Mount Kilimanjaro, snow-capped with her moorland slopes running down to the rain forest below, was now partially hidden by low cloud or mist drifting across her foothills. A pinkie hue encompassed her so early in the morning, but like us, why should she be at her best first thing? Why should a mountain have such an effect on me? Although she wouldn't know it, she had changed my life so much, just from me succeeding to climb her. It was something I had wanted to do for so many years, and almost five years ago to the day I had returned to give my best wishes. She had changed me, made me so much more positive in my outlook and what I wanted to achieve in life. She gave me the confidence to write a book, or two, or three, and the confidence to realise that the only person who could snap me out of my coma, my depression, was myself. Yes, this lump of rock, even if it was the highest lump of rock in Africa, had changed my life for the better, and so I had bonded with her, she meant so much to me.

As I stood there, an American couple approached, camera in hand and said good morning. They started chatting about Kili, what it must be like to climb, and be at the top. I could tell them, so I was only too willing to relate to them my experience of five years ago. I told them the best pictures would still be to come, especially as there was now a Japanese family charging around in the foreground, and however you tried, you couldn't do the mountain full justice without including them in the photo.

"Give it a few minutes and the mountain will be clearer, the mist will have lifted and the reflection of the sun will give some great photos," I advised.

We went in for breakfast, joining some of the others who were up. I sat where I could keep an eye on the light, and after some 20 minutes had to excuse myself from the table. Those clouds that had hidden the lower slopes and the mist and clouds that had drifted across the upper slopes had all gone. I had a clear view of Kilimanjaro, and Mawenzi to one side. She looked magnificent in the rising sun, it gave her the slightest 'tan', and there was a background of blue sky.

As I stood there in admiration, I was joined by more of my table, and the Americans were now also watching in awe at the sight of the mountain, which was as clear as you could get.

Knowing I would be feeling a little emotional, I felt a touch on my arm.

"You said we would see her clearly in the morning," Geraldine said, and smiled.

A few photos, and it was time to finish our breakfast and get ready to go to Amboseli Game Park. It was amusing to see a large stuffed leopard toy perched on top of a pillar at the entrance to the restaurant - an anti-monkey deterrent, which we were told was very successful.

The National Park was further along the dusty path we had followed to the hotel, and we had a 25-minute drive through bush to get to the gate we would enter through. We passed Maasai children on their way to school, enchanting us with their waves and smiles, though some stood by the side of the road asking for sweets. They all seemed so small, so cute in their school uniforms. When they were older I wondered how many would just work the land and look after their herds, and how many would move away and get city jobs. All I knew was that which Boniface had told me about the structure of their schooling, and the fact that if they attended they would have the beginnings of a good education. I guess the rest would be up to them.

I was also surprised to see a large field of tomato plants, laden with ripe fruit. I thought they required a lot of water, something evidently lacking around here looking at the dry soil surrounding us.

At last we reached the gate to the park, and waited while Ibrahim and Abdullah sorted out our paperwork with the guards. We were of course hounded by the usual gang of Maasai sales people, men and ladies here, trying to sell us what every one of them had tried to sell us throughout our journey through Kenya. No change, no Kenyan shillings, only large dollar notes, but even showing them that we had got some of these souvenirs already did not deter them from trying to make a sale.

More interestingly, we were shown where the toilet was - we wouldn't see any happy bushes in this park and were told: "Go now while you have the opportunity!"

We were in. This was another park where we would have to remain on the made-up tracks, again it was a different sort of Reserve to the Mara. We had spotted the odd giraffe in the bush before we reached the park, now we waited in anticipation for what we would see today. A male lion? Ibrahim did say that Penny would be unlucky today in her wish to see a leopard, but all else was possible. We would wait and see.

Amboseli National Park is one of the smaller National Parks in South East Kenya, occupying an area of 392 sq. km. This is a small percentage - about 5% - of the large 8,000 sq. km ecosystem which spreads across the Kenya-Tanzanian border. Lying 240 kilometres south-east of Nairobi, it is probably the second most popular of Kenya's Game Parks, even though it has the larger parks of Tsavo East and West close by. Its attraction is the sight of big tusked elephants, set against the backdrop of Africa's largest mountain, Kilimanjaro. But we hoped to see an array of animals on our visit.

It is Kilimanjaro and volcanic activity that has played a large part in the development of this ecosystem, starting with violent eruptions through the earth's crust some million years ago when Kilimanjaro was formed. Some of the rocks in this intriguing geological story date back millions of years to the formation of Earth. In time, these rocks would have been subjected to intense heat and metamorphism, leading to the formation of Pre-Cambrian metamorphic rocks such as granulite, gneisses and crystalline limestones, which were hurled out over the surrounding plains and hills in northern parts of Amboseli. Laval flows from the mountain would also have had a big influence on the geology of the area, bringing such rocks as basalt into the area. Some of Kilimanjaro's eruptions would have caused lava flows that blocked the ancient Pangani River, creating Lake Amboseli, and a basin which would fill with volcanic debris, and later other rocks and sedimentation. Lake Amboseli is now very much a dry lake unless there is very heavy rainfall, and this is seasonal.

The generally flat topography of Amboseli is dotted with several extinct volcanic hills including Noomotio, Kiturua and Ilmerishru, formed in the Pleistocene period. Because of their volcanic origin, the soils of this area are powdery, loose and nutrient deficient, contributing further to the fragility of the ecosystem. In the dry season this means that sometimes the volcanic ashy soil is blown into dust devils and dust storms - the harbinger of impending rain.

At 1,150 metres above sea level, we therefore have in this bleak dust bowl an ecological masterpiece, with animals converging to graze and drink at the park's permanent swamps and lakes, oases in a dry savannah. The swamps are entirely derived from the melt waters of the mountain and from the rainfall - which high up will fall as snow - seeping through the pervious volcanic rock, and then springing up in these swamps all through the year.

Historically there was a huge Maasai reserve set up at the turn of the 19th century, stretching from Nairobi down to the Mara River, and to Kilimanjaro. In 1948, the Amboseli Reserve was established, focusing on wildlife but allowing the Maasai to graze and water their herds. At this time, wildlife and livestock could been seen drinking from the waters of the swamp at the same time.

In 1961, it all came under the control of the Maasai, but with an increase in tourism, and more and more encroachment onto the Reserve lands.

In 1974, President Kenyatta withdrew local control and the National Park became an exclusion zone for Maasai herdsmen to graze and water their animals. An area of 400 sq. km. The Maasai were enraged and retaliated by a slaughter of wildlife, wiping out the black rhino population, and most noticeably the larger of the Amboseli lions.

In time, the Maasai came to realise the importance of tourism and relented, seeing the benefits to the local economy and the opportunities of jobs for them, enabling them to live in harmony with the park's residents.

In 1991, the Reserve became a UNESCO Man and Biosphere Reserve and a big tourist attraction for the country.

Surrounding the park lie a series of ranches, mainly administered by the Maasai elders. These are small holdings with an ever-increasing population – 30,000 Maasai live in the Amboseli ecosystem together with over a million livestock. The potential for encroachment is still, therefore, very real, and the balance between humans and wildlife hangs as ever - a problem which will continually have to be dealt with.

The swamps are the only permanent source of water in the ecosystem, stretching over to the Chyulu Hills near Tsavo West.

Nature hangs in the balance here, especially with the return of the predators as the local inhabitants recognise their worth - but Ibrahim told us they were also expecting compensation from the Government if they took their livestock, at one stage slaughtering a whole pride till the authorities relented. The spread of the wildlife out of the park during the wet season to outlying grazing was another source of possible conflict, as was damage caused by elephants, there were so many examples. A balance was needed between the Maasai farming practices, the economy from tourism, and the needs of wildlife. One to ponder.

For now, we had come to enjoy the wildlife, and as we entered this dusty park, the road bordered by tall yellow barked Acacia trees and a feast for any passing giraffe, we hoped it would yield its true worth to us.

We entered the park in anticipation of seeing something special, for me, my elephants, for Penny, her leopard and for us all, a male lion. It wouldn't be long before we got our first treat, although in the distance. A couple of real big tuskers ambled along at the edge of the woods, noticeably brown compared with the elephants we had seen on the Mara, but then this was the colour of the soil, and they were far larger.

An early sighting gave us encouragement for what we may see later, though from a distance. In this park again, we were confined to the official manmade tracks.

Impala grazed near the side of the track, not overly bothered by more passing vehicles, they saw them every day. As long as we were not noisy, and therefore not disturbing them, they were quite happy to be close enough for us to get some good photo shots. Thompson's gazelles who were more timid grazed in the background, and then we spotted two giraffes (Masai giraffes in this park) a fair way off on the other side of our vehicle.

Here it looked dusty and barren, with only the odd bush and acacia tree standing out in this bare landscape. The giraffes were coming our way, slowly but surely, the male in the lead and the female ambling along further behind, still interested in anything she could feed on from the surrounding vegetation. What the male did show us is how giraffes manage to feed off the ground as he stopped, spying something on the ground he fancied. But to get his mouth down to the ground was an intricate manoeuvre of widening the stance of his front legs and stepping sideways with each foot bit by bit until he had reduced his height to such that when bending his neck down, he could easily reach the grass he was trying for. Then the reverse procedure took place to stand upright again, then down again.

I guessed he would be very vulnerable to predators while carrying out this process. He gave up, and with his slow lolloping stride, crossed the track in front of us, making his way over to the taller acacias close to the elephants. Here, among this green foliage, he could browse comfortably on the branches at his height. The female, she followed in due course, in her own time as women do - there was no hurry.

The backdrop of all this was Kilimanjaro, still clear in the sky towering above us, with Mawenzi clear close by, but there was the threat of cloud building over my beloved mountain. Between us, Ibrahim and I imparted as much information as the rest wanted, but Ibrahim was also learning from my first-hand knowledge of the mountain.

We were soon to arrive in a green pastureland, a far different environment from that which we had driven through so far. Lush grasslands, and with such an offering of food to grazers, the area was abundant with wildlife. We had arrived close to the first of the swamps, and with it we saw a far greater diversity of wildlife, and a far greater interaction around this huge waterhole than we had seen so far on safari.

There were huge numbers of zebra, wildebeest and ante-lope of different sizes, from the small Thompson's gazelles to the large eland and the warthog, all grazing alongside each other. A freshwater source in this dusty plain. Zebra were looking to water, some disappearing down from our view to the water's edge, oth-ers standing vigilant above them. The sentries didn't look totally comfortable with their situation, their heads suddenly raised and their ears were pricked and startled. Ibrahim wondered if there was a lion down there, resting, but still worrying these sentries. They suddenly ran away, followed by a herd of warthog, who would run a fair distance and just stop.

Was it true what Ibrahim had told us? Would they would forget what they were running from and just stop? They turned and walked back to the water, only to come scuttling out again a few minutes later. But all this made the plains seem so much more real; different scenery, a diversity of animals mixing, feeding together, and predators - who knows if there were any about, but one of these animals in front of us would be supper tonight. That is nature, and that is Africa.

We departed from the Olokenya swamp, leaving behind this beautiful scene to explore deeper into the National Park. Back onto dusty plain again, and soon we would be watching an alpha male and female ostrich patrolling their territory. They were searching the ground with their necks curved, when a female – with a shuf-fling of her long legs – created a dust storm around herself. The lushness around the swamp, and now back to this parched plain.

Kili was behind us now, but we could see the odd mini-tornado, dust devils - a spiral of dust rotating up into the air then suddenly disappearing, rising in thermals of hot air. This dust bowl stretched on forever on our left-hand side, but on the other side of the track there was longer mature grassland, and we started to see some of the 400 species of bird that the park boasts.

Grey crowned cranes stood in the long grasses – standing tall, these would have to be the most spectacular birds I saw. They're usually found in pairs, and even though it was outside of breeding season, there were many of them. They strutted (and they were entitled to in their elegance) around on their long legs, a distinctive golden-yellow tuft on their crown, bold white patch on their cheeks and a black forehead and red wattles. A grey neck led down to paler underparts, and they had black wings, but with a white-tinged chestnut patch along their borders. These birds, as we had now seen, are found around swamps, lakes and on grasslands. Again, they were oblivious to our attentions and just got on with their own business.

As we were about to drive off, Ibrahim spotted some movement in the grasses no more than five or six feet away from us. There, hidden bar his head, was a small bustard. He was not going to show us anymore of himself than that, and in the fronds of grass, had disguised himself very well.

We also saw plovers roaming the dry plains, often solitary. But they were quite happy to keep their distance from us, just minding their own business and keeping out of the way of their far larger ostrich neighbours. Some of these birds we were seeing were similar to those back home, but the larger birds - we have nothing like them. It was an experience to be seeing them.

Back to the more arid savannah where you could almost persuade yourself that this well eaten grassland was slightly green. Grazing wildebeest, and zebra. How many of these had very young foals, busily following mum, catching a drink of her milk while they could before she moved on for her next few blades of grass.

Then, in the middle of nowhere, a solitary hyena walked past our vehicle without even looking at it, crossing in front of us and continuing his journey across the plains. This was the third hyena we had seen, one in each park, and if I had thought they lived and hunted in packs, all we had seen were individuals – there wasn't another in sight. But this was one solid boy, well-muscled, full-bellied and mean looking. As he walked across the plain, his short neck and head pushed forward and his lips pulled back as if in a permanent snarl, you would not want to come face to face with him – especially not alone and out of the vehicle. One could only ponder one's fate if there had been a pack of them, and you were a solitary wildebeest and surrounded. He was definitely one of the ugly five.

He would continue his journey, oblivious of his watchers, from the safe confines of a Land Cruiser.

From these dry plains we were suddenly driving beside another swamp, the Enkongo swamp, and again here we were spoilt with an abundance of wildlife, both birds and mammals.

Our first sightings were of buffalo wallowing in this fresh water oasis, and then searching into the distance over this water-laden landscape, there were elephants and hippos. This was a massive swamp, with views of the snow-capped Kilimanjaro in the background giving some wonderful opportunities to take some great photos. Africa, real Africa, animals, birds, wetlands, drylands and its highest mountain, all in the same picture.

One assumes that the tracks we were driving along had been made up, for either side of the slightly raised road was water, sedges, reeds. In places, the water was surprisingly clear, in other places it was looking more muddied, and in other places I could see gas bubbling up to the surface through the water. I guessed this came from an underground spring, seeping off through the mountain slopes we could easily see in the distance.

The elephants were in their element, half submerged in fresh water, cool in the ever-increasing heat of the day. The park was laden with foliage for them to feed on, and water to drink, play with, and spray over their backs from those prehensile trunks to keep themselves cool. And the numbers of them, if I tried to count them all, even in the distance because we weren't going to get any closer to them because of the swamp, there were 40, 50, even more. An elephant's playground. As I said, they were some distance away - the best part of 100 yards into the swamp - so we could only admire them from a distance, and try to differentiate them from hippos. We could identify them mainly from their heads, but even this far away it was fascinating just to watch them, and to wonder what the bottoms of these swamps were like to support the weight of such massive animals. The heat of the day was upon us, but the animals were in the perfect place to enjoy it.

On these wetlands there was an abundance of birdlife, and they were quite happy to be feeding in the shallower waters close to our track. Wading birds, geese, moorhens, terns, herons and egrets all used these rich feeding grounds.

The best picture was of a small group feeding in the swamp near the roadside. There was a dull brown hadeda ibis, the unmistakable sacred ibis - mainly white but with a black neck and head, and black tail feathers - and the distinctive spoonbill - all white but with a flattened spoon-shaped bill. With them was the colourful Egyptian goose, foraging through the shallow waters just in front of us. Further out and standing on their long legs were numerous herons and white egrets, and in the distance you could see these birds perched on the backs of their large mammal neighbours - elephant and hippos.

As we drove further along the borders of the swamp, with drylands now stretching out to our right, not far off was a brown eagle, standing preening itself. A large bird, half a metre tall with an owl-like face, watching us before heading off to the water's edge himself.

So many different species, and so close to each other was a real treat as we continued along this ever-enjoyable nature trail.

There were no happy bushes out here in this barren landscape as we left the shores of the swamp, very few bushes at all, and there was no way we would be getting out of the vehicle, so after a conversation with Abdullah, Ibrahim was going to follow them for a comfort stop at a nearby airstrip. There was a small clump of trees in the other direction surrounding a few buildings, this was apparently an elephant research camp. It had been established back in 1972 when there were about 800 elephants in the park. But with prudent management and community support, by 2008 this number had increased to 1,600. But from the results of a severe drought in 2008/9, more than 300 had died, mainly matriarchs and their calves, so the number now in the park was around 1,200 spread over 60 families.

There was now an ongoing study to establish the impact of that drought on the families and their social lives. One of the researchers I saw on my return had written a book, *The Amboseli Elephants*, something I must put on my wish list.

We headed off in the other direction towards the airstrip, but as Abdullah sped off in front of us, we turned and in the distance we could see a family of elephants heading our way. A long line of them, in single file, about 20 in total. We stopped to watch them as they got ever closer. Younger females led the way, then calves, and in the middle a couple of huge matriarch elephants. A few of them were very distinctive as they carried egrets on their backs, and the older girls had some seriously long tusks sticking out in front of them. Their trail was relentless across the short grassed green plains, anything in their way they ignored. Grazing wildebeest had to scuttle out of their path, as with a shake of their massive heads and ears, the lead elephants gave their warning that the wildebeest were in their path. It was a common purpose to the herd as they continued their trek, getting ever closer to us, and crossing the road no more than five yards from us. I think if we had been at that crossing point it would have been us moving, not them altering their path to avoid us.

We remained parked, watching in awe as the largest of the land mammals carried on across the plains, creating a little cloud of dust behind them until all we saw was a trail of elephant rear ends disappearing away from us.

This had to be another of the most memorable sights of my time in Kenya, an unforgettable sight, seeing these creatures so close at hand.

Again, the others had missed this as they waited for our arrival at the airstrip for our comfort stop. When we got there, they were ready to leave again, but waited for us to get out of the vehicles, relieve ourselves in the facilities and stretch our legs.

A couple of signs made interesting reading, one on the history of the area, the other giving some park rules:

- Animals are wild and dangerous, maintain your distance, stay in vehicles unless in a designated walking area
- A maximum driving speed of 40 kph
- Give the animals a break - noise irritates them, so keep as quiet as possible
- Use litterbins
- Don't feed wildlife

All sound advice so that we could continue to watch these wonderful animals in their own environment without them becoming timid to human intrusion, and then disappearing from view at the sight of an approaching vehicle.

A monument made from mammal bones had been erected near the car park, it was bleached in the sun, but for a vet it was an interesting exercise in spotting which bone had originated from which animal. The length and width of some of these long bones was amazing, and I was guessing they were from an elephant.

Our next port of call was Observation Hill, 'Normatior' in Swahili. But first, our journey to this site would take us around another swamp. We crossed a small concrete bridge, below us were the signs of another spring rising, and the sight of another two fascinating birds - one because of its looks, the other for its actions.

The hamerkop - I thought Ibrahim said hornbill when he pointed it out to us – was an unmistakable dull brown water bird, characterised by its hammer-shaped head, with a large thick crest and a large black bill. It looked like a brown duck with a large crest stuck on the back of its head. These birds build very large, dome-shaped nests in the forks of trees, or occasionally on rocks, with the entrance often pointing east.

Then we saw the African jacana, a bright chestnut bird with long legs and very long toes, giving the impression that it was

walking on water as it strode across the water on any floating vegetation. Very distinctive with a black crown and hind neck, it has
a white face and fore neck, with a golden-yellow band at the base,
and a blue bill and frontal shield on its forehead. It was fascinating
watching these birds flitting across the surface of the water looking for food.

But again, this swamp was heaven for elephants and hippos
wallowing in the shallow waters, their calves almost submerged as
they tried to stay with mum.

There were bull elephants at the side of the swamp, and
youngsters play fighting, learning the rudiments of a fight because
one day they would have to be the strongest to win over the females
of the herd and ensure their hereditary line would continue with
the birth of their progeny. Tusks interlocked, ears flapping, pushing, shoving at the water's edge, one was a lot larger than the other
and so always getting the upper hand, but there was no spite or
malice in this 'mock fight' , and when over they would stand side
by side covering each other with dust. It was wonderful to watch
as they interacted in their social structure, teacher and student
in the art of elephant fighting, but something that may prevent
injury in later life.

On the other side of us stood a small family group, alone on
this harsh landscape. It was dry here, bare and with only a few tufts
of grass visible. Mum stood with her two calves, one was about six
months old, the other probably about four years old. I watched the
bonded family group. When mum wanted to move on and baby
was a little reluctant, big sister was there to nudge her on. She also
offered shade behind mum, because now in the middle of the day,
this did look a hostile and hot environment.

Dust stretched as far as the eye could see towards Kilimanjaro, which now as I had predicted, was lost in cloud cover. The
horizon was filled with more and more of these dust devils rising
high into the sky, twisting, turning, moving along the ground and
collecting more and more of the dust from this arid, dry plain, until
they would burn themselves out and disappear. But now as soon as

one was gone, another would form elsewhere. A disco of twirling twisters! Me on the dance floor!

One last bird of note, the black crane - far smaller than the magnificent grey crowned cranes we had seen earlier. All black except a distinct yellow bill and red legs, another bird with long feet that could 'walk on water'.

The others were now way ahead of us, and by the time we reached Normatior, Observation Hill, they were disembarked and wandering around to the toilets and starting to climb the steps up the hill. A result of a small volcanic eruption, this small pyramid shaped hill sticks out of the flat plains, a lookout spot from which one could see for miles. Some of the native elders say Normatior means 'place with inward hollow curved rocks which can hold water', others say it means 'the place of water pans'. I was going to climb it, after all it was a hill and I hadn't climbed anything for nearly a week now, so I set off up the steps, taking one in each stride. The others said they wouldn't, but looking behind me, they too were following. I'm glad they did, for from the top of the hill the views were wonderful, a panorama all around us.

Looking across the plains to Kilimanjaro, and in between, directly below us, another swamp, stretching away from us until it met the dry savannah. Green, vibrant green colours danced on the water and its surroundings.

Hippos wallowed, and below us a matriarch elephant with calf in tow walked around the edge of the swamp. On the other side were pink tinges of birds standing at the water's edge, more flamingos, and pelicans as well. A picture of life. Turning to look behind us there was nothing but dry plain, yellowy brown, with a solitary tree in front, now dead standing as a branched statue in this picture of death. A stark contrast to the harshness of the ecosystem we were in, water and desert, life and death. That tree really did paint a picture to me. But this hill, Normatior, was a well-defined stop for us tourists.

With a covered observation hut encompassing a large part of the perimeter of the top of the hill, and with very informative boards about the history of the park we were in, about elephants, about lions, it was a real experience to be up there, hence why I was pleased the others had followed me. Above us in the rafters of the hut were muddied nests of swallows, and we could just see their offspring through the entrance of their nests.

I could have spent some time up here, but as with this type of safari we had to move on, so it was back down the steps to our waiting vehicles. As we went down, walking up the hill were a couple of Maasai, a box being carried between them - they were about to set up shop at the top of Observation Hill, we had escaped, but the next lot of tourists would be collared as they reached the observation points.

Geraldine and I couldn't resist, we were supposed to ask any tribesmen if we could take their picture, and they would almost certainly want some recompense for it, but as they walked away from us, snap, snap, we had them - two salesmen who had lost a sale.

I was glad I had made the effort to climb this hill. The views and the picture of the National Park were fantastic. We were close to Lake Amboseli, but it was only a lake by name now, more a dust bowl which would only have water in when the next exceptional rainfall arrived. It wouldn't be soon, so the lake was just a part of the barren landscape in front of us.

As we returned to the vehicles, our trip and our safari in Amboseli National Park was almost over. We drove around the edge of the swamp, close to the flamingos we had seen from the top of the hill, past a few isolated wildebeest and zebra, and back past the group of ostriches we had seen earlier, until we were again nearing Olokenya swamp.

When we had passed earlier it was like it was elevenses, and all the animals close by had an appointment there, a gathering. The whole focus at that time seemed to be that every living being was converging on the swamp. Now, they were all dispersing away from it to seek grazing elsewhere. Who knows, maybe it was to get away from any predator that may be lurking in the long undergrowth!

Now, as we saw, it was the turn of the Maasai herdsmen to lead their stock to drink from the plentiful waters of the swamp. Herds of cattle were all heading in one direction, to the water. This was the balance that had to be reached, where the local tribesmen could feed and water their stock, living alongside the needs of the wildlife on the park. If the two can live in harmony, if the Maasai can see the value of this rich resource they have on their doorstep, then they will develop jobs from tourism, benefit from the increase in local economy, get involved in conservation for everyone's benefit, and the area can prosper.

There is little migratory passage from this park as on the Mara, a small number of wildebeest and zebra will follow their brothers, but in the main Amboseli, inhabitants stay put. They may wander outside the confines of the park, especially in the rainy season when there may be some destruction of local crops and vegetation, especially by elephant, and perhaps the odd kill by predators of herdsmen's stock, but overall, they can live together to their mutual benefit. This is something that is achievable through education and by government initiative, and I hope that this vision is reached so that for my grandchildren, Africa still exists as I have seen it, not as something from history. I had spent but a few hours in this wonderful Game Park, but to me it was, and is, very special. It was well worth my journey, and I would certainly like to return one day with Jane.

We had seen so much, so much that was special, the interaction of species in such a diverse environment, a herd of elephant crossing in front of us, the quantity of elephant we had seen - we must have seen nearly 200 scattered amongst the different swamps. We had seen their social interaction, calves, youngsters, old big tuskers and even a research station to monitor and observe them; it was possible for visitors to enter if pre-arranged.

The backdrop was my old friend Kilimanjaro, and all these animals living off the waters which she provides them played an important part in their lives, just as she had done for me in helping me overcome depression. One fantastic photograph of a Masai giraffe standing tall with a background of forest and the snow-capped mountain. A picture to blow up and frame, Amboseli.

20

A Farewell To Amboseli

WE HAD SPENT but a few hours in Amboseli, but it had been a real experience. Those memories I have just mentioned - the acacia trees in front of a mountain – were the cover for *Kilimanjaro. My Story*.

As we made our way back past the swamp and towards the gate, our safari was over. We were to have a cooked meal in the bush - I think that was the description on my itinerary. I had images of a barbeque under one of the aforementioned acacias, but in reality the hotel had a tent and kitchen in an enclosure just outside the park.

We were dropped off in a clearing and made our way round to be seated all together under canvas, and of course accepting the offer of a Tusker. A three-course menu was provided for us, a menu to choose from, and then it was for us to enjoy the delights of our meal in the bush. It was a shame Ibrahim and Abdullah could not join us, but it was still Ramadan. In a couple more days it would be finished, and they would have a big family celebration. They did seem to like their soup here, and with it came some lovely bread rolls.

What we didn't eat was given to the local birds and wildlife, thrown on the grass, and from nowhere, squirrels, and an array of birds appeared from all around. The most striking of these was the red-billed hornbill - a black and white spotted, winged bird with a red bill; these birds fed happily on the ground, almost aggressively fending off other birds. Sparrow-like birds, swallows, crows and the three squirrels, one as bold as you like and ignoring all around, stuffed their face with bread. There was a timid squirrel who would feed when allowed, and a bully who pestered the second one more than eating.

While we ate, they filled their bellies as well until both our respective meals were over.

We returned to the vehicle and headed back towards the hotel. There was a talk and demonstration taking place by a local Maasai tribesman on herbal medicines and cures, if we were interested.

By now, everyone knew of my experience in the Maasai village, and I had told Ibrahim about it and how uncomfortable I had felt. No one was that keen to have another Maasai experience, which was probably a shame as it would have been interesting - if there was no commercialism involved. We all expected they would try and sell us something again.

It was coming back from school time, so all the children lined the roads waving and smiling at us again, until we turned down the hotel drive to be greeted by a host of monkeys playing in the trees along the drive.

Monkeys were something we hadn't seen in great numbers on the whole trip. The greatest numbers we had seen were in the more wooded Nakuru reserve, there were more there in total than anywhere else we had been put together.

There were also plenty of monkeys in the hotel grounds, and I decided I would enjoy the facilities of the hotel pool while the sun still shone. As I made my way through the gardens and the pool, again there would be more monkeys, on the ground, in the trees, grooming, feeding, or just lounging about, almost human like.

I was amused as I entered the pool surrounds that there was yet another toy leopard sitting on a stone pillar, 'guarding' the entrance to the pool, and the hospitality tea that had been laid out for a conference in one of the hotel rooms bordering this area. I would have liked to explore further, towards the Ernest Hemingway bar, for was this not the place where the ideas for *The Snows of Kilimanjaro* may have originated from.

But after a hot day on safari, the cool waters of the pool beckoned me. Joined by Michael, Ula and later Janet, we enjoyed the late afternoon sun, braving the chilly waters in a very picturesque pool, with its rocky waterfall at one end and surrounded by trees.

The conference appeared for their afternoon tea. I gleaned it was a conference on Nature and Environmental Conservancy, it would have been nice to chat with some of the delegates. The chance didn't arise as they obviously had some project that in groups they had to come up with an answer for during their break. When they had gone, the hotel staff kindly offered us what was left.

When the sun did start to set, falling behind the trees, it suddenly became quite cool. It was time to go back to the room and think about starting to pack, to shower and then get ready for dinner. Showers, which in these areas of water shortage, took an age to get hot, but the water did eventually come.

I explored the hotel shop while the ladies bartered with Maasai women who had a small market on the hotel veranda. A few books were of interest, I finally found and bought a book on Kenyan birds. I chatted to the attendant about my book and my visit to the mountain overlooking us five years ago. It was good to talk to some of the locals, they were interesting.

Then to the bar, and a beer, a glass of wine and my last dinner with these lovely people that I had spent the last few days with.

Michael and Ula were in the bar after the meal, as usual the ladies had gone to find some internet reception to contact home. Geraldine and I joked about the British Lions rugby team in New Zealand, who, if doing okay, were doing better than I thought they would do, and were now only a few days off the First Test Match. It would happen when I was back in England and on my stag weekend with Dave and Anthony, two of my three best men. But for now, I expected defeat, and the Kiwis were making the yachting America's Cup look easy as well, they were well happy.

I join my German friends with another beer, perhaps these Tusker and Kilimanjaro brews were okay, and the happy memories of Africa that go with them.

The German couple had kept it very quiet, but like Jane and I, they were soon to be married back home in Germany. It was the second time round for both, and like us, they were getting married in a castle. Also like us, they were wondering how their children, or to be precise, Michael's would react to it all. We talked wedding ceremonies, receptions and honeymoons for some time, before they called time on the day, and retired to bed.

I was left alone. In the garden outside the bar and the restaurant, there was a piece of grass which had a large area cut out and excavated to make a place for a large fire. Surrounded by chairs, and a bit reminiscent of my scout camp fires all those years ago in my youth, it was a place to sing, chat, reflect.

Tonight, there was a large log on the lit fire, slowly burning and giving off a pleasant heat from its leaping flames. No one was there, it seemed a nice peaceful place to finish my wine, a place to enjoy some of my last few moments close to the now hidden Kilimanjaro - hidden in the darkness of the night, but I knew she was watching over me.

It was a time for me to stare into the flames and dream, to reflect on my fortnight in Kenya. I didn't quite make it up Mount Kenya, but I had tried, and two charities would benefit from my efforts.

More importantly, on a personal note I had got to see the African wildlife that I had longed to see for so long. Those wonderful sights I had seen today, that procession of elephants, that mean looking hyena, a vast array of Kenyan birdlife, the swamps. That memorable picture of life and death at Observation Hill, the greenery of the swamp, the desert going in the other direction, the irony of Lake Amboseli being a 'desert'. So much, so good, and of course those fantastic pictures of all those animals with the backdrop of my mountain behind.

I had fallen in love with Africa and its people five years ago during that personal triumph of climbing its highest mountain, and now that love could only be reinforced having seen more of the treasures that East Africa has to offer.

There was time also to reflect briefly on some of the issues I had seen in my stay, matters which I would concern myself more with later: conservation, man's role in the balance of nature and feeding its own population, global warming (the retreating icecap on my friend behind me, now covered in darkness), drought, the ivory trade, and the potential for food growth in a country that has so much potential if only water could be used better.

I knew I would be returning next in 2018 to help my chosen charity Send a Cow. I would offer advice to poor farmers on better animal husbandry over a two-week period - but would politics with the upcoming election allow that to happen? And what good could I do? Without water, most advice would be irrelevant.

In those dancing flames were so many happy thoughts, and as the flames retreated into glowing embers, and as the last of my wine passed my lips, it was time to retire to my bed, and my last night in an African lodge, surrounded by my mosquito net.

Jane had said she would try and get me on messenger, but sleep was foremost on my mind, tomorrow would be a long, long day, leaving here, travelling back to Nairobi, a couple of visitor attractions, and then a long time at the airport to kill before boarding my flight and heading home via Amsterdam. I would get up early to finish packing, then have breakfast and we would be gone.

21

Reflections On Amboseli
And Its Elephants

M Y FIRST SIGHTING of elephants, in the flesh as it were, had been in the Masai Mara reserve, it had been a bit coinciden- tal as we had heard of the whereabouts of the black rhino not far away, and seeing them was a distraction from elephants.

The first view was a baby emerging out of the bushes looking for mum who was with the rest of the group a little way off. We would see more on the Mara the following day, firstly a herd in the distance, then after seeing the lions and a leopard, we came across two groups in quick succession. But it was to see the elephants in Amboseli that had been my main aim. Why? I think I had heard about them here (as well as my childhood reading of *The Orphans of Tsavo* not far away), as being the place to view African elephants in Kenya.

Here were the big tuskers, here they were a bit more used to seeing humans and just got on with their lives as we watched. My fascination with elephants had stretched back years, and I guess the reason I had come back to Africa was mainly to see these mag- nificent animals in their natural habitat while they still existed.

The African elephant, Loxadanta africana, is the largest land mammal in the world, living to an average age of 60 years. A mature bull weighs in at 6,000 kg, that's nearly ten times the weight of the modern cows I see in my day to day life. They will drink over 220 litres of water a day, consume 300 kg of foliage a day and pass some 150 kg of waste daily. No wonder the quarters on the Mara were such a mess after elephants had broken in during the night. Elephants have a gestation period of 22 months when the female has reached sexual maturity at about 20 years old. They breed every three to five years, and a female may have up to seven calves in her lifetime.

Here's something that would make any girl weep - but perhaps not an elephant, a male's genital equipment can weigh up to 27 kg. Surprisingly, what looked like cumbersome animals, can move at speeds of up to 30 kilometres per hour. Their social structure means they all look after each other, and the tales I had heard in the past about elephant grave yards (do they exist?), were just some of the reasons I had always had this fascination with them.

Our first sighting of them as we entered Amboseli was a way off, skirting the acacia trees, sandy brown in colour from their frequent dust bathes, but what did look obvious even from a distance was that they did seem bigger than on the Mara, and their tusks were considerably longer. That was our intro to Amboseli elephants, but the best was still to come.

Our drive around the arid lands of the first part of the park were full of sightings of other more familiar wildlife: wildebeest, zebra, antelope, and I guess with the absence of much woodland, I wasn't expecting to see many more. But when we arrived on the road bordering the swamp, we were positively spoilt by the abundance of pachyderm flesh in front of us. There were cool waters for them to lounge in up to their midriffs, and they were grazing on the lush vegetation growing so freely in these freshwater lakes. They mixed with hippos, buffaloes and the array of wildfowl that I have already described.

As I toted up how many I could see, the number went up and up, but I couldn't get bored with the more I sighted. Sucking up water, spraying it out through their trunks and over their bodies, they looked as if they were thoroughly enjoying their present environment. I was fascinated by how they didn't sink, what the bottom of the swamp consisted of, and how they knew when to stop when their calf was starting to get out of its depth. But in the hot, baking African sun, with no protective hair to speak of, what better place could there be than this to try and keep cool, and feed at the same time.

The real sighting was the troop that appeared in the distance, that group of 20 odd that moved in their determined way towards us, and then passed us in our transport, in a line - the social order of the procession, young females in the lead followed by their elders and the herds matriarchs, the real long tuskers. Babies kept pace, but then in their protective way it could have been that they set their pace at that of the young so they wouldn't get left behind. That everlasting picture in my mind was of them, then they passed and were gone as their backsides went further from view. Equipped with their egret passengers, that is what I had come to see.

The stop at the airstrip, and the sculpture made from bleached bones of various species gave an insight to the strength of the skeleton of these heavyweights, as we saw the long bones of the fore and hind limbs made into this creation. More swamp, and more elephants, now I was well past 100 and still counting. Mums and calves stood half submerged, while babies enjoyed these cool waters. Elder elephants could take full advantage by lying, some nearly submerging themselves fully, periscopes raised, as their trunks curled upwards out above the surface.

Bulls were play fighting on the water's edge, but on the other side of the road was a female elephant with her last two calves, a completely different environment as they showered each other with dust from this baked landscape. It was a tight family group, the elder sister was helping baby sister, cajoling her in the direction mum wanted to go, and then pointing her in the direction of mum's teats for a drink of her milk. Maybe here, we humans could learn from our animal brethren as to how they look after each other. Yes, they will fight, but that is usually the males, and it is about sex and the right to father the herd.

The Amboseli elephant experience was fantastic, a dream

come true for me to see so many of them in such a short space of time, doing what elephants do. They may seem a bit old world in their appearance, but I find them fascinating, majestic creatures, and it had been an honour to see them in their natural environment.

On the Mara, with the absence of these huge swamps, they were impressive, but to me, not as awe inspiring as these wonderful beasts in Amboseli. But sadly, the elephant population is severely under threat.

This threat comes from two sources. Firstly, there is the conflict between man and animal for that natural resource, land. Conflict between elephants and the growing human population has become a major issue in conservation. As man looks for more land to grow his crops - and this isn't helped by the drought conditions - then the more he encroaches on the natural habitats where elephants live.

The amount of food an elephant will eat in a day means there will be conflict, as their food supply is compromised by farming. Ways to drive elephants away from areas of agriculture have been sought, such as playing the sounds of angry bees, which will discourage these huge animals and reduce conflict. But with all wildlife, as we had seen on the Mara with the encroachment of Maasai herds onto the reserve, this conflict will always persist - especially in the Game Reserve and park areas.

Education is essential in getting the local people to accept the importance of these animals to their local economy, for the benefit of all. There must be a balance between nature and farming, so that all can survive together in harmony. Hopefully, there will be some success in this process, but the conflict between man and animal's needs will always go on.

However, secondly, and far more importantly, is poaching and the ivory trade, and although they are not present in Amboseli, this also applies to the black and white rhinos we saw on the Mara and at Lake Nakuru.

The keratin horn of the rhino, and those two large incisor

teeth protruding in front of an elephant, have become valuable commodities in the world, especially in the Far East and China. Ivory has been around for years but is now keenly sought after as conservationists put more and more pressure on the trade being banned internationally.

A crisis is developing for the elephant. In 2014, the World Wildlife Fund (WWF) estimated there to be in the region of 700,000, and although in some areas of Southern Africa the population is large and expanding, it is estimated that over 23,000 elephants are being slaughtered by poachers for their tusks annually.

With less than 20% of the elephant's range being under formal protection, this is worrying. It could be that there has been a 30% reduction In the elephant population in the past five years, with more being killed than are being born. The species, though not down to the low numbers of rhinos left in the world, are becoming more and more endangered.

The ivory trade (though it would be more honest to call it illicit trade) is now a $10-20 billion business, along with gun running, drug cartels and the trafficking of people - the worst side of humanity, and a wonderful example of man's intent on destroying the world he lives in by seeing himself as the superior being.

Through circuitous routes, the tusks - the source of the ivory - end up mostly in China, where they are sold to dealers to augment their stocks, or to speculators hoping their value will increase, and to workshops where the tusks will be made into a variety of ornaments.

The poor rhino, for having a growing keratin horn on his nose, is persecuted for what is basically the same material as our hair. In traditional medicines in Asia, and especially Vietnam, the horn is ground up and consumed - the thought being that it has specific therapeutic properties.

It would seem that the old idea that it is an aphrodisiac is a fallacy, but that doesn't stop the desire for it. It can sometimes fetch as much as gold on the black market. With their sought-after horns, rhinos, and not just those in Africa but also the Javan, the

Sumatran and the Indian in Asia, have become endangered, and the black rhino critically so.

Over the past few decades it has been recognised that numbers of these species are diminishing, along with much other wildlife in Africa as the needs of humans encroach onto what was wildlife territory. Over the past 30 years there have been many attempts to try and reduce and eliminate much of this illegal trade.

In 1989, CITES (Convention of International Trade in Endangered Species of Wild Fauna and Flora) banned international trade in ivory in an attempt to fight the illegal trade. Major ivory markets were eliminated, and as a result, there was a reduction in killing elephants, especially in areas where they were protected. Elephant numbers recovered, but in countries where wildlife conservation authorities are short of money, poaching persisted. In countries where there are still significant elephant numbers, such as South Africa and Botswana, this is largely due to there being large numbers in well-protected areas.

In 1989, the Kenyan Wildlife Service burned a stockpile of tusks to protest against the ivory trade, and this is something that has been repeated from time to time since then. But now, is it counterproductive in creating a shortage so that the need for poaching persists. The need for ivory would again create a large upsurge in poaching, with most of the ivory still heading towards China.

Poachers have continued to slaughter elephants, whether it be for the need of money to support their families, whether it be by warlords to enable themselves to fund the purchase of arms (and many of these would be crossing borders to poach), or just as part of a well-oiled industry. Carcasses are found where the only sign of damage are the wounds where the tusks have been removed from the unfortunate elephant. Brutality unbounded. Whether by shooting, snaring or poisoning, the elephants continue to die. Kenya has made some progress in reducing poaching in her own country, though the problem has been the enforcement of law for the traffickers.

Shipments of elephant tusks have been found by Thai Customs which have originated from Mombasa, the booty being disguised as 11 tonnes of tea heading for Laos. Singapore has seized tons of ivory, rhino horns and big cat teeth on route for Vietnam from Kenya. Kenya has obtained the dubious distinction of becoming the leading transit route for ivory trafficking in the world, with ivory being transported through Malaysia, Cambodia, Vietnam and the UAE, on route to China. Of those caught, very few are convicted and go to jail, instead they are given paltry fines which amount to little. Cargoes are disguised as tea, coffee beans and marble carvings, and with stories such as these and the misplacement of evidence, rhino horns are stolen from authorities' safes and police headquarters. The will to convict and enforce perhaps is debatable but is something that needs to be addressed as Governments realise the importance of these endangered species on their economy, they are what tourists come to see.

Organisations are trying to highlight this trade and the transport routes taken out of the African counties by tracking marked tusks - a long and laborious process. Sometimes tusks will be hidden for some time before being moved on, so bringing this research into fruition may take some time.

Here, one would have to point out that here in Britain, we are no angels in this illegal trade. Between 2009 and 2014 nearly half of illegal wildlife products seized entering the UK were ivory products. According to CITES figures, between 2005 and 2014 the UK was a significant re-exporter of ivory for commercial purposes, representing nearly a third of the EU's total. There has been a dramatic increase in the amount of ivory being re-exported from the UK to China since 2005.

But over the last couple of years there does seem to be some political will to do something about this illegal trade, to try and do something about the needless slaughter of these wonderful animals. Political leaders such as our own former Prime Minister David Cameron, while still in office, tried at international conferences to push forward the plight of these unfortunate creatures before it is too late.

The Chinese government in 2015 started several changes concerning the future of the ivory trade. Firstly, and probably most importantly, they stated that they would strictly control ivory processing and trade until the commercial processing and sale of ivory and its products were eventually halted. No dates were given, but it was a formal announcement that at some time in the future the government would stop the legal trade in China. They went further to reduce the number of officially licensed ivory factories from 37 to 34 and the number of officially recognised outlets from 145 to 130.

The new policy of licencing factories started in 2004 with nine factories and has increased every year since then. The same has happened in the number of retail shops, from an original 31, to 145 in 2015 - a result of the Chinese government actively promoting the cultural heritage of their ivory-carving industry.

Next, the government imposed a one-year ban on the import of ivory. This regulation closed legal imports of some European pre-CITS Convention (1975) tusks that had been given export certificates, and worked ivory items for personal use, notably from Zimbabwe. Lastly, they restricted the number of mainland visitors to Hong Kong, hoping this would affect the number of shoppers who would buy ivory items. Strangely, these changes made no difference to the price of black-market ivory back in 2015, after a four-fold increase since 2010.

With Chinese officials no longer supporting the ivory industry as an important part of the country's cultural heritage to the same extent as before, and a clamp down on corruption in accepting ivory bribes, the demand for ivory back in 2015 had stabilised if not decreased. At last a positive move.

At this time in the United States was the symbolic crushing of one ton of illegal and confiscated ivory in New York's Times Square - sending out the message that they were not only crushing ivory but crushing the trade for good. They were sending out a strong message that the United States wanted no part in this trade which was so devastating to wildlife. In September 2015, both

China and the United States said they would enact a complete ban on the import and export of ivory. This meant that Chinese consumers would try to source their ivory through Laos. Pressure needed to be applied to try and stop this route.

At the end of 2016, China announced they would ban all domestic ivory trade and processing by the end of 2017, a move hailed as a game changer by activists for the future of the African elephant. By the end of 2017, a government statement announced: China will gradually stop the processing and sale of ivories for commercial purposes by the end of 2017. This announcement followed a move to widen the ban on imports of all ivory products. China was praised for its move and called upon the Chinese territory of Hong Kong to bring forward its plan to end the ivory trade by 2021. There were concerns that with the Chinese market closed, Hong Kong would become the preferred market for traffickers to launder illegal ivory under cover of the legal ivory trade.

It seems that progress has been made. I think it is unfortunate that our current government dropped its support for the banning of the ivory trade in its 2017 election manifesto, but perhaps now there is a political will among world players and especially China to at last ban this trade. However, in October of 2017, our Environment Minister at last seemed to be doing something about the ivory trade, in banning the sale of ivory goods in this country. Petitions were drawn up in support of this, I have signed one on behalf of the World Wildlife Fund. But will it go far enough? Exceptions may be made for historical items, but will this provide the loophole for a trade to continue? At least it's a step in the right direction and I hope, like many more people, that it will create an end to this trade, and the needless slaughter of elephants will come to a stop.

Conservation bodies work very hard in their own countries to save their valuable assets, their elephants, their rhinos, all their wildlife. We saw evidence of this ourselves in the rangers at Lake Nakuru doing their round the clock surveillance on the mum and baby rhino we saw. Mum really did have one impressive horn on her. People have tried 'knocking out' the rhinos and removing the horn at the base in order to try and save them. Some poachers have now turned conservationist, there is a whole army of the country's people trying to ensure the survival of these endangered species.

Bodies like the David Sheldrick Wildlife Trust have for the past 40 years collected and nurtured orphans, elephants and rhinos especially.

Whether they have been orphaned through the death of their mothers from poaching, or death from natural causes, these wonderful 'babies' have been hand-reared and integrated back into the wild, the aim being by the time they are 10 years old. They have researched findings of the perfect elephant milk formula and investigated complex husbandry needs.

The aim is to eventually release the orphans back into the protected Tsavo Parks, where they will integrate back into herds. Over 150 infant elephants so far have been successfully hand-reared. I would have loved to have had the chance to visit while in Nairobi, to see the Orphan Project. I gather feeding time for the baby elephants is a real treat before they go into playful mood with their wardens, spraying water about with their trunks.

I took time to read about the charity online on my return. Their website gives a fascinating insight into the work they carry out, and especially how they train the baby elephants into a routine. Firstly, in bottle feeding the milk formula, then as they get older and more confident, teaching them the interactions and social structure of an elephant group. Swopping attendants from time to time so that the bond of baby jumbo doesn't get too strong with one handler, and even disciplining them when necessary as to what is acceptable in an elephant community, and what is not.

As they are moved down to Tsavo they are taken out into the wild for days, integrating with other elephants that have been returned to their natural habitats. Next, they allow them to stay out at night, but with a handler close by until they are confident enough to join a herd for good. When this happens it is their own choice. It makes fascinating reading and I would love to see it in action.

Rhinos are returned to the wild into fenced reserves like at Lake Nakuru and into reserves in Laikipia where these rare animals can be protected.

Areas like Ol Jogi in Laikipia County, where 85% of the sub-species Eastern black rhino exist have proved to be a success story in the breeding of these rhinos, to the extent that rhinos taken from here are used to repopulate other areas where their numbers are dwindling. A hope by the Kenyan government to grow the population to more than 2,000 means there must be co-ordination between Laikipia rhino sanctuaries to try and achieve this. Great success has been achieved over the years since its early beginnings, but now with an increase in poaching, the security expenditure has increased. Ol Jogi tries to work with local communities to identify and investigate wildlife criminals and suspected poachers and bring them to justice.

A growing success story, but one which needs support in terms of funds. Other charities like 'Rhino Ark' are trying to raise funds to create rhino sanctuaries or build fenced national parks as they have done in Aberdare National Park. These charities are so desperate for our help in funding, encouraging us to adopt an orphan elephant with the David Sheldrick Trust.

Organisations like 'Save the Elephants' and 'Amboseli Trust for Elephants' have worked tirelessly in trying to understand these animals and help their conservation. While the number of elephants may have risen from a low of about 5,400 in 1989, at least in Kenya, poaching has been to some extent defeated. However, this work in conservation needs to continue along with world pressure to make sure that the ivory ban happens and is enforced.

The conflict between man and wildlife and their individual needs like the continuing drought, puts pressure on both sides of the battle as they seek food and water from new sources. It may be now that there is a growing realisation that both need each other. The animals attract tourists, create jobs and build their own economy around this trade. Respecting their National Parks, their protected areas can be of benefit to both sides of the equation.

There will still be obstacles that threaten this status quo. For instance, there's talk of a bypass and railway that would encroach on the Nairobi National Park and talk of a 'Serengeti Highway', as it is quickly becoming known - a major highway that would cross the northern Serengeti to bring development to people living in the west of Tanzania. The highway would be built across the great migration routes of all those wildebeest and zebra, despite the annual migration being described as one of the wonders of the world.

It will be an international effort that will hopefully solve these problems facing man and nature in these parts of the developing world. We must all strive to make sure this happens.

If I had started talking of my reflections of Amboseli, seeing all those elephants and wildlife around the waterholes and swamps living in some sort of harmony, then to me, that only emphasised the importance of what we have, and what we must protect. I could not do this without mentioning ivory or rhino horn because these are two materials which directly threaten the existence of two of our most wonderful creatures. I had wanted to see them in the flesh since I was a boy.

Shortly after my return, I became a grandfather for the second time. It would be nice to think that when my new granddaughter is an adult, that at some stage in the future she might be able to visit Kenya and Tanzania and see the wonderful sights that I have seen, looked over by a snow-covered Kilimanjaro. I hope she gets that opportunity, I really do, but that depends on us, on mankind and our will to preserve what nature has given us. Amboseli was only a short experience in my life, but a real joy to visit and to see all those elephants and wildlife in the park. A memory that will stay with me forever, and I am only too pleased that my itinerary included this wonderful game park.

22

Time To Go Home

I SLEPT OKAY and was up bright and early to shower, finish packing and be ready to depart. If the shower had been slow to get hot before, after a night with the generator turned off, it was ultra-slow first thing in the morning - but I got wet in the end. A final check around the room for tickets, passport, car keys for when back in England and I was ready.

Having given away a considerable number of clothes on my travels through Kenya, my bag was considerably lighter now than when I had arrived at Naro Moru nearly two weeks ago. Even at this early hour, as I looked outside the window of the lodge, a porter was waiting for me and my soon to be given tip. There was no way they were going to miss out just for a few minutes extra sleep. But if that small reward would get them more food and allow them to help their family, then I would not begrudge it to them (though after breakfast I wasn't going to pay for carrying the bags the two yards from where he left them for me to the vehicle waiting to take us home).

I wandered slowly through reception, paying my room tab as I went. I was finished here now and so could check out before going into breakfast. But first, as I wandered past the stuffed leopard sitting on the pillar outside the restaurant, I had to say goodbye to my mountain. The orange/pinkie hues of the reflection of the sun rising on the mountain made her stand out again in all her glory, and it was a picture I wanted to keep in my mind. It was sad saying goodbye again, but I went and stood in front of her, just like on the previous morning, but this time me and my mountain were alone together. I could again reflect on the effect she had on my life, and how she changed me for the better those five years ago, and so would always have a place in my affection. I enjoyed my last few moments in her company before Michael and Ula appeared. They took their last few pictures of the mountain before their breakfast, and knowing my attachment to her, offered to take mine again in front of her - without the Chinese running around in front of her this time.

Today the cloud shrouded her lower slopes so that only the alpine moorland and the diminishing snow-cap could be seen. It was a different view from the other side of the mountain from that which had been my departing view five years ago, when her icecaps stood out against a blue background. I promised to come back, I hoped I would have the opportunity to see her again, and that when that did happen, she would still have her white cap on top. It is such a distinguishing feature of her in my memory. It would be a shame if man's affect on his environment destroyed my happy memories of this, the tallest peak on this continent. I can only hope that it stays as it is (but I doubt it) and that I will someday be back.

We went in to breakfast, a quiet breakfast for me, I was leaving my mountain again and it was the end of my adventure. It was another mountain, but at last I had got to go on safari and at last I had seen elephants in the wild (along with so many other animal and birds). It was a dream come true. I hoped one day I would be back, but other places in Africa also have a draw: the Okavango, the Serengeti, and perhaps some of the reserves further north in Kenya where there are more rhinos, and more spectacular scenery. Another time, another place.

It was time to go, having eaten well and gone out to put my bags into the now waiting Land Cruiser. Ibrahim and Abdullah were waiting outside for us. I thought that since Abdullah wasn't going back to Nairobi, and all the others bar Janet and I were going to the Tanzanian border, that perhaps he would take the six, and we, the remaining two, would be taken straight back to the Kenyan capital. But no, I guess somewhere in the small print of the entry permits into the Park it stated who was in which vehicle, and it would stay like that. We would all go to the border, then Ibrahim would take Janet and I back to Nairobi and Abdullah would head home to Mombasa. Our farewells would wait a little longer.

Everybody loaded their luggage onto their respective vehicles, and we were ready to leave. But not before being given a farewell by our massive Maasai warrior who worked at the hotel, in his tribal costume. He assured us he was six feet four inches tall, but to see the top of his head was like staring up into the sky. I would not have wanted to meet him on a rugby pitch. He was however, one of those gentle giants, happy and smiling as he waved us goodbye from the Amboseli Lodge. It had been a nice location with good food, good facilities and quaint lodges.

Our journey would take us back through the National Park, one more running the gauntlet with the local Maasai salesmen at the gate. The sun was shining, even if Kili was quickly being shrouded in cloud, even at 6.30am. It would be gone I guess by 9am today. Already the Maasai children were out and about in their school uniforms preparing for another day. By the roadside, they waved us goodbye, and even a couple of giraffes wandered our way to wish us a safe journey.

When we got to the gate, surprisingly we were too early to be bombarded with more souvenirs to buy - not that I was complaining, but we were quickly checked in again and waved on our way, entering the park before heading west. Arusha, which is where the others were heading, was almost directly opposite us on the other side of the border, but we would have to drive for a couple of hours before they crossed and then retrace their steps back in the other direction.

Our permit had allowed us access to the park for 24 hours, so we had to be out of it the other side by nine, a minute longer would incur heavy penalties, so we headed off along the hard, dusty tracks at a good speed. Elephants came to see us go, as did a few wildebeest and zebra, but otherwise this was barren land, even more so than we had seen yesterday.

Close to the 'lake' of Amboseli, which was dust of course, and out in the remoteness of this place - so dry, so yellow - we continued to see the odd grazer, usually solitary, in this wasteland. Why here, when there were pastures so lush near the swamp? But amongst this arid land, we were treated to two more species we hadn't seen before, plus any number of guinea fowl - a native bird here, unlike the domesticated ones I would see on farms back home. Chuck chucks they came to be known as in our vehicle, as when we first saw them on the Mara, they were soon followed by dik dik as our silly alphabet went on, ele ele, and perhaps best to pass over F!

Our next treat was to see the tall secretary bird just across the road. It was an unmistakable bird, with a long, slim grey body, black wings and a long-graduated tail, an orange-red face and very long legs. Africa's largest flying bird was here, strutting across the grassland in search of food; it's a snake eater and that gets my vote. I thought I had seen one when we first saw a lioness on the Mara, but wasn't sure, and our first lion was exciting, but here on Amboseli, having found one, we then found several. They were magnificent looking birds, looking their part on these expanses of savannah.

Next, the gerenuk, the giraffe antelope. We just saw one to begin with, but the closer we got to the other side of the park the more we saw of these rare animals. Browsing in the bushes at the side of the road, they were quite timid, though as we stopped to photograph them, they weren't going to hang around long in our presence. They were a distinctive dusky yellow colour, with longer necks than the Tommies and Grants' gazelles we had seen. I had to admit, with what I thought was a good knowledge of African wildlife, I had never heard of them before.

We were reaching the far edge of Amboseli. Here, there seemed to be many deserted Maasai villages, the circles of their huts and the mud walls now falling into disrepair as the Maasai had moved on in search of fresh grasslands for their stock.

Huge termite mounds were now being eroded by weather as the inhabitants had left them. They were tall earthen towers, striking in the red soil they had been made from, which would have contained thousands upon thousands of these industrious little insects within them.

Sadly, we did hit one small bird that then fell through the vent in the roof of the Cruiser, which even with my veterinary skills I wasn't going to save. But what a beautifully coloured little bird this was, blues, yellows, I wish I knew what it was, and even more so that we could have seen it fly away.

That was Amboseli, we reached the gate with 30 minutes to spare and as the roads improved and we saw more and more Maasai with their cattle, bigger herds as well, we would soon reach the border town of Taveta. Here, there would be proper roads, a town built on both sides of the border, and big lorries waiting to enter the crossing area to have their papers checked before continuing their journey. Ibrahim had never been here before, meaning we had to ask a few locals where we were supposed to be going to find the Control Point.

We were there, and as Ibrahim took Penny and Geraldine off to have their papers checked, Janet and I waited by the vehicle, only to be pounced upon by another Maasai woman with her bracelets and bangles. We did persuade her that we didn't have any money that was of any use to her - too big denominations. She gave up, instead starting up a general conversation with us, thinking we were as one, man and wife.

The others returned to get their bags; it was time to say goodbye, and to the others in the second vehicle. Their luggage was loaded into another truck, they would all be travelling companions now together as they continued their adventure into Tanzania, the Serengeti and Ngorongoro. Geraldine and Penny had been lovely companions, I hoped they would keep in touch, I hoped Penny would see her leopard.

We were to pick up another passenger and take her back to Nairobi, a niece of the owner of the tour company, a teenage Indian girl. With her, we would be back on our way, the final stage of our journey before flying home late at night. We had a lot of time to kill before our respective flights, Janet's was due to leave at just before midnight direct to Heathrow, my own at midnight to Heathrow via Amsterdam. It was still before 10am, and there were 14 hours to occupy ourselves. I had pre-booked a couple of trips in Nairobi, Karen Blixen's house, and a trip around a giraffe sanctuary to kill some of those hours. Janet had arranged nothing so had decided to join me, partly for the company and partly for the same reason as me, to kill some time.

The road to Nairobi would take us about three to four hours (surprise, not four to five), I had worried whether I had enough time to fit these trips in as it seemed the tour operators would be dropping me off at the airport at 6pm regardless. Thankfully at least, Ibrahim had said earlier that he would be our transport, until we arrived back at Kenyatta Airport. First, we had to get back, so headed out of Taveta on, for once, a good road - though at this time of day it was largely deserted.

Another stop on the edge of town at yet another souvenir shop for a comfort break, our last, and it was then a straight run up to the capital. This area we were driving through was still classed as part of the Masai Mara, and we were still in the Rift Valley. To begin with there was a mixture of undulating land, some forest, some farming. For once, very few cattle and other stock grazed the sides of the road, instead, there was just one solitary hyena corpse lying on the verge, soon decomposing as the heat of the day increased. Kenyan roadkill!

Progress was good for some time, but the further from the border and the closer to Nairobi we got, the more traffic we started to pick up, with more and more lorries trundling towards town. The Indian girl was very quiet, and so Ibrahim started asking us both about our respective families, and our own relationships. He had two divorcees with him, and wanted to know why we were separated, about our links with former partners, our children, and where we would go from here. I was getting married in just over two weeks, my course of action was clear.

One got the impression that divorce was an uncommon event in his country, different cultures I suppose. We chatted a lot as our journey continued, about our police, about corruption and their police stopping traffic and fining motorists for anything, even if there was nothing wrong. This was perhaps how they supplemented their income into a decent wage - our police were paid better so there was no need to take the law into their own hands. That discussion of course took us to the subject of the upcoming election, and as we neared Nairobi, the posters and billboards became more and more common. After the troubles following the 2007 election, would all the tensions resurface again this time round? Ibrahim hoped not, the country needed stability and that wouldn't come with tribal warfare. Fingers crossed everything would work out alright, and everybody would accept the result. This was a developing country with rich resources, now open to Chinese investment which was improving the infrastructure of Kenya, but a country suffering from tribal tensions, and from an ever-worsening drought problem. This was especially true in the north of the country, which was having serious effects related to the supply of the country's staple diet, maize. Six weeks off, all would soon be decided by the people.

The outskirts of Nairobi brought us into the most industrialised part of Kenya that we had seen to date, and with this industry came wealthier looking housing estates - those you would suspect to be the homes of middle management. There were some massive factories, some smaller, lining this trunk road into the city. Roadsides were tidier, and there wasn't as much litter or refuse abandoned there, an altogether more prosperous area than we had seen to date - bar perhaps Naivashu.

But the volume of traffic just went up and up until we were virtually at a standstill, only making progress by weaving in and out between lorries. Imagine doing this journey every day - it would drive me mad, but I had to admire Ibrahim's confidence in his own driving as he continually changed lanes to propel ourselves forward. He arranged a drop off point for the Indian girl to meet her uncle - Ibrahim didn't want to leave this road then have to get back on it again. Dropping her off, his ferrying job was done and there was just us two, Janet and I, left now.

We still had an eternal journey through Nairobi to get to our tour of the Karen Blixen house and museum in the Karen suburb on the edge of the Ngong Hills. Approaching Nairobi from the south, we had to cross over to the north-west part of the city, but thankfully after a time the traffic did ease considerably, with many lorries stopping by the roadside near the city centre. I wasn't sure whether we should stop for lunch, or just get there so we had some time to look around this museum, which is famous for the book, and the Meryl Streep/Robert Redford film - now over 30 years old. At least as we got closer, the suburbs were more attractive, there were more trees, and most of all there wasn't as much rubbish littering the road.

While we were driving there, we asked Ibrahim what he wanted to do with his life. We knew he was very keen on nature - every chance he got when we were driving around the parks, he would be looking up topics in his books. This is to what he would like to devote his life, nature and nature conservancy. We had seen some of the effects of global warming, Lake Amboseli, the snow-cap on Kilimanjaro and my experiences on Mount Kenya, and I especially had seen the amount of litter lying around in streets, in both the capital and other towns we had driven through on our travels. Cattle picking through this waste looking for food on the roadside is not something I would want to see in England. It became apparent from what Ibrahim told us that there was no refuge collection here, the rubbish just sat there until someone did something about it, which may be never.

He hoped that with education, which was becoming more prominent in schools now, the effect that man was having on his

environment would have an enormous impact on future generations, their health, their sustainability.

"What about recycling?" Janet asked.

"At the moment, it's minimal, and this is where education
comes in," replied Ibrahim.

Janet told him about the recycling of plastic bags back home,
and how it was reducing the amount of wastage of non-recyclable
materials.

"Couldn't this come in over here?" she asked.

"Education again," said Ibrahim. "People are starting to realise the impact they are having on their surroundings, their local
environment, but, like all things it will take time."

We pulled up into a car park surrounded by trees, leading onto
a vast lawn. There through the trees we got our first glimpse of the
Blixen house, a colonial style building standing in the centre of its
large grounds.

Ibrahim led us to the reception to sign in as it had all been
prepaid, and to introduce us to our delightful guide called Millie.

Ibrahim would wait for us in the car park until we were
ready to leave.

Millie took us onto the lawn and gave us a quick history of
Karen Blixen and her farmhouse. She delivered her speech as if
pre-learned, word for word, we dared not interrupt her in case she
lost track of where she was.

Karen Blixen, (her writer's name was Isak Dinesen) had lived
here between 1914 and 1931, arriving in Africa to marry her fiancé
and to grow coffee. They had been sold this land to start a plan-
tation, but coffee growing land it was not. Her husband, bored
with farming, went off to be a game hunter, returning from other
parts of Africa from time to time, and giving poor Karen a venereal
disease, which meant she would never have children.

She was left at home to develop the farm and bring about
several improvements to the lifestyle of her native staff, mainly
Kikuyu. Eventually she was divorced and had a love affair with this
Robert Redford character, Denys Finch Hatton, a British playboy

who loved her but didn't want to settle down. He would take off in his plane for long periods, only to return to Karen's loving arms. It was during one of these flying trips from Tsavo National Park that he was involved in a plane crash and killed. Her heart was broken, and the fortunes of the farm went from bad to worse, with fires in the coffee buildings, failed crops on these poor soils (not like the rich soils in the Aberdares, the Central Highlands where the rich coffee plantations are all located). In the end the farm was forced into bankruptcy. She was forced to return to Denmark, where she would continue her writing career, and writing of her Kenyan experiences in the book I was now reading, *Out of Africa*.

A sad tale, but she had left her mark on the country she had fallen in love with, improved the lot of the local tribes, given them land, built schools for the Kikuyu and had had a hospital erected next door to the farmhouse in her memory. Denmark had, in the not too distant past, bought the farm and given it to Kenya as a museum to this notable lady.

Millie had finished her speech and led us into the house for our guided tour, pointing out the different rooms, the paintings that Karen Blixen had done and the styles of furniture of this colonial age. She showed us the separate rooms of her and her husband, her writing desk, the kitchen and the wonderful wood panelled walls of some of the rooms. This was a step back in time, the Empire and white rule.

Millie gave us a fascinating tour before crossing the grounds and showing us some of the old coffee making equipment. These were old machines where the coffee beans would have been separated and then fermented, before being put into tubs for 24 hours, dried and bagged for sale. It was too cold here for coffee growing and her plantations had failed!

But these were the lands that Karen loved – a two-hour drive in those days from the colonial centre of Nairobi. It was where she farmed, gardened and would often ride up into the Ngong Hills.

Our tour was finished, and we asked Millie what she wanted to do, this was a part time job for her while she was studying at university in Nairobi. From Mombasa, and living in a student hostel in the city, she at the end of her studies, like Ibrahim, wanted to go into Nature Conservancy to become a guide. Hopefully this would have a positive effect on the future of her country and the rich resources that Kenya had.

We wished her luck and went for a quiet walk around the grounds of the house, we saw shrubs, tall trees and flowers, all well-manicured. A lovely place to sit and relax. I also went for a look around their collection of rather old farm machinery and tractors, most of which had seen better days.

Janet and I sat peacefully enjoying the surroundings before returning to meet Ibrahim and go on our next visit. He told us the history of Kenya, the Empire, the Mau Mau uprisings, and the political uncertainty now with another election so close.

The subdued lighting of my tent on Mount Kenya didn't offer the greatest encouragement to get stuck into her book, *Out of Africa*, but I tried, and continued to on safari. I found it hard going, and as much as I had enjoyed the film many years ago I really struggled with the book. Some four months on, I am finally coming to the end of it. I have persisted mainly for the joy of recognising the places that Karen Blixen travelled all those years ago in colonial Kenya, and that I saw on our travels. I could say we would have travelled faster, but there was so much traffic on the roads around Nairobi, much more built up than in her day, that I couldn't say that she wouldn't have got there faster on an open road.

"I had a farm in Africa, at the foot of the Ngong Hills," this line from the book sticks in my mind and has done ever since I saw the film. I have been lucky enough to enjoy some of the sights that Karen Blixen saw herself all those years ago.

23

Giraffes And Conservation

W E HAD A short drive to our next stop, the Giraffe Centre where the aim was to re-establish the future of the Rothschild giraffe. The route would take us past some very posh looking houses, mansions even, which belonged to senior politicians and one to the vice-president of the country. These large houses in walled gardens and a lot of trees wouldn't look out of place in London. We arrived at the centre, a large car park leading us into the attraction itself. Again, Ibrahim signed us in as we had prepaid, and we were directed towards a helper who I assumed would show us around. He led us up some steps to where people were feeding giraffes with food pellets.

During the Ugandan civil war, the Rothschild giraffe (for Uganda was its real home) had been hunted and slaughtered for food for the warring armies. Some had crossed the border, from where the need for conservation of this species was recognised. The centre was set up in Nairobi to breed these beautiful creatures, with the hope of being able to introduce them back into the wild. The chosen place, as I have already mentioned, was the Lake Nakuru National Park. The sub-species was re-established and is now doing well, so much so that these giraffes we were now seeing would probably remain here, bringing attention to the public of a success story in conservation.

Started in 1979 by Jock Leslie-Melville and his wife Betty, they started by raising a baby giraffe here at Langata, at a time when there were no more than 120 Rothschilds' in existence - numbers have now reached over 300. The centre borders a hotel, where Janet told me she had heard tales of giraffes sticking their heads through the hotel windows to help themselves to the guests' breakfast. We passed this colonial looking building just before entering the grounds of the centre.

It was only on going up these steps that I got the feeling of how big these giraffes were, now being at eye level with them and their very large heads. They would gently take food from your hand, and if you were feeling brave enough, if you put one of the pellets in between your lips, they would gently take it from you - a soft gentle 'kiss' while they helped themselves.

What you did have to look out for was if they were swinging their heads from side to side, looking for the next person to feed them, for if in swinging they caught your head with theirs, you would certainly know about it.

A large male, a few females and a couple of babies dwarfed us, they took it in turns to come to the rail to be fed, then got bored and would wander off into the trees before soon returning for more titbits. They also had the company of a few warthogs, scouring the soil for any pellets which may have been missed by the giraffes, usually from people getting scared as these magnificent beasts tried to take the pellets from your hand, and dropping them in fear that they might be harmed. A reflection of some people's confidence in the company of wildlife.

That very much was the attraction here, it was lovely to be in close contact with a once endangered sub-species, but one would only want to spend so much time doing it. The guide pointed out the difference in this sub-species, there was no patterning below the knee. Kenya is the only African country that has three kinds of giraffe, the Masai, the Rothschild and the Reticulated giraffe. He wouldn't have told us if I hadn't asked!

That hadn't killed a lot of time for us, but there was an art exhibition here as well, and a display of some of the conservation that has gone on in the past. The art exhibition was very good and made by local schoolchildren on the topic of conservation, the environment and global warming - something I will come back to.

Having spent some time viewing this, I found Janet having a cup of tea in the centre's café area. I joined her, and it is strange that, the same as with Neil at Addis Ababa airport when returning from Kili, in those last few hours of a brief acquaintance you really get to know the person you have been travelling with for the previous few days.

Over the course of that time, she had told us a lot about her work in care for the elderly charities, how it had affected her with the death of her mother, and then how she was caring for her father when needed. She had said a lot about her children, holidays, where she had been in the world, but one always got the impression she was hiding the real her behind her loud and extroverted appearance. She had flattered me in saying I was too nice for all the things that had befallen me in the past, but what about her?

In the tranquillity of the tea garden under a huge tree we chatted, and she told me about her past relationships with her former husband and then a lover who she thought she would settle down with, but it was not to be. She was a woman now defining the direction she wanted to go in life, trying to find out whether she needed anyone else in her life, and a woman looking for new goals. She knew of the disasters in my life and how I had tried to put myself back together again, she was doing the same, and being a far bolder person than me - I know she will succeed. I was glad we had chatted now; one can rebuild one's life on seeing other people's disasters as well as your own.

Ibrahim re-joined us, and we sat and chatted for a while, me feeling a bit guilty that we were keeping him from his family he had been apart from while guiding us around on our safari. Ramadan had nearly come to an end, and at the weekend he would be able to enjoy a large family meal and celebration. For now he was still very conscientious and knowing our drop off was supposed to be at 6pm, he would honour that – so he was happy to sit and talk to us now about what our futures held.

For me it was an impending marriage, writing and a trip back to Kenya the following year. For Janet, she would soon be off to the

States with her children on holiday. For him, he awaited his next trip, to guide more of us around his beloved country and nature, and of course to spend time with his four children that he doted on. It was finally time to leave and cross Nairobi to the airport.

The skies opened on the journey as we passed the Nairobi National Park again, with large, massive drops of rain falling on the cruiser, some making their way through the viewing roof and wetting the two of us in the back of it. The roads were quieter now, and we were soon going through the routine we had before, leaving Ibrahim and the vehicle to go through security while we funnelled through ourselves on foot. They hardly bothered with us this time.

Before long we were back outside the departure buildings where we unloaded our luggage ready to fly home. Janet paid for a waiting courier for the travel company on our arrival, and there he was to greet us. I was somewhat staggered and embarrassed by the amount she had needed to pay for today's activities, especially as she had done them on my suggestion. It was extortionate.

We thought we would be leaving from the same building and would therefore at least have some company until we had to board, but no, I was in Terminal 1A, Janet in 1B.

It was time to part, firstly our goodbyes with Ibrahim, giving him a large tip, he had been great, very helpful, informative, and always with a smile on his face. Then Janet - Ibrahim seemed most insistent that we should hug before we departed, we did. Gathering our luggage we set off in our separate directions, she with 5 hrs 55 minutes to kill, me the full six hours.

What to do in an airport for six hours, check in then...

Time dragged, I hadn't eaten properly all day since we had departed Amboseli, and now I would eat despite knowing we would be fed on the plane, but that was some time away still. I found a Chinese, ate it in solitude then .... killed time, pacing, reading, having a beer.

At last we were called to our boarding gate, then the long flight began.

24

Home

IT WAS JUST past midnight, now Thursday and my two-week trip to Kenya was about to end. Safely aboard KLM flight KLM566, I had my seat belt on and was sitting in seat number 61H. I had the aisle seat, first occupied by some man who moved into the middle seat of three when I arrived, and after a while moved to the central row of seats, moving again when someone claimed that seat as well. There seemed to be a mix up of seats, with people sitting where they felt like, some not wanting to move, some, the true incumbent, happy to move. The couple in front of me, one who was in the wrong seat but unwilling to move, claimed there was something wrong with his wife and he should be moved into First Class. The stewardesses were having none of it, he would stay where he was, they even showed him the lack of available seats on their computer. There were no spare ones, bar one opposite me. He shut up at last.

My fellow passengers were a Dutchman with the window seat, and between us, a young Kenyan lady bound for the States who had never flown before. She was somewhat apprehensive about it all, and very keen to know where the sick bag was. This could be a fun journey! The Dutchman patiently explained all about flying to her, the take-off, the flight, the landing and the meals. He explained the difference in time zones and advised that as she was going so far, it would be best for her to try and sleep.

All checks done, we were ready to go and taxiing down the runway, then full throttle, we were off and up in the air. So far so good as far as my fellow passenger was concerned, fingers crossed it stayed that way. We ascended into the African skies.

Unlike both my previous trips to Africa, it was dark, so there were no final views over the plains, or of Mount Kenya like I had with Kili five years ago. There were no views over the highlands of Ethiopia or the deserts of Egypt, just darkness. This eight-hour flight would take me over Kenya, Ethiopia, Sudan, Egypt, the Med, then Greece, the Balkans, Austria, Germany, and finally to Holland. With the time difference, I would be there at 7am in the morning, and in Europe it would be light.

First though we were served our evening meal: chicken curry, which would go well with my Chinese of earlier - I really was eating international cuisine today. I sipped a glass of wine, and when all was cleared away it was time for sleep, or to try to anyway. The lights were dimmed, I closed my eyes.

Unfortunately, the lady passenger was more than a wriggle bottom and seemed to be trying to take possession of my seat as well as her own. Sleep could be wishful thinking, again, but if I couldn't then I would just reflect on my previous few days in her country. Wonderful memories, and the fulfilment of another dream, another personal ambition. I had failed on the mountain, but so what, at last seeing African wildlife for real was far bigger to me than the mountain. Through the continual poking and prodding from beside me, I enjoyed my thoughts, I dozed and enjoyed them again.

Time passed slowly to begin with, but then we were close - I must have slept somewhere along the route. Sunrise over Europe, and as we started to descend, this was my first look at Holland, the flatlands, the straightness of the dykes, the agriculture and horticulture below.

Then the seat belt lights came on, though I had never undone mine other than a quick walk up the corridor in search of the happy bush. We had landed smoothly, my fellow passenger had been fine, though for her, like me, it was off one plane only to find her connection and board another again across the Atlantic.

For me, it was a rush to disembark and find the next terminal for my connection to London. I ran, I didn't have much time. I asked the Dutchmen about Schiphol Airport and how easy it was to find my way about, he said it was a big airport with several terminals, follow the signs and don't dally.

Being towards the back of the plane, getting off was slow, but I did find a notice board telling me flight details, terminal and gate number. A brisk walk would see me eating up the yards, sorry, metres towards my flight gate. I was doing well until I found I had to go through security which I wasn't expecting, and as always I was directed into the slowest moving queue, the one where someone had a query or had lost some documentation. Frustration!

Finally, I passed through security and continued along a couple of long aisles. I arrived with about five minutes to spare, and was very hot and sweaty.

I was soon on board having spoken briefly to Jane, giving an estimated ETA for my arrival back home, barring any delays. It would be an easy flight back to the UK, breakfast and landing at Heathrow at much the same time as I had taken off, with the different time zones meaning I would lose an hour. Through our different routes, Janet would have landed an hour ago, and would be nearly home by now.

The rest was routine: disembark, security and immigration, baggage collection and then to summon my car park taxi. There was a delay waiting for that, but I was soon back in my car and driving home. We had heard there was a heatwave in Britain, with temperatures reaching the low to mid-30s, but today was a typical English summer day - humid, dull and drizzling.

But for a journey that had started deep in the south of Kenya, close to the Tanzanian border some 24 hours ago, in another three hours I would be safely home, in time for a late lunch.

It was an adventure, a real adventure, but it was over now, and I was back home in Jane's arms. Unpack and unwind. Tonight, her sister and niece would be staying, going around viewing prospective universities. Jane would fix up the media card from my camera so that all could view my photos - all 800 of them - on the television. In high definition, they were very good, I was really pleased with them.

But it had been a long 48 hours when bedtime approached. Tomorrow I was being picked up at 10.30am by Dave, he was taking me on my stag do, a trip up the Shropshire Union Canal on his barge, along with Anthony and several bottles of beer.

In two weeks' time I would be getting married, I had turned around on the mountain for Jane, but there would always be that nagging question in my mind: Could I have reached the top?

Maybe, maybe not, but it was the right decision, so we could spend the rest of our time together.

Two weeks later would see us at Shrewsbury Castle with my nearest and dearest friends, a small ceremony in the grounds of this beautiful place, then a boat trip on the Severn on the Sabrina, and finally a meal at Renaissance - my favourite Shrewsbury restaurant. A chance at last to say a big thank you to all those who had helped me through depression, to declare my love for Jane, and ...... to live happily ever after. There was one missing guest, a certain she who had been instrumental in being the trigger for my cure, but we wouldn't have got my beloved Kilimanjaro in the room!

I hope one day I will see her again.

25

Thoughts

I GUESS IT was turning out to be a big year for me, and it was only July. An eye operation, a marriage and my trip to Kenya. What effect would all this have on my life? Well, for a start I could see better, and I would now have to adapt my life to live with Jane and share a future with her, giving up some of the independence I had given myself since overcoming depression and setting my own goals to achieve. I would continue as a vet for a while longer; I enjoyed the country life, meeting farmers and working outside. Was that not where my life had started, on my father's farm all those years ago?

If all went to plan, I would be returning to Kenya in 2018, this time as a vet helping the Send A Cow charity to improve farming and allow workers to benefit more from their livestock and be more productive in milk and meat production, even on a small scale. In doing this, the hope is that they will have more food, more money and be able to support fellow countrymen - in short it should improve their lot in terms of food production and hopefully reduce poverty. The charity is the one I had tried to raise money for, as well as a local hospice, in my attempt to climb Mount Kenya. But during my trip to Kenya, and it was only a short trip of a few days, I had seen things that worried me in the country's development, and I'd seen how successful these projects could be.

Anything I write can only be my opinion of what I saw and what I learned from the people I met, but I could see problems that needed to be addressed in the country, problems that may already be attended to. I saw a country rich in potential, with a developing infrastructure, road and rail systems being supported by Chinese investment. A booming floriculture industry around Naivashu and a coffee industry, both supplying a good income from exports. And of course, there was tourism and ecotourism, an industry that had a vast potential providing tourists were willing to travel there. But tourism depended a lot on wildlife, of which Kenya and East Africa has in abundance. But this is where there must be a clear strategy for the future.

Areas like the Central Highlands offer rich, fertile lands that can produce ample food supplies, the coffee plantations, but there are other areas where the land is not so productive, and where the co-existence of farming and human needs must compete with the needs of wildlife. Every living thing must eat, everything must drink and for a successful tourist industry there must be a balance between nature and farming.

In some ways in my microcosm of life I can see similarities between myself and the problems of Kenya. I had depression, caused by a combination of events, and realised the only person who could solve everything was me. Some of those things were out of my control but I had to find answers on how to cope with the situation. Kenya, I found to be similar, there is a lot of good, some bad and some things she has no control over, namely climate change and global warming. If there were two topics that the people I spoke to talked of, it was of that and the impending election and what effect the result would have on the stability and future of their country. The people all seemed so proud of being Kenyan, and accepted there were things wrong with their Government, but hoped for a better future where they could better themselves.

Fears of violence and tribal warfare which followed the 2007 election were real. But as I had to address my lack of confidence in myself, and lack of direction in my life, then Kenya too must develop so that people have the confidence to visit and to conserve their wildlife, which is what people want to see on their visits, to find a balance between that and the needs of farming, and somewhere along the line there needs to be some sort of water policy. My visit was supposed to be shortly after the rainy season, but what I saw were dried up water courses, arid, parched grazing land and struggling crops, with the question: When would it rain next?

Sub-Saharan Africa was in crisis with drought, and that extended into Kenya and the Lake Turkana region which I have already mentioned earlier. Areas need a tourist industry to improve their economy, to be able to sustain their farming and grow their crops. They need to be able to grow maize as their stable diet, but crops failed in the drought conditions and that was if they could plant in the first place - an effect of global warming, almost certainly, but it was creating an emergency. We frequently hear of troubled areas in the world, of hurricanes, earthquakes and other natural disasters, but here in Northern Kenya, in Sudan, they only get the occasional mention, but it is never a news headline.

As I travelled out there, it was election day in the UK. In Kenya, their election would be on August 8th. After the troubles of 2007, Uhuru Kenyatta had come into office in 2011, and there had been some stability in the country since then. What would happen now?

On my arrival in Nairobi, the election was very much in your face, even though it was still eight weeks away. There were billboards, advertising on workmen's clothing, it was everywhere. Bilal had bought me a paper to read for my journey to Naro Moru, half of it was about the election, local violence and local rallies. Boniface, a Kikuyu like Kenyatta, talked much of the politics in the country and the money that was ploughed in to get elected as a local official, an MP. Some of it, he thought, seemed unsustainable from the income one would receive if elected, but the money kept being poured into the campaigns. There was a large fund-raising event in the Safari Park Hotel by the President just before my stay there. I guess I lost contact with what was happening out there after my return until the election date, it wasn't exactly making the news back home.

But I was aware that the result could influence my future trip, especially if Foreign Office advice would be to deter people from travelling if the violence of 2007 re-occurred. I hope that doesn't sound selfish, but my concern was that any forward movement in the development of the country would come to a halt, and any good done by the charity would be wasted if the country erupted into violence again.

Fingers crossed, I went online to find out what I could on election day and for the following days. Election day was monitored by outside sources, so that the events of 2007 hopefully would not reoccur – there were over 1,000 deaths in post-election violence, and over 600,000 people were displaced. It would be a presidential vote between the main participants, Uhuru Kenyatta, the incumbent president, and Raila Odinga of the NASA. This would coincide with the election of 47 governors, 47 senators and 290 members, for the lower house Odinga had feared a rigged election and his supporters and Rights Activists wanted to ensure that all Kenyans felt secure and could cast their vote. There were fears of fraud, even in the last election, and an electronic system was being set up to aid the vote - but this could be abused or switched off on a whim by the electoral officer of any polling station. People were voting in constituencies where they didn't live to boost a vote there, and the names of many dead who were still on the electoral role were also used, all possible ways to alter the vote of the twenty million voters.

Outside agencies who would try to monitor the vote, including Obama himself, all called for a fair election, calling for 'an election and aftermath which is peaceful and credible, reinforcing confidence in the new constitution and the future of the country'.

However, days before the election there was the abduction, and later torture and murder of one of the chief Election Commission Officers, Christopher Msando. Odinga hinted at interference in the election, and people took to the streets in protest. Kenyatta in turn accused Odinga of trying to divide the nation. The vice-president, William Ruto, had his house attacked by protesters shortly after the murder.

August 8th, and the election took place under a cloud but with Kenyatta stating that if he lost, he would step down and accept the will of the people. He called on Odinga's party to do the same. The two men represented different ethnic communities, Kenyatta the Kikuyu, and Odinga the Lua, whose rivalry with the Kikuyu has defined most of Kenya's post-independence history. A close race was expected.

I tried to follow the election results online over the following days, and early indications were that Kenyatta was taking an early lead and had secured some 54% of the vote, to Odinga's 44%. By now, Odinga was claiming the election had been hacked, with riots breaking out in opposition strongholds like Kisumu in western Kenya. This is of significance for me because that is the area I thought I would be going to with Send a Cow the following year. Worryingly, with Odinga rejecting the preliminary election results as a fraud, and his supporters taking to the streets chanting: "No Raila, no peace", trouble was looming.

The next I heard was that the administrators had stopped publishing results, but it did look like a Kenyatta victory. I thought as I had heard little further news of violence or any different result, that all had been settled and that a peaceful future would now follow in this country.

I was somewhat surprised therefore to find that in September, the Kenyan judiciary had declared that the election should be re-run on October 26th (they had stated within a 60-day period of which this date was within), but even this date seemed to evoke some opposition from the Odinga side. The Courts had ruled that without some areas being able to submit documentation of the election, of the counts and citing irregularities, they could not rule that all had passed above board. In that event they could only call for a re-run, the August 8th election was declared null and void.

However, by late September as NASA supporters had taken to the streets again to protest, Odinga accused the IEBC Independent Electoral and Boundaries Commission) of being puppets of Kenyatta. He was demanding the sacking of election officials, though the courts had said it was not an individual responsible but rather institutional failings that led to irregularities and illegalities in the transmission of election results. Despite calls for the protests to be called off, and the chief prosecutor ordering investigations into 11 board members, including its chief executive, Ezra Chiloba, Odinga felt that the election could not be fair while these officials remained in place.

With death threats against the judiciary and members of the commission, Kenya remained in a position of political turmoil. By the beginning of October, Odinga had withdrawn from the presidential race, citing that it could not be a fair election while members of the electoral commission were still in office. A call for more demonstrations on a regular basis was made, and there was chaos. Kenyatta claimed that if the one other candidate had withdrawn, then he should be elected by right, but then another of the minor candidates got a court judgement that he could stand again. Along with a constitutional argument about whether the election should be nullified with the withdrawal of a candidate, the political future of Kenya remained very much up in the air.

A big surprise to me, again it was a 'watch this space' type of event, and I wondered how the people I had met, especially in the Kikuyu region, were feeling now. The uncertainty of the political future of this country was still very much up in the air.

26

Conservation And Climate Change

A S I HAVE said many times during my discourse, the topics of conservation and global warming/climate change seemed to be on the lips of everyone that I spoke to, perhaps more so than the election. Kenya's wildlife was a rich resource, to attract ecotourism and enhance the country's economy, in the process providing a lot of jobs to Kenyan natives.

From the moment I had entered the country and been taken up to Naro Moru with Bilal, the subject was always close by: on the mountain with Boniface and the porters, and with Ibrahim and Abdullah on our safari. This ended with the trip to the Giraffe Centre in Nairobi on the way to the airport, and the art exhibition I have already mentioned, but said I would come back to.

The exhibition was a competition for primary and secondary school children to paint, draw or create a picture from materials, with the theme of conservation and global warming. The effect it had on them and their future was depicted in art form, and I was staggered how much common sense and reality was shown in those so young. Okay, some of the art was basic, and some very mature, but the messages coming out of virtually every exhibit were very meaningful.

There were images of wildlife, of life and death as habitats diminished. The effect of man's waste on the environment, pollution, rubbish, how it affected the fine balance of nature, toxifying water courses and killing fish (the staple diet of some of the birdlife I had seen) also appeared.

The interaction between farming and the needs of the wildlife was essential not only for their survival, but also for the generation of ecotourism.

As deforestation takes place, the natural habitats of some animals will be destroyed, putting their survival at risk. The needs of the nomadic herdsmen and their stock will stray into the habitats of what is potentially Africa's richest resource. Their stock has to feed and drink, but the reserves are protected and although we had seen Maasai herds impounded at the park gate, no doubt their stock would soon be returned to them, and transgression would no doubt repeat itself soon.

What I thought would be a quick whizz around a few pictures to kill time actually turned out to be a more than interesting 40 minutes looking at the next generation's view of the problems that were facing their country, and that needed to be addressed. Okay, especially in the pictures of the younger children there may have been some input from their teachers, but a message stood out, they feared for the future, and they cared. This exhibition had made a real impact on me, but only brought in to perspective everything I had seen and thought in my brief stay in this country.

My initial trip out of Nairobi was in the outskirts, where suburbs intermingled with grazing land for the nomadic herdsmen, sometimes along the roadside, sometimes in larger areas of pasture - even here everything looked so dry and dusty. Through the lusher farmlands of the Central Highlands before we entered the Mount Kenya area, where even though there seemed vast areas of fenced farmland, as well as much scrub where nomadic herds grazed - everything was so arid. Not the fields of green, lush grass I had expected so soon after the big rains which I thought should have been finishing now, but low dried grass waiting for a hungry goat or sheep to graze it off. These should have been the times of plenty, they were not, and I was surprised looking at the emaciated state of some of the cattle that they survived at all, let alone managed to produce any milk to rear a calf, or provide sustenance for their owner.

On Mount Kenya itself, the rainforests were struggling so much to survive now, there were not the lichen covered branches I had expected to see, though that may have been different if we had managed to descend on our intended route on the other side of the mountain.

Boniface himself had said that this wasn't the rainforest he had seen as a child not that many years ago, and he was worried that in 20 years the mountain would be a desert. The journey from Nairobi to the Mara looked lush until we entered the Great Rift Valley, but I remembered looking down from the viewpoint of our first comfort stop, looking down into the vast expanse of the valley and thinking how dry everything looked.

This thought was reinforced as we then drove across this terrain towards Narok and saw dried-up river beds and the barren acacia covered scrubland, again with its nomadic herdsmen, but little sign of water. And from Narok to the Mara on that to-be made up road was dust, bare soil, some scrub and acacia again, but very little evident pasture. Red soil and dust, yellow vegetation, and that would be the same when we entered the reserve itself.

We did find the wonderful grazing grounds they had travelled for, but not the pictures and films I had seen of the migrating animals swimming the Mara River, risking life and limb to get to the other side and scrambling up the far bank while crocodiles waited for them. Where was the water now? The riverbed was barely covered in places, and though the banks are steep, perhaps this year they will have an easier passage.

The lakes at Nakuru and Naivasha did look low judging by the bare earth we had to walk across to reach the water's edge and view the flamingos there, but the true impact of the lack of rains would hit me most when we reached Amboseli and I saw my beloved mountain again.

In the five years since my last visit, I was surprised at how much the ice cap at the summit of Kilimanjaro had retreated. In *Kilimanjaro. My Story* I wrote of the forecasts predicting the disappearance of the cap in 30 years - from my view in 2017, I cannot sadly see it lasting that long. There is something majestic about the free-standing mountain with its snow crown. Would it have the same appeal without it? Time will tell.

Back in 2011, the drought in East Africa was described as the worst in the region for six decades, threatening the lives of millions of people with food shortages. Thousands fleed Somalia to seek food in Kenya and Ethiopia. The normal rains of October to December in parts of the region had failed to arrive, and the spring rains were inadequate, meaning that the area had missed out on two growing seasons. Even then, the predicted trend was that the amount of precipitation would diminish leading to food prices becoming unaffordable and food shortages.

It is thought that as the world has warmed over the last century, the Indian Ocean bordering these countries has warmed especially fast. The resulting warmer air and increased humidity over the ocean have produced more frequent rainfall in that region. As the air rises, loses its moisture as rainfall, and then flows westwards, it descends over Africa causing drought conditions in Ethiopia and Kenya.

By June of 2017, the time of my travel, the national Drought Management Authority had issued an early warning bulletin indicating that the long rains had finished, and that many parts of the arid and semi-arid lands were still experiencing long distances between home and water sources, unusually high food prices, and worryingly high levels of malnutrition.

Scientists concluded that, after examining the regions' weather and climate data, most of that warming was caused by greenhouse gas and aerosol emissions. But here, the East African situation was an example of how climate change and global warming was impacting on human populations, and it was the world's poor who were paying the heaviest price. The future then was predicted as weather dependent, if the rains fell it would be necessary to ensure famers had seeds to sow as previous crop failures had left some without seed. If the rains didn't appear the situation would worsen, creating hunger and more displacement of people.

If the rains were too strong, then falling on the baked ground, they could wash away crops and create flooding.

Move forward three years to 2014, and the situation was repeating itself. By 2017, there had been four years of reduced rainfall and drought, especially in the northern regions of Kenya, the Lake Turkana area.

By February 2017, the Government had a declared a national drought emergency, with 23 of the 47 countries affected. The number of food insecure people had more than doubled, from 1.3 to 2.7 million. Over 350,000 children and lactating mothers were considered malnourished. Maize production in the coastal areas had decreased by 99% compared to the long-term average; people were having to travel further to access water, and there were reports of large numbers of livestock deaths as farmers' stock starved. The impact of the drought meant that large numbers of primary school children were not attending school.

By May, the situation was deteriorating rapidly, with high levels of malnutrition prevalent in the arid and semi-arid lands. Water resources had dried up in half of the 47 counties, and it was estimated that three million people lacked access to clean water. Recurrent droughts have destroyed livelihoods, triggered local conflicts over scarce resources and eroded the ability of communities to cope. Children needing educational assistance, and the outbreak of multiple diseases, cholera, diarrhoea, and measles are just a few of the problems being created.

Being the third consecutive below-average rainfall season, the modest recovery conditions were likely to be short-lived, therefore, the June to September dry season would be difficult for these areas, in terms of malnutrition and access to water. On top of that, an infestation of African armyworm was threatening crops in marginal areas, further reducing the potential harvest. All this caused the price of basic food commodities, including the Kenyan staple diet of maize, to soar. Food inflation was running at over 11%. People are reducing what they eat, with many families only eating once a day.

The election has added to the anxiety of people which may politicise the problem. All in all, the crisis is dire, and far worse than the drought of 2011, with the failure of three rainy seasons in a row.

In November 2016, the Government pledged Ksh 210 million as a drought response, but this took some time to be put into full use. By February 2017, the Government declared the drought as a national disaster, and appealed for international assistance, with an appeal from United Nations agencies and partners for $165.7 million dollars.

Ibrahim told me that maize was being bought from neighbouring countries to feed the population, with a limit on the price that shopkeepers could sell it to the people, meaning they would make no profit on it but at least there would be some supply of the people's staple diet.

During the years of sufficient rainfall there was a period of economic growth, and there had been the emergence of a new class of 'cattle barons', who had boosted the numbers of cattle greatly. Ranches owned by white and black farmers in times of plenty had been poorly managed, leading to insufficient grazing in the north. Historical land issues were now being raised in areas like Laikipia, now that there was a shortage of grazing and water supply.

Many ranches were acquired during the period of British colonial rule, with others purchased after Kenya became independent in 1963 - but now there was conflict between the white 'haves' and the black 'have-nots' who thought the lands in this region were their tribal historical right. They thought that if they occupied them, acquiring them through violence, then they could reclaim their heritage. Farmers, both black and white, were being murdered as these herdsmen thought they could reclaim what they thought was rightfully theirs. This was especially so during a period of shortage of pastoral grazing and was exacerbating that which was already a dire situation. This, along with the serious drought further north, was having a critical effect on livestock populations. Forage was short or non-existent, meaning animals were becoming emaciated and therefore worthless to sell, or they were dying. Being weak, they were vulnerable to disease, especially pneumonia which was proving fatal to them.

The Kenyan government introduced a livestock insurance programme, using satellite imagery in drought-hit areas to offer a safety net to vulnerable farmers. This monitors forage conditions through rainy seasons, triggering payments to farmers when vegetation dies back to critical levels. These payments are aimed at enabling families that depend on their livestock to purchase animal feed to keep their herds alive. It's hoped that this 'Klip' programme may bring relief to thousands of families on the brink of hunger.

Animals have been dying in the thousands over the past months in the drought affected regions of the country with the shortage of forage to feed them with. Even when some rains occurred, this had caused flash flooding, destroying the crops on these parched lands. Perhaps the Kenyan government detected the drought earlier than other countries, and to some extent mitigated the effect of it, but in what some locals describe as the worst drought they have ever seen, the numbers of people approaching malnutrition levels worsens with time.

A crisis that is ever deepening. The effects of global warming, a man-made problem, is something that affects these poor countries more than the affluent west, and China. The Kiyoto agreement was set up to try and slow down this process, to give some hope to these countries, and those Kenyans I spoke to were only too aware of it - and of President Trump's intention to ignore it, saving the jobs of thousands of Americans in its industrial heartland. But that is of no help to these people who are starving and trying to eke out a living to survive, to live.

I suppose it created some feeling of guilt for the food we ate, and the food I didn't want on the mountain. But I suppose one should weigh that up with the money tourists bring into the country to boost the economy, and to create local jobs.

27

Send A Cow

I F MY WISH to go back to East Africa was driven by me making a promise to myself five years previously when I climbed Kiliman-jaro, but when I had seen no wildlife to speak of, then it was also encouraged by having another go at a mountain. This time it would be Africa's second highest peak, Mount Kenya.

Five years ago, a friend had suggested that if I was going to do the climb I should try to raise some money for charity as well. Although the trip was entirely self-financed, I did raise a good sum of money for a local hospice. This time around I decided to do the same again. The mission was of my own volition, but again I wanted to try and help a charity. This time, having finally arranged the trip, I decided to try and help the local hospice again, and a charity called Send A Cow.

I had already volunteered my services to them in Kenya in a project organised between them and an organisation that the practice I worked in was part of. They had sent a pair of veteri-nary surgeons out to Kenya, Uganda and Rwanda in rotation to impart some of their knowledge on African farmers. This would occur over the latter part of 2015 through to late spring 2018. I had been asked to go in October 2017, which would have meant going to Rwanda, but instead I had chosen Kenya in 2018. It only seemed fair that some of my fundraising should go to this char-ity and having contacted them, the encouragement and support I received from their Bath base was tremendous. I hope in the end that I will have funded my trip with them, for they are dependent on donations to keep their good work continuing.

Quoting some of their own literature: 'smallholder farming is the backbone of Africa, with 70% of people reliant on the land to feed their families, and to make a living. However, poverty has seen traditional farming knowledge lost, forgotten or replaced with more intensive technologies.' Even on my trip, I had seen a vast difference in the types of farming, the intensive and high tech farming I had seen at the base of Mount Kenya, and the subsistence farming of smallholders just up the road. Tending their crops (usually the women) by hand, some looked healthy, some didn't. That wasn't in the drought torn north of the country - I would have no idea what it looked like there in those arid lands. The nomadic herdsmen compared with those smallholders who grazed their cattle, goat and sheep locally, and had them stockaded up by night. I compared these with the Delamere Estates we had passed outside Naivashu. Climate change challenges all forms of production. There are too many families that no matter how hard they work, cannot make ends meet. Our project is to enable farmers to learn innovative techniques to boost production while working in harmony with the environment. The result is a sustainable, thriving farming business resilient enough to survive drought and hardship. Families need a low-input, low cost solution to improve their own lot and to benefit their neighbours. With knowledge, skills and the encouragement of natural fertilisers like manure, they have everything to take back control of their land.

With the training Send A Cow is introducing, people are taught natural farming practices that work in harmony with all of nature's resources: people, land, water, and livestock. They help communities start to reverse the impact of environmental degradation and become more resilient in the face of climatic 'acts of god' such as extended periods of drought, or of flash flooding. Being capable of growing more and producing more means a more diverse diet and improved nutrition. Increased biodiversity means there is a reduction in risk for families if one crop were to fail.

Sometimes, as poverty has depleted their assets, there is a need for new resources to kick-start the farm again, whether it be the gift of livestock, seed or other assets. It can have a huge impact on a poor farming family. Animals - a source of manure, milk and eggs - give growing children nutritious protein, and hopefully a surplus they can sell. Livestock in times of emergency can be sold. But with this there is a need for the farmers to learn how to give them the very best care, food and shelter.

The farmers that Send a Cow help are often marginalised in their communities, labouring on neighbouring farms for exploitative pay. Families will be helped to develop rural businesses that enrich the lives of their customers and workers. Successful farms not only provide food and income for the families who own them, but also offer employment and food for local people too. The aim is to produce aspiring and confident farmers who knit their communities together and bring lasting wealth and confidence to their region.

For me it's a chance to return to a country and its people which I thoroughly enjoyed meeting. In the final years of my career, having myself started as a dairy farmer's son some 50 years ago, it gives me the chance to give something back from the knowledge I have picked up both from books and more importantly from experience. My career has been a learning curve throughout, as they say, 'you are never too old to learn'. This is my chance to say thank you to all those who have given me knowledge, and I hope that can be of benefit to others to improve their health, wealth and to help along a developing country to improve its lot, to the benefit of all.

I hope I can be of help. I wish I could make it rain more for them. I think I will be based at Kisumu on the shores of Lake Victoria, there is water there. But what about the areas I had visited? That is something the Government will need to address at some time in the future, and it needs to be soon. This is just a personal opinion of what I have seen, but somewhere along the line the authorities and aid agencies need to work together to water the country.

Time will tell. All I can say now is that from the people I met, the likes of Boniface, Bilal, Ibrahim and others I spoke to, I hope the future of their country turns out how they would like.

For me, there are many happy memories. I at last saw my beloved African elephants, and how will I ever forget the sight of that herd trooping from afar, across our path in Amboseli, or the young bulls play fighting, mum and two generations of offspring all tending to each other? They are wonderful animals, but I shouldn't single them out just because I have always wanted to see them in the flesh since being a kid. The birds - small and big - the lizards, antelopes, wildebeest, zebras – I loved all of them. How lucky I was to see the start of the migration - the greatest show on earth - when we visited the Mara, with those vast open plains of grassland waving to and fro in the breeze, that solitary acacia breaking up the landscape.

I witnessed the different landscapes of the Nakuru park, and that gorgeous rhino calf with mum. The flamingos and the setting sun over the lake, the giraffe, the tree lions, where does it end?

Amboseli is a memory in itself, especially the social structure and interaction around the swamp. The funny warthogs, the gangly ostriches, Observation Hill and its stark landscapes, and of course Kilimanjaro. How pleased I was to go back and see her again, standing so majestically over the African plains. The mountain that will stay in my heart and in my memory forever.

Of course, I mustn't forget the wonderful company I had on safari, and in climbing the mountain. Everybody was real fun and it was a privilege to spend time with them.

Kenya itself has so many problems to deal with, but from what I saw of the younger generation, they do seem to care about their future, the future of their wildlife, and how they can live in harmony while becoming more self-sufficient in their own food production.

Drought, famine, people migration, disease, there is so much for a developing country to cope with, but again I must emphasise that this is my opinion of my observations. I get the feeling there is so much potential in the country to be released and harvested. How good it would be for Africa if there was a stable and developing Kenya. A land of opportunities.

I hope I can offer a little help myself in 2018, but mostly I wish Kenya, and Tanzania from my visit five years previously, all the best for the future.

To quote Karen Blixen again: "When you have caught the rhythm of Africa, you find out that it is the same in all her music."

I also hope that if I were to be lucky enough to return in a few years' time, Mount Kenya won't be the desert Boniface is predicting, and most of all I hope that Kilimanjaro has kept her snow-cap, and that the picture will be of that which is emblazoned in my mind.

There is something very beautiful, very calming and very peaceful about the places I have visited, and on my previous visit to the foothills, and then the slopes of Mount Kilimanjaro. Peace amongst the chaos and turbulence of African and of world politics. That peace comes from the country's wildlife, where within its own, there will be the daily savagery of any ecosystem where there are hunters and the hunted. Animals can be brutal, but so can man. But again, I hope that they can co-exist to each other's benefit, so that in future years, many more people can enjoy the sights and sounds of the Mara, Amboseli, Nakuru and the many places I didn't have the chance to visit. Let man capture the importance of this gift he has been given in his 'back garden'.

Those memories of 2012, and of 2017 are now firmly etched in my mind, it has been a privilege to visit and see all these wonderful animals in their natural habitat. I may have repeated myself a lot, but that can only be a reinforcement of what good I hope will come to this region.

Again, good luck for their future.

Finale
– and what about me?

ON 8TH JULY 2017, just after 2pm in the afternoon, I walked through the streets of Shrewsbury from the Lion Hotel to Shrewsbury Castle accompanied by some very dear friends and of course my fiancée, Jane. The weather was kind to us as we took ourselves to the place where we would soon be married.

An hour later, standing at the doors of the castle, we were man and wife and now with a life to look forward to together. Jane had at last got her man, six years after we had first gone out, though we had at one point parted as I fought my depression. Wasted years in Jane's mind, but time I needed to sort myself out - something I realised that I alone could do.

We enjoyed the grounds of the castle before the ceremony, and then walked down to the quay by the Welsh Bridge to board the Sabrina for a trip on the River Severn. This gave us the chance to see Shrewsbury by boat and to relax before our select band of invited guests would dine at our favourite restaurant, Renaissance (now sadly closed as the proprietors have retired).

Less than a month earlier I had started my climb of Mount Kenya, a promise to myself to return to Africa. Climbing Kilimanjaro and the achievement of reaching the highest peak in Africa, as I have so often said, has had such a profound effect on my life. I have become a different person and am now transformed into someone who thrives on success, on fulfilling what he sets out to achieve. I have acquired a new found confidence with real goals in place that I want to achieve after the effects of depression wasted so much of my life.

My farmers often stop to ask me what my next challenge will be as if I have some sort of eternal youth. But it's lovely that those that have seen me suffer (not really knowing me for the person I really was), have now taken on board the new me and are so interested in what I want to achieve. The veterinary profession and the farming community have a track record of taking their own lives because of mental health problems like depression, but my farmers were so pleased to see someone they know come out the other end, and for me to have become the real person I am.

I set off to Kenya to climb a mountain and to see the wildlife, especially elephants, something that I had wanted to see all my life. It was another personal challenge, especially as I went to Africa by myself and didn't know if I would be climbing alone or with others. I knew I would meet new people on safari at least, as the tour company wouldn't take me by myself. Another challenge for me was to accommodate the needs of other people on safari, along with what I wanted to get out of it.

Where I was now, I didn't accept failure anymore, though Mount Kenya seemed by all accounts harder than my beloved Kili. I was going to climb it and see the magnificent scenery the other side on my descent via a different route.

I didn't make it. How would I cope with that 'failure'? It was a big one. People had invested in me to climb Mount Kenya to raise money for two charities.

While deciding whether to go up or back down the mountain the way I had come, there was definitely a rationale in my thinking that I had never possessed before. I had to get home to marry Jane and I had to be able to give the proceeds to charity and I had to see my children again.

On reflection of my trip, I asked myself why I had gone to Africa in the first place. That five-year promise was to fulfil my ambition of seeing Africa's treasures, its wildlife and my desire to see elephants.

As I walked back down the mountain with Boniface, I realised that not reaching the summit was but a minor setback. I found out far more about myself in not making it to the top than I would have if I had made it. The opportunity to chat long and hard with Boniface and the other porters about their country became so much more important to me.

I had questioned Chunga on my descent of Kili about his home of Tanzania, but I now wish I had started that conversation far earlier on the trip to gain more and more information about his country. As a result of my depression I didn't have the confidence in myself to do so, not until I addressed Chunga at our final meal on behalf of my fellow climbers and gave him our vote of thanks. The change in me had begun, followed by the writing of the book on Kilimanjaro. Until then I had never enjoyed writing, but now I had a tale to tell - even if only to myself.

I had fallen in love with Africa, and that descent with Boniface gave me the opportunity to develop that relationship and since then to continue in my pursuit of knowledge of this great continent, but more specifically the region of East Africa. It is likely that if I had continued the climb in the rarefied air above 15,000 feet, I would have had to concentrate on breathing and pole, pole rather than talking.

The experience of climbing Mount Kenya in 2017, as with Kilimanjaro, was life changing. I did see my wildlife, and it was unbelievable seeing it in the flesh as opposed to on TV or in photographs. Those memories will remain with me forever. But equally important to me now are the issues a country like Kenya must address, some of which I have discussed in this book, others I will pursue at a later date. It gave me the incentive to want to research these issues more and more. To be honest, would the old Rod, pre-Kili have had the confidence to put his thoughts down on paper? The answer to that is a strong no!

No, I didn't summit, but by no means was this trip a failure. New boundaries have been opened for me that I will pursue with interest, and I have a desire to visit this country - along with Tanzania - again and again. This is now very much instilled in my blood. The trip turned out to be a triumph for someone who had lost themselves for years, but had now discovered who they really are. Someone who could now differentiate between the things in life that mattered and those that didn't, and that there was no point in losing sleep over those that didn't. I returned to my wife-to-be and to a future together. I returned knowing that in less than 12 months I would be stepping onto Kenyan soil once again, helping Send a Cow teach its facilitators to go out and improve the lives of smallholder farmers, and help them to develop their wealth and health. Could old Rod have done that? Certainly not.

In 2018 I will return to Kenya with a new confidence in myself. Developing farming, wealth creation and finding out about other issues in this developing country: the role of women, gender violence, what drives the Kenyan person, what they enjoy and how they see their country. That will all be the subject of another book.

This trip was not a failure, but a stepping stone in my journey to become the real me. I spent a day in a tent resting, thinking, worrying about my immortality, but Kenya 2017 turned out to be a success in my life as I continue to try and fulfil my potential.

Back to the wedding day, and not only was it a chance to marry a woman who loved me dearly (and I her), but it was also a chance to thank at last all those who had stood by me in my dark years that came before. If the theme of my speech was friendship, then those present have my eternal gratitude for helping me through the bad times through my depression, and offering help when they thought necessary - but never being intrusive. Dear friends, special friends, I raise a toast to them all.

My friend Graham, in particular, greatly encouraged me to climb Kilimanjaro. Now in his speech he had mentioned my bad times but at the end he wished Jane and I a happy future together and finished by welcoming back the real Rod.

A mountain to climb, I can now feel I have achieved many summits, and will no doubt find others to reach for.

Kenya is a country I have now come to love. She too has her own mountains to climb, and those are far more difficult than mine. Her people deserve the same success that I have achieved.

Postscript

I GUESS AT some stage there must be a finish point, to draw a line under certain issues.

But as I come to a conclusion, much is still up in the air as to the election in Kenya, the ivory trade and the elephant population.

The election was re-run on October 26th, with one candidate standing against the incumbent president, Uhuru Kenyatta, and with a 98% share of the vote (on a 38% turnout), he won again. But again, a petition was filed in the Supreme Court as to the legality of the election. The result was upheld in Kenyatta's favour, but still the opposition will not recognise the new government.

At the same time, Mugabe in Zimbabwe is having his status challenged. Politics in Africa! I can only wait and see what happens with my proposed trip in 2018.

The UK government is at last proposing to ban the sale of ivory, regardless of its age, and as the largest exporter of legal ivory, one hopes this will have a significant effect on the trade.

In the meantime, there are encouraging reports of a rise in elephant numbers in East Africa, though sadly not in the whole of the continent, with further drops in their numbers in Southern Africa. One can only thank those working so tirelessly to ensure their future is successful.

Lastly, I did eventually get to see my own GP. If I had genuine concern about the old ticker on the mountain, then I didn't need to. He gave me a clean bill of health, so I guess my struggles were perhaps a touch of overdoing it on day two, especially at that altitude.

So, would I like to try again, even at my ripe old age? I think that can be answered in the affirmative, though I will be getting fitter before I go, and sticking to the original route plan.

Something to look forward to in the future. *KENYA: A MOUNTAIN TO CLIMB*!!

Acknowledgements

*Sue Kinton for sorting the trip out for
me and making it all happen.*

*To Boniface, Bilal and Ibrahim for
looking after me in Kenya.*

*To Janet, Stephan, Viv, Penny and Geral-
dine for many hours of company on safari.*

*To all those, especially Shropshire farmers who supported
me in raising money for Severn Hospice and Send a Cow.*

For the support from Send a Cow.

*And lastly to Jane, for her support in the background
and waiting for my return to marry me - she said she
would have killed me if I had died on the mountain!*

A Note From The Author

Thank you so much for reading Kenya: A Mountain to Climb.

I poured my heart and soul into this book, and it would mean the world to me if you could leave me a brief review on Amazon to let me know what you thought. Reviews from readers like you help others to find the book and decide whether they want to read, so your help in spreading the word is greatly appreciated.

Just head to www.amazon.co.uk and search for 'Kenya A Mountain to Climb Rod Wood'

Thank you,

Rod